Reading the *Lives* of Poets:

Discovering the self and the World

Hyangil Kim · Yeongyu Kim

Shinasa

🕮 Preface

In today's rapidly changing world, university students need more than basic English communication skills; they are increasingly called to develop creative thinking, self-reflection, empathy, and critical thinking. *Reading the Lives of Poets: Discovering the Self and the World* was created to move beyond the traditional focus on the four language skills, guiding students to explore poetry and stories alongside their historical, social, and philosophical contexts. This book serves as an integrated liberal arts English resource designed to help learners reflect on their personal direction, explore possible career paths, and deepen their understanding of themselves and the world.

Through reading, students are encouraged to cultivate the following core competencies:

- **Creative Thinking**: Interpreting and reimagining themes through poets' lives and works
- **Self-Reflection**: Relating the messages of texts to personal experiences and values
- **Empathy**: Gaining emotional insight into diverse historical and social settings
- **Critical Thinking**: Analyzing and discussing themes from multiple perspectives
- **Communication Skills**: Expressing ideas effectively through recitation, dialogue, and writing

These competencies are developed through a rich variety of activities, including pre- and post-reading exercises, poetry paraphrasing, in-depth discussions, and essay writing. This approach invites learners to go beyond language acquisition, discovering their identity, clarifying their values, and experiencing meaningful connections with others.

Ultimately, *Reading the Lives of Poets* goes beyond the scope of a traditional textbook by guiding students on a path of self-discovery and growth. By engaging deeply with literature and the humanities, readers will have the opportunity to integrate language learning with intellectual curiosity and cultural awareness, making this book a valuable resource both in the classroom and for personal study.

2025. 10.

Hyangil Kim · Yeongyu Kim

Table of Contents

Chapter 3: Living in Harmony

Chapter 4: Self-Awareness in the Community

Reading the Lives of Poets:
Discovering the Self and the World

Chapter 1:

Creative Thinking and Imagination

Warm-Up!

Talk about the following questions with your partners.

1. What is meant by “remote interaction” or “contactless life”?
2. How would you define imagination?
3. How does imagination shape our dreams and daily life?

Poetry is the oldest and most universal form of expression, deeply bound to human imagination. In every age and culture, people have used poetry to enrich their lives beyond simple amusement. Film director Lee Joon-ik once remarked in an interview about his film *Dongju* (2016):

"When you admire a poem, it is important to consider the life of the poet as well. To appreciate a poem without recognizing the circumstances of the poet's life and death is, in fact, to admire only your own emotional response rather than the poem itself. Without empathy for the historical context and the struggles that gave rise to Yoon Dong-ju's poetry, one cannot truly claim to understand or appreciate his work."[1]

His point is clear: to understand a poem, we must also look at the life and background of the poet. Poetry is not only a source that nourishes imagination but also a window through which we gain insight into the poet and the world that shaped their voice.

Today, we stand in an age of rapid transformation—one defined by hyper-connectivity, super-intelligence, and super-convergence. With the rise of conversational AI, advanced interfaces, and immersive digital realities, people now interact with machines in entirely new ways, using their voices to shape their surroundings, collaborating with AI on creative tasks, and blending physical and virtual experiences into daily life.

At last, we have entered a new world where what we imagine and dream can truly be turned into reality. In such a transformed society, what we need most is imagination—a quality that poetry, as an inexhaustible source of creativity, continually nourishes. Through poetry, let us reflect on the world we hope to imagine and create together. In doing so, we can shape a clearer vision for a better self and a better world.

What We Will Read

Unit 1: What Is Imagination?
Unit 2: We Dream!
Unit 3: What Are We Creating?

Further Reading 1: Excerpt from "I Have a Dream"
Further Reading 2: Excerpt from "Pale Blue Dot"

Unit 1

What Is Imagination?

"Imagination is the beginning of creation. You imagine what you desire, you will what you imagine and at last you create what you will."

—George Bernard Shaw

Preview 1. Main Ideas

1. Imagination is the ability to give form to something that does not yet exist in reality.
2. No one can directly look into or fully understand another's imagination.
3. Innovators around the world are still interested in and actively discussing this topic.

Preview 2. Keywords

Define the words below in your own words. Then, search online for example sentences that show how each word is used. Share your definitions and sentences with your partner.

1. imagination:

____

2. artistic creativity:

____

3. truth and beauty:

____

4. envision:

____

5. hyperconnected society:

____

6. technological revolution:

____

Preview 3. Talking About

Look at the following questions and discuss your ideas with a partner.

1. Do you agree with the saying "Imagination is the beginning of creation"?
2. Can you think of a real-world example that illustrates this saying?
3. What do you think are some of the major features of today's technological revolution?

Preview 4. Further Discussion

1. What kind of future do you imagine?
2. What do you think is the role of imagination in our lives?

People often associate imagination with artistic creativity and expression. For the English poet John Keats, imagination was closely linked to truth and beauty. He believed that what the imagination recognizes as beautiful must also be true. For him, imagination was the only force that could lead us to discover both truth and beauty. Today, imagination remains an important topic of discussion among artists, thinkers, and influencers around the world. If you search for the word "imagination" on YouTube or Google, you will find countless videos, songs, and talks dedicated to it.

So, what is imagination, and why is it so important? In simple terms, imagination is the ability to create mental images or ideas of things that do not exist in reality. It allows us to give shape to something new, build a story in our minds, and explore possibilities beyond our immediate experience. Although imagination belongs to the realm of individual thought and varies from person to person, it is something we all share as a universal human ability.

Long ago, the philosopher Thomas Aquinas explained that we perceive the world through our senses, imagination, and intelligence.[2] This shows that imagination plays a key role in connecting what we sense with how we think, paving the way for understanding the human world.

With the development of science and technology and the rise of artificial intelligence, the world is becoming increasingly interconnected. This rapid change, often called the technological revolution, is transforming the way we live and work. In this hyperconnected society, no one knows exactly what the future will look like. To adapt to and thrive in an uncertain future, we must be able to envision a world we have not yet experienced. Imagination helps us think flexibly and prepare for possibilities we cannot yet see. As far as we know, humans are the only species capable of using advanced imagination, making it both our unique gift and our responsibility.

In this unit, we will explore the power of imagination and understand why it is such an essential part of our lives.

1A: George Bernard Shaw

Pre-Reading 1. General Questions

1. Search for information about George Bernard Shaw online.
2. Talk about the Pygmalion effect.
3. Have you heard of Received Pronunciation (RP)?

Pre-Reading 2. Vocabulary

Guess the meaning of each underlined word and choose its definition from the list below.

1. Ireland was still suffering dearly from the aftermath of the potato famine. ________
2. He was self-taught and eventually pioneered his own literary world. ________
3. Despite these setbacks, he became one of three great Irish writers. ________
4. Higgins' stubbornness eventually causes their relationship to fall apart. ________
5. Shaw satirizes the world as pursuing only outward appearances. ________

A. (n) the quality of refusing to change your opinion or behavior
B. (a) acquiring skills or knowledge by oneself without instruction
C. (v) to use humor, irony, or exaggeration to criticize people or ideas
D. (n) extreme shortage of food
E. (n) something delaying or impeding progress

George Bernard Shaw

George Bernard Shaw, commonly called Bernard Shaw, was born in Dublin, Ireland, in 1856. Having lived for nearly 100 years before he died in 1950, he witnessed many of the major historical events from the 19th to the mid-20th century. When Shaw was born, Ireland was still suffering from the aftermath of the potato famine. About one million people died during the famine, and another one million emigrated to Britain or the United States as people sought to escape hunger and starvation. Due to poverty, Shaw received only an elementary school education, after which he was self-taught and eventually pioneered his own literary world. Despite these setbacks—or perhaps thanks to them—he became one of the three great Irish writers alongside William Butler Yeats and Oscar Wilde. He published more than 60 plays and novels, pointing out problems in society with extraordinary insight. In 1925, for being an outstanding writer who left an indelible mark on the history of Western literature, he was awarded the Nobel Prize in Literature.

Among Shaw's works, *Pygmalion* (1912) is probably the most well-known. According to Greek mythology, Pygmalion is a man who falls in love with one of his female sculptures called Galatea. Unable to endure the sadness of unrequited love, he earnestly prays to Aphrodite, the goddess of love, and eventually the sculpture transforms into a real woman who reciprocates his feelings. In Shaw's play, however, Pygmalion appears as an arrogant phonetics professor named Henry Higgins, and Galatea is represented by Eliza Doolittle, a girl from a lower class who sells flowers on the street. Professor Higgins accidentally overhears Eliza's poor English pronunciation and grammar. He decides to teach her to speak 'proper' English, which would be acceptable in the high society of London, allowing her to pass as an upper-class lady.

As indicated above, certain features of English pronunciation had come to be viewed as a mark of the speaker's class. The pronunciation used by the upper class in the past is today called Received Pronunciation (RP), the traditional standard of British English. With modern advancements in media, most people today are familiar with RP, but in the past it was limited to the upper-class society of central London. In the movie *My Fair Lady* (1964), adapted from Shaw's *Pygmalion*, there is a scene where the female protagonist, played by Audrey Hepburn, walks in a white dress and a large-brimmed hat, politely greeting everyone with a repeated "How do you do?" This highlights the fact that, at that point in the story, Eliza had mastered only this one phrase in flawless RP. Everyone she meets considers her an upper-class lady. The audience might wish that Eliza could meet a similar happy ending with Professor Higgins, as Galatea did with Pygmalion in the Greek myth.

The ending in Shaw's original work, however, is quite different. Higgins' stubbornness eventually causes their relationship to fall apart, and Eliza finds a place in society as a pronunciation teacher. She tells Higgins that although she has a finer ear than he has, she knows how to treat people with politeness and kindness—something he doesn't.[3] Eliza's lines show that the accuracy of pronunciation or the appearance of luxury alone does not represent true nobility. By borrowing an ancient tale, Shaw, with his unexpected ending, satirizes the world that pursues only outward appearances and gives us a lesson on what really matters in life. What drove Shaw to conceive of this brilliant work? As he said, it came from his own imagination: "Imagination is the beginning of creation. You imagine what you desire, you will what you imagine, and at last you create what you will."[4]

The Search for Dr. Livingstone, 1872. Wellcome Library, London

Shaw's Poem:

Imagination

I used to play at Pirates,
And sailed the seven seas.
Then I was a cowboy,
These simple things did me please.

I had a vivid imagination,
Adventure was always on my mind.
I discovered the joys of reading,
And escaped the daily grind.

Once I lived with the Eskimos,
In the land of ice and snow,
Went hunting and a fishing,
My fantasy was all aglow.

I read a book of Jules Verne*,
And went off to the moon,
It was just to take a look,
Then it was time to return.

I spent time in the forests of Africa,
With Dr. Livingstone** as my guide,
Then off again to America,
With Huckleberry Finn*** I did hide.

---

* Jules Gabriel Verne (1828–1905) was a French novelist and poet, best known for his pioneering works of science fiction, including *Around the World in Eighty Days, Journey to the Center of the Earth, and Twenty Thousand Leagues Under the Seas.*

** Dr. David Livingstone (1813–1873) was a Scottish physician, Christian missionary, and explorer known for his extensive expeditions throughout Africa.

*** Huckleberry Finn is the protagonist of *The Adventures of Huckleberry Finn,* a novel by the American author Mark Twain.

In my world of fantasy and imagination,
I performed such wonderful deeds.
A Hero of all the Nations,
I was the one that did succeed.

Then I grew up my childish world at an end.
I had become serious it nearly drove me around the bend.
I still do like the mysterious,
This is the message I am trying to send.

HUCKLEBERRY FINN.

Huckleberry Finn with a rabbit and gun, from the original 1884 edition of the book

Post-Reading 1. Review

1. Who is George Bernard Shaw?
2. What is the main plot of Shaw's play *Pygmalion* (1912)?
3. How is the story of the movie *My Fair Lady* (1964) different from *Pygmalion* (1912)?

Post-Reading 2. Paraphrasing

Rewrite Shaw's idea as seen in the lines below in simpler, everyday English.

I spent time in the forests of Africa,
With Dr. Livingstone as my guide,
Then off again to America,
With Huckleberry Finn I did hide.

Post-Reading 3. Discussion

1. Do you believe in the Pygmalion effect? Why or why not?
2. Do you think using so-called "standard" English pronunciation, such as RP, is important? Why or why not?
3. What role does imagination play in Shaw's poem "Imagination"?

Post-Reading 4. Critical Thinking

1. What do you think is the role of the kind of imagination that Shaw mentioned at the end of the reading passage?
2. Do you think borrowing ideas from the past is an effective way to build the future? Why or not?
3. What do you think is an effective way to develop imagination?

1B: Phillis Wheatley

Pre-Reading 1. General Questions

1. How much do you know about slavery in America?
2. What do you think about the fate of gifted slaves?
3. In what ways can imagination help someone in need?

Pre-Reading 2. Vocabulary

Guess the meaning of each underlined word and choose its definition from the list below.

1. Thanks to her innate intelligence, she was able to read classics. ________
2. Her most prolific period coincided with the peak of the American War of Independence. ________
3. We hold these truths to be self-evident that all men are created equal. ________
4. She desires to tear down all obstacles that were suffocating her and her clan. ________
5. It is undeniable that what Wheatley had dreamed of became law. ________

A. (a) something that is definitely true and cannot be denied
B. (a) existing naturally from birth; not learned
C. (v) making it hard to breathe or feel free
D. (a) producing many works or results; very productive
E. (a) clearly true and needing no proof

Phillis Wheatley

Phillis Wheatley, whose exact age remains uncertain, is believed to have been born in 1753. Poor record-keeping was not the only reason for her inaccurate birthdate. She was born in West Africa and sold in the United States as a slave around the age of seven or eight. Even the surname Wheatley did not come from her parents but from her enslaver. Back then, slaves often adopted their master's surname—when required. After being bought, they were forced to endure inhumane treatment, including forced labor on farms as well as domestic work and in many cases, even sexual exploitation.

However, Phillis Wheatley's experience differed from that of most slaves. Her owner, Mr. Wheatley, had a daughter named Mary who taught her to read and write. Her aptitude for learning soon caused her owners to recognize her talent and further invest in her education. This was highly unusual for slaves at that time. Thanks to her innate intelligence and the support of her owner's family, she learned the Latin and Greek classics and began composing poetry by the age of 14. In 1773, at the age of 20, she visited England with Mr. Wheatley's son, where her first collection of poems was published by a British publishing house. Her volume was highly acclaimed by contemporary reviewers. Despite her success, which was remarkable in light of the times, she still could not break free from her status as a slave.

Her most prolific period coincided with the height of the American War of Independence. In 1775, the thirteen colonies in the United States went to war against Great Britain to free themselves from British colonial oppression. In 1783, the British finally surrendered, fully granting American independence.

The Declaration of Independence,* issued in July 1776, declares that All people are created equal and are endowed with inalienable rights—among them life, liberty, and the pursuit of happiness. These ideals, asserting that government derives its power from the people and must protect their rights,

* The original Declaration reads, "We hold these truths to be self-evident, that all men are created equal, that they are endowed by their Creator with certain unalienable Rights, that among these are Life, Liberty and the pursuit of Happiness. That to secure these rights, Governments are instituted among Men, deriving their just powers from the consent of the governed, That whenever any Form of Government becomes destructive of these ends, it is the Right of the People to alter or to abolish it, and to institute new Government, laying its foundation on such principles and organizing its powers in such form, as to them shall seem most likely to effect their Safety and Happiness."

must have deeply influenced Wheatley, who lived both as a slave and as an intellectual. Her poem "On Imagination" expresses her yearning for freedom and equality. It also reveals her determination to overcome the oppressive barriers of her time and to transcend the harsh reality suffocating her and her people.

It took nearly 80 years after Phillis Wheatley's death in 1784 for her vision to be recognized in law. In January 1863, during the American Civil War, President Abraham Lincoln issued the Emancipation Proclamation.* It declared that all enslaved people in the rebelling states were to be "forever free," and that the U.S. government—including its military and naval forces—would "recognize and maintain their freedom" and take no action to oppress them.

In the days of Phillis Wheatley, an equal world was merely a figment of her imagination. Yet through the sacrifice and perseverance of those who imagined, hoped, and fought for the vision she had once conceived, it eventually became an undeniable reality in law. While we still have a long way to go before we achieve true equality for all, her poetry offers a glimpse into the power of the imagination to move society forward.

Cargo of newly released slaves on board HMS London

* The original Proclamation reads, "That on the first day of January, in the year of our Lord one thousand eight hundred and sixty-three, all persons held as slaves within any State or designated part of a State, the people whereof shall then be in rebellion against the United States, shall be then, thenceforward, and forever free; and the Executive Government of the United States, including the military and naval authority thereof, will recognize and maintain the freedom of such persons, and will do no act or acts to repress such persons, or any of them, in any efforts they may make for their actual freedom."

Wheatley's Poem:

On Imagination

Imagination! Who can sing thy force?
Or who describe the swiftness of thy course?
Soaring through air to find the bright abode,
Th' empyreal palace of the thund'ring God,
We on thy pinions can surpass the wind,
And leave the rolling universe behind:
From star to star the mental optics rove,
Measure the skies, and range the realms above.
There in one view we grasp the mighty whole,
Or with new worlds amaze th' unbounded soul.

- thy: they, imagination
- th': the
- thund'ring: thundering
- pinions: wings (of birds)
- the mental optics: imagination

A formerly enslaved woman sits outside the plantation home where she had once been held in bondage. Photo by Jack Delano, May 1941

Post-Reading 1. Review

1. Who was Phillis Wheatley?
2. What is the main idea of the Declaration of Independence?
3. How was Phillis Wheatley's life and experiences as a slave different from those of other enslaved people in her time? What factors contributed to these differences?

Post-Reading 2. Paraphrasing

Rewrite Wheatley's idea as seen in the lines below in simpler, everyday English.

> Soaring through air to find the bright abode,
> Th' empyreal palace of the thund'ring God,
> We on thy pinions can surpass the wind,
> And leave the rolling universe behind.

Post-Reading 3. Discussion

1. Describe what kind of world Wheatley envisions in her poem, "On Imagination."
2. Discuss the impact of imagination on Wheatley's life and success.
3. What factors may have nurtured or inspired Wheatley's imagination and creativity in her writings.

Post-Reading 4. Critical Thinking

1. Do you think an individual's imagination can help change the world? Provide a specific example to support your opinion.
2. Is it hypocritical or kind that Mr. Wheatley gave Phillis Wheatley a chance to develop her talent as a poet while still owning her as a slave?
3. Do you think the goals of the Emancipation Proclamation have now been realized? Provide examples to support your view.

Unit 2

We Dream!

**But I, being poor, have only my dreams;
I have spread my dreams under your feet;
Tread softly because you tread on my dreams.**

—William Butler Yeats

Preview 1. Main Ideas

1. Through dreams, we are free to explore and turn our ideas into reality.
2. Dreams become a motivating force that helps us shape the future we desire.
3. As long as we keep dreaming, our future will never grow dark.

Preview 2. Keywords

Define the words below in your own words. Then, search online for example sentences that show how each word is used. Share your definitions and sentences with your partner.

1. dreams:

2. fantasy:

3. a motivating force:

4. *The Chronicles of Narnia*:

5. proverb:

Preview 3. Talking About

Look at the following questions and discuss your ideas with a partner.

1. Discuss various meanings of the word "dream."
2. Share an example of a dream that became reality for someone.

Preview 4. Further Discussion

1. What dreams do you have for your future?
2. Do you have any specific plans to achieve your dreams?
3. Do you agree that dreams have the power to change our future? Give an example or a reason.

All humans dream. Dreams are our silent hopes and wishes, unfolding on the endless stage of our minds, where we see reflections of our ideal selves and our views of the world. In this limitless space, we are free to explore and shape any idea or fantasy, no matter how impossible it may seem in real life.

In her poem "We dream—it is good we are dreaming," Emily Dickinson suggests that dreaming is comforting. However, she also implies that if we were fully awake, our dreams might actually hurt us. Dreams offer an escape from the pain of reality, yet they can also make reality feel even harsher by contrast. The more clearly we become aware of life's difficulties, the stronger our desire grows to retreat into dreams. This shows the deep contrast between the world of dreams and the world we live in.

Despite this contrast, Self-Discrepancy Theory suggests that even when dreams seem far from reality, recognizing the gap between the two can become a motivating force to create the future we desire. Dreaming is not just wishful thinking—it is an essential first step toward making concrete plans. That is why we need to dream.

C. S. Lewis once said that we are never too old to set another goal or to dream a new dream,[5] emphasizing the power of imagination to keep us young at heart. Lewis himself lived by this belief. Rather than settling for the familiar, he imagined and created entirely new worlds. In his fifties, while working as a professor of philosophy and Renaissance literature at the University of Cambridge, he published *The Chronicles of Narnia*, a beloved fantasy series that continues to inspire readers around the world to explore their own imagination and sense of wonder.

Dreams are a driving force that can improve both our lives and the world when we imagine, believe, and take action. Everyone has different dreams. Some hope for a better future for themselves, others for happier relationships, and still others for a better world for future generations. There is a Greek proverb that says, "A society grows great when old men plant trees in whose shade they shall never sit." As long as we continue to dream, our future will never lose its light. What are you dreaming of today?

2A: William Butler Yeats

Pre-Reading 1. General Questions

1. Search for information about William Butler Yeats online.
2. Explore the historical relationship between Ireland and the British Empire.
3. Find a song or poem about dreams. How is the dream described in it?

Pre-Reading 2. Vocabulary

Guess the meaning of each underlined word and choose its definition from the list below.

1. Unlike his <u>illustrious</u> writing career, love was a bitter thing. ________

2. Yeats was concerned that her reputation would be <u>tarnished</u> by scandal. ________

3. His love for her hardly <u>wavered</u> despite the hardship. ________

4. He must have felt <u>betrayed</u> by her. ________

5. Yeats' literary world became even more mysterious and <u>profound</u>. ________

A. (v) To make something lose its shine or good reputation
B. (a) highly distinguished; famous; renowned
C. (a) having or showing great knowledge or insight; deep; very thoughtful
D. (v) to hurt (someone who trusts you) by not helping or doing something morally wrong
E. (v) to become unsteady; begin to give way

William Butler Yeats

William Butler Yeats, one of Ireland's most cherished writers, was born in Dublin in 1865. He is one of the major poets who holds a significant place in the history of English poetry, alongside William Wordsworth and T. S. Eliot. In 1923, at the age of 58, he won the Nobel Prize for Literature. He did not stop there; he continued to develop a unique worldview in his writings until his death in 1939, demonstrating his sharp intellect and imagination.

Unlike his illustrious writing career, love was a bitter thing that caused him great disappointment in life. He first met Maud Gonne, an Irish independence activist and theatre actress, when he was 24 years old. At first glance, he fell in love with Maud who he regarded as passionate and lively. Despite his contemplative personality, he devoted himself to the independence movement in which she was involved. His love hardly wavered even after Maud had a child by another man. Yeats was more deeply concerned that her reputation might be tarnished by scandal than he was distressed by her choice of another man. He willingly proposed to be the guardian of her and her child, but Yeats' proposal was rejected. This occurred when he was just 26 years old. He went on to propose to her three more times by age 51.

In the meantime, Yeats saw another woman but eventually returned to Maud. He must have felt betrayed by her, as she turned down his proposals and finally married John MacBride, a leader in the Irish independence movement. Unfortunately, MacBride was arrested in 1916 and executed for leading the Easter Rising in Dublin against the British Empire. Soon after, Yeats visited Maud and once again offered her his hand in marriage. When even this proposal was rejected, he finally abandoned all thoughts of marrying her. The following fall, he married Georgiana Hyde-Lees. With her, Yeats' literary world became even more profound and symbolically rich. However, it seems that his love for Maud Gonne never completely faded.

If there was one thing that Yeats loved as much as Maud Gonne, it was his homeland, Ireland—a country filled with mysterious legends. Surrounded by the sea and facing its dangers, Ireland remained somewhat isolated from the European continent, which helped its people preserve a unique way of thinking and traditional culture. Even today, the Irish "are accustomed to thinking fondly of medieval or early Ireland."[6] Yeats was deeply connected to his roots and fascinated by the mystical folktales passed down through generations. According to an anecdote he told, when he was a child, he once saw a mysterious light moving over a river where the waters rushed fiercely.[7] To him, it looked like someone was walking in the water carrying a bright torch, although he knew such a thing was impossible. Even as an adult and a man of letters, he continued to draw creative inspiration from the traditional culture and history of Ireland.

Maud Gonne

Back then, Ireland was in a dire situation. Irish aspirations for independence from the British Empire came to a head, and an era of turmoil against the oppression of the Empire began. Many were publicly executed for leading uprisings against British rule. Under such circumstances, Yeats wrote about the Golden Age—the first era of humankind in Greek mythology—when people were peaceful, happy, and complete. According to Yeats, the present world feels imperfect and fragmented compared to that ideal time, yet he believed that the kindly and perfect world still exists somewhere beyond our reach. This reflects not only the sorrow he felt for this reality but also his hope for the future. Let us reflect on the world he dreamed of.

Yeats' Poem:

The Lake Isle of Innisfree

I will arise and go now, and go to Innisfree,
And a small cabin build there, of clay and wattles made;
Nine bean-rows will I have there, a hive for the honey-bee,
And live alone in the bee-loud glade.

And I shall have some peace there, for peace comes dropping slow,
Dropping from the veils of the morning to where the cricket sings;
There midnight's all a glimmer, and noon a purple glow,
And evening full of the linnet's wings.

I will arise and go now, for always night and day
I hear lake water lapping with low sounds by the shore;
While I stand on the roadway, or on the pavements grey,
I hear it in the deep heart's core.

- rows: long narrow lines of soil prepared for planting crops
- glade: an open space in the woods with no houses or fields
- a purple: a purple glow or bloom, often from heather-covered hills

The Lake Isle of Innisfree. Photo by Kenneth Allene, licensed under CC BY-SA 2.0 via Wikimedia Commons

Post-Reading 1. Review

1. Talk about the historical background in which William Butler Yeats lived.
2. Talk about the women Yeats loved.
3. What do you think had the most significant influence on Yeats' literature?

Post-Reading 2. Paraphrasing

Rewrite Yeats' idea as seen in the lines below in simpler, everyday English.

> I will arise and go now, and go to Innisfree,
> And a small cabin build there, of clay and wattles made;
> Nine bean-rows will I have there, a hive for the honey-bee,
> And live alone in the bee-loud glade.

Post-Reading 3. Discussion

1. Was the love between Yeats and Maud Gonne impossible from the beginning?
2. Talk about how his love for Maud Gonne influenced Yeats' literary work.
3. Describe Yeats' reality at the time and how it might have influenced "The Lake Isle of Innisfree."
4. Yeats' dream in the poem seems like an escape from reality. What effect do you think the conflict between his reality as an independence activist and his dream had on the public or himself?

Post-Reading 4. Critical Thinking

1. How much do you agree that imagination is the driving force that transforms our reality into the future we desire?
2. Discuss the influence of Yeats' literature on Ireland's independence movement.
3. As long as we keep on dreaming, never will our future grow dark. Do you agree with this? What dreams are you dreaming of?

2B: Lewis Carroll

Pre-Reading 1. General Questions

1. Search for information about Lewis Carroll online.
2. Search for the storyline of *Alice's Adventures in Wonderland* written by Lewis Carroll.
3. Describe the key cultural, scientific, and political changes of the mid-19th century that influenced Lewis Carroll and his work.

Pre-Reading 2. Vocabulary

Guess the meaning of each underlined word and choose its definition from the list below.

1. The world was preparing for a new era and for new ideas to unfold. ______
2. The atmosphere in his house was conservative but not restrictive. ______
3. Boys should be brought up conforming to the social norms of the time. ______
4. He showed an extraordinary talent for mathematics. ______
5. Carroll did not see it as insurmountable and eventually solved it. ______

A. (n) a standard of behavior or mindset that is considered normal or expected.
B. (a) too great or difficult to overcome
C. (a) limiting one's freedom to act or think; placing controls or constraints on behavior
D. (v) to become known, revealed or developed
E. (a) having very special, unusual, or remarkable talent or quality

Lewis Carroll, 1856

Lewis Carroll's real name was Charles Lutwidge Dodgson, famous for *Alice's Adventures in Wonderland.* He was born in January 1832, between Charles Darwin's historic journey to explore new worlds on the HMS *Beagle* in 1831 and the first general election after the Reform Act in Britain a year later. The former marked the beginning point of Darwin's theory of evolution, and the latter is an event that was a significant step in the development of political democracy in the country. It was a time when the world was preparing for a new era and for new ideas to unfold.

His family was not aristocratic but upper-middle-class who had long ago settled in the northwest of England. The atmosphere in his house was conservative but not restrictive enough to hinder Carroll's free intellectual development. He acquired most of his basic knowledge at home and read many books considered advanced for his age. Through this habit, he broadened his imagination beyond the familiar and enjoyed the freedom to imagine a world he had never known.

This freedom came to an end in 1846 when Carroll entered Rugby School, one of the most famous private boarding schools. He spent three years there under strict day-and-night discipline. Mid-nineteenth-century British society, often called the Victorian era, valued gentleness, moral virtue, and religious respectability over physical vigor. As a result, education focused on producing mild and well-mannered gentlemen rather than encouraging individuality or strength. Under such conditions, students faced heavy academic pressure and strict regulations, sometimes even physical punishment. Although Carroll achieved good grades and made friends, the oppressive atmosphere of the school made him weary. He later recalled that he had no fond memories of those three years and never wished to experience them again.

In 1850 he was admitted to Christ Church, Oxford, where he gained a newfound sense of freedom. He showed an extraordinary talent for mathematics, enough to receive first-class honors in Mathematics Moderations, an examination assessing students' academic performance in their first year. Three years later, he was appointed to the Christ Church Mathematical Lectureship. He went on to build a solid reputation as a mathematician. Especially during the last decade of his life, he published several notable essays on mathematics. One of these, titled "On a Method for Finding the Day of the Week for Any Date," explained how to calculate the day of the week for any given date without relying on an almanac. At that time, it was difficult for anyone to determine a day and date in the past or future because there were no calculators or computers. Although many considered this inconvenient, few could find an easy solution. Carroll, however, saw it as an insurmountable challenge and eventually solved it because he was deeply interested in mental calculation methods.

Carroll began his literary career in 1856, a period that also marked the start of his successful journey as a mathematician. During this early phase, he published his first poems and also ventured into writing short stories, although these initial literary efforts were met with only limited recognition. Finally, he gained international fame with the publication of *Alice's Adventures in Wonderland* in 1865 and *Through the Looking-Glass* in 1871. Many literary works for children were published during his time, but Carroll's books stand out for being original, experimental, and free from the moral lessons common in his era. For example, when Alice asks the Footman, "What am I to do?" he simply replies, "Anything you like."[8] In another scene, the Cheshire Cat explains that the direction Alice should take depends on where she wants to go. Since their publication, these books have posed numerous questions for readers, encouraging them to think, dream, and imagine.

88

"The Queen of Hearts she made some tarts
All on a summer day:
The Knave of Hearts he stole those tarts,
And took them quite away!"

"Now for the evidence," said the King, "and then the sentence."

"No!" said the Queen, "first the sentence, and then the evidence!"

"Nonsense!" cried Alice, so loudly that everybody jumped, "the idea of having the sentence first!"

"Hold your tongue!" said the Queen.

"I won't!" said Alice, "you're nothing but a pack of cards! Who cares for you?"

At this the whole pack rose up into the air, and came flying down upon her: she gave a little scream of fright, and tried to beat them off, and found herself lying on the bank, with her head in the lap of her sister, who was gently brushing away some leaves that had fluttered down from the trees on to her face.

A page from Lewis Carroll's original handwritten manuscript and illustration for *Alice's Adventures Under Ground*, the early version of *Alice's Adventures in Wonderland*

Carroll died in 1898, just as Modernism was emerging. Yet his works continued to be loved. In fact, their popularity has steadily increased since. Perhaps that is why it makes you exclaim as Alice did, "What a curious feeling!"[9]

Carroll's Poem:

Life is but a Dream

A boat, beneath a sunny sky
Lingering onward dreamily
In an evening of July

Children three that nestle near,
Eager eye and willing ear,
Pleased a simple tale to hear

Long has paled that sunny sky;
Echoes fade and memories die;
Autumn frosts have slain July.

Still she haunts me, phantomwise,
Alice moving under skies
Never seen by waking eyes.

Children yet, the tale to hear,
Eager eye and willing ear,
Lovingly shall nestle near.

In a Wonderland they lie,
Dreaming as the days go by,
Dreaming as the summers die;

Ever drifting down the stream
Lingering in the golden gleam
Life, what is it but a dream?

Photograph of the Liddell sisters—Lorina, Alice, and Edith—taken by Lewis Carroll. Alice Liddell (center) is widely believed to have inspired the character of Alice in *Alice's Adventures in Wonderland*

- linger: to stay somewhere longer than necessary because you don't want to leave
- nestle: to sit or lie in a warm, comfortable position, often close to someone or something.
- phantomwise: in a ghost-like manner

Post-Reading 1. Review

1. Briefly summarize the characteristics of the era in which Carroll was born.
2. Describe Carroll's life, highlighting the differences between his childhood and school years.
3. Why have Carroll's novels remained popular for so long?
4. What key themes did Carroll intend to convey in his poem "Life is but a Dream"?

Post-Reading 2. Paraphrasing

Rewrite Carroll's idea as seen in the lines below in simpler, everyday English.

In a Wonderland they lie,
Dreaming as the days go by,
Dreaming as the summers die;

Ever drifting down the stream
Lingering in the golden gleam
Life, what is it but a dream?

Post-Reading 3. Discussion

1. Which part of Carroll's life most influenced the world he created in works like *Alice's Adventures in Wonderland*.
2. Why do you think Carroll became a children's novelist while living a successful life as a mathematician.

Post-Reading 4. Critical Thinking

1. Do you think the era in which a person was born affects the way they think, imagine, and dream? If so, how do you think it affected Carroll?
2. Discuss whether or not a repressive school environment can be effective in fostering creativity.
3. Do you think fantasy novels like *Alice's Adventures in Wonderland* help foster children's dreams and imagination? Why or why not?
4. When thinking about the future, is it more beneficial to set realistic goals or to aim for ambitious, even seemingly impossible, dreams? Discuss the potential advantages and disadvantages of both approaches.

Unit 3

We Create Reality!

Creativity is seeing what others see and thinking what no one else has ever thought.

—Albert Einstein

Preview 1. Main Ideas

1. Creative thinking emerges from our everyday experiences.
2. Dreaming of new ways to approach everyday problems marks the true beginning of creative thinking.
3. We all need sufficient flexibility to avoid limiting the scope of our thoughts.

Preview 2. Keywords

Define the words below in your own words. Then, search online for example sentences that show how each word is used. Share your definitions and sentences with your partner.

1. groundbreaking:

____

2. sophistication:

____

3. formula:

____

4. flexibility:

____

5. adaptable:

____

6. threshold:

____

Preview 3. Talking About

Look at the following questions and discuss your ideas with a partner.

1. Give some practical examples of creative thinking that you used or observed in your daily life.
2. What are the results or effects of flexible thinking in problem-solving?

Preview 4. Further Discussion

1. What do you think is the greatest invention in human history?
2. What do you think are the main factors that have shaped K-culture worldwide?
3. What are your future goals or plans?

Through creative thinking, people come up with groundbreaking inventions that have had a tremendous impact on humanity, or outstanding works of art that have ushered in new eras for culture and society. Is creative thinking something extraordinarily far from us? Not at all! One of the first tools made by humankind was a hammer. These early hammers were undoubtedly primitive and lacked sophistication. Nevertheless, they were a monumental and practical invention. Why did human ancestors make a hammer? They must have experienced discomfort in their lives and dreamed of better ways to solve the problems of everyday life.

Let's look at another example around us. According to a Netflix show, *Seo Taiji & Boys* are now seen as a cultural symbol that represents major changes not only in Korea's music industry but also in its wider social and cultural environment.[10] The show also explains that South Korea became a pop culture powerhouse by turning the group's unique style into a successful formula. Few people at the time expected that Seo Taiji & Boys would later receive such recognition or that their debut would be viewed as a turning point in Korean cultural history. They achieved this influence by challenging traditional musical formats and norms, creating a style uniquely their own.

Creative thinking begins with the simple wish to improve our current lives. Dreams guide us toward a better reality, and imagination drives every step of the process. To make our dreams come true, we need a flexible mindset—one that keeps our thinking open and free from limitations. Flexibility, in most cases, develops through learning and experience. As we gain knowledge and connect new ideas with what we already know, our thinking naturally becomes more adaptable. This adaptability not only helps us navigate change in every aspect of life—from work and relationships to society—but also enables us to turn challenges into opportunities for growth and creativity. Engaging in activities such as reading, discussion, and critical thinking further strengthens this capacity, stimulating our minds and preparing us to imagine and shape new possibilities. Standing at this threshold, we are invited to step forward into a world shaped by creativity.

3A: Emily Brontë

Pre-Reading 1. General Questions

1. Search for information about Emily Brontë online.
2. Talk about the main characters and plot of *Wuthering Heights* (1847).
3. Why did female writers often use pseudonyms?
4. Talk about the social atmosphere in the 19th century in which Emily Brontë lived.

Pre-Reading 2. Vocabulary

Guess the meaning of each underlined word and choose its definition from the list below.

1. Her only <u>companions</u> were her sisters. _______

2. We can <u>infer</u> that she lived a life full of passion and imagination. _______

3. It was common for female writers to use <u>pseudonyms</u> when publishing books. _______

4. *Wuthering Heights*, unlike her <u>reclusive</u> life, was full of passion and love. _______

5. It is regarded as a <u>masterpiece</u>. _______

6. This space <u>evoked</u> her infinite imagination. _______

A. (n) people or animals with whom one spends a lot of time or travels
B. (v) to bring a memory, feeling, or image into the mind
C. (n) fake names used by writers instead of their real ones
D. (n) an artist's or writer's greatest and most outstanding piece of work
E. (v) to deduce or conclude something based on evidence and reasoning, not explicit statements
F. (a) tending to keep away from other people; preferring solitude

Emily Brontë was born in 1818 and lived only to the age of 30, but her legacy endures to the present and will certainly continue for ages. Shortly after her birth, her father Patrick was appointed perpetual curate in Haworth, where the Brontë family settled. Emily was never married and kept a very small social circle; her closest companions were her sisters, Charlotte and Anne, who were also well-known writers in their own right.

The Brontë sisters,
by their brother Branwell Brontë in 1834

Emily began working as an assistant teacher at the age of 17 at Roe Head School, where Charlotte was employed. However, she soon came back home due to poor health and homesickness. Charlotte kept teaching and later got married. Emily, on the other hand, spent most of her life in Haworth with Anne. The two lived modestly and supported each other, taking care of their brother Branwell, who suffered from mental illness and alcoholism. Anne, nearly two years younger than Emily, died in 1849—one year after Emily. The two were known for being inseparable.

It seems that her life must have been utterly quiet, even dull. However, her inner world was certainly not. Through Emily's only novel, *Wuthering Heights* (1847), we can infer that she lived a life full of passion and imagination that no one, except for her sister Anne, could have guessed. When Emily first published her book, she used the pseudonym 'Ellis Bell.' At the time, it was common for women writers to use pseudonyms when publishing books, as it was believed that their works would be undervalued because of prejudice against female writers. The famous novel *Frankenstein: Or the Modern Prometheus,* written by Mary Shelley, was also initially published anonymously. Emily, however, used a pseudonym out of consideration for the reputation of her religious family and her father's social status, and likely because she did not want to be noticed by others.

Emily Brontë's *Wuthering Heights* is very different from her quiet, reclusive life. The novel is full of passion. It tells the story of Heathcliff, an orphan adopted by the Earnshaw family, who falls deeply in love with Catherine Earnshaw. However, Catherine chooses to marry Edgar Linton, a wealthy neighbor, for social status. Feeling betrayed, Heathcliff leaves but later returns rich and determined to take revenge on everyone who hurt him. His obsessive love for Catherine and his thirst for revenge drive the story forward. Heathcliff is passionate, proud, and often cruel. His deep love for Catherine drives both his happiness and his hatred. Catherine is torn between her love for Heathcliff and her desire for a comfortable life, which ultimately leads to tragedy.

When it was first published, *Wuthering Heights* shocked many readers. A review at the time noted that "readers are shocked, disgusted, almost sickened by details of cruelty and inhumanity."[11] Its daring exploration of themes such as destructive passion, revenge, and social inequality challenged Victorian ideals of morality and feminine virtue. Nothing like it was published before, and it still remains one of the most passionate and intense novels in English literature, now universally regarded as a masterpiece. From a literary perspective, *Wuthering Heights* is considered a tragedy because the characters' intense love and desire for revenge destroy their own happiness and bring suffering to everyone around them. For this reason, it is often listed alongside *King Lear* and *Moby-Dick* as one of the three greatest tragedies ever written in English.

What led Emily Brontë to this new and shocking path of creation? Perhaps the wilderness surrounding Haworth became a space that evoked her boundless imagination—like a sketchbook where she could draw anything she wished. Anne, who published two novels as sensational as *Wuthering Heights*, must have supported and encouraged Emily's imagination. We know that imagination can grow even further when it is shared, as was the case with Emily and Anne's relationship. Regardless of where Emily's imagination came from, her mind transcended the physical boundaries of Haworth and created an entirely new world and history. This helps us see more clearly how imagination fuels creativity.

A scene from the 1939 film *Wuthering Heights*

Brontë's Poem:

To Imagination

When weary with the long day's care,
And earthly change from pain to pain,
And lost and ready to despair,
Thy kind voice calls me back again:
Oh, my true friend! I am not lone,
While thou canst speak with such a tone!

So hopeless is the world without;
The world within I doubly prize;
Thy world, where guile, and hate, and doubt,
And cold suspicion never rise;
Where thou, and I, and Liberty,
Have undisputed sovereignty.

What matters it, that, all around,
Danger, and guilt, and darkness lie,
If but within our bosom's bound
We hold a bright, untroubled sky,
Warm with ten thousand mingled rays
Of suns that know no winter days?

Reason, indeed, may oft complain
For Nature's sad reality,
And tell the suffering heart, how vain
Its cherished dreams must always be;
And Truth may rudely trample down
The flowers of Fancy, newly-blown:

But, thou art ever there, to bring
The hovering vision back, and breathe
New glories o'er the blighted spring,
And call a lovelier Life from Death,
And whisper, with a voice divine,
Of real worlds, as bright as thine.

I trust not to thy phantom bliss,
Yet, still, in evening's quiet hour,
With never-failing thankfulness,
I welcome thee, Benignant Power;
Sure solacer of human cares,
And sweeter hope, when hope despairs!

- thy: (archaic) your
- thou: (archaic) you
- Liberty: the goddess liberty
- canst: can
- oft: often
- Its: of it; of the suffering heart
- trust not: do not trust
- never-failing: not changing; infallible or constant
- thee: (archaic, in the objective case) you
- benignant: kind-hearted and generous

The Bronte Way descending from Penistone Hill, Haworth.
Photo by Humphrey Bolton, licensed under CC BY-SA 2.0 via Wikimedia Commons

Post-Reading 1. Review

1. According to reviews at the time, how did readers react to Emily Brontë's novel *Wuthering Heights*?
2. Emily Brontë used the pseudonym Ellis Bell. Why do you think she did this?

Post-Reading 2. Paraphrasing

Rewrite Brontë's idea as seen in the lines below in simpler, everyday English.

> When weary with the long day's care,
> And earthly change from pain to pain,
> And lost and ready to despair,
> Thy kind voice calls me back again:
> Oh, my true friend! I am not lone,
> While thou canst speak with such a tone!

Post-Reading 3. Discussion

1. Discuss why we can say Brontë displayed remarkable creative thinking in her work.
2. What aspects of her life suggest that she lived a secluded life?
3. What powers does imagination have in Brontë's poem "To the Imagination"?
4. Talk about how Anne's relationship with Emily Brontë influenced their writing.

Post-Reading 4. Critical Thinking

1. Why is a book that once created a sensation in society now considered a masterpiece?
2. How can sharing imagination with others lead to its further development?
3. Do you agree with Brontë's idea that imagination comforts and heals despair?

3B: William Wordsworth

Pre-Reading 1. General Questions

1. Search for information about William Wordsworth online.
2. What do you think Romanticism is about?
3. What do you know about the French Revolution?

Pre-Reading 2. Vocabulary

Guess the meaning of each underlined word and choose its definition from the list below.

1. We often refer to an emotional overload or a state of losing contact with reality as *romantic*. _______
2. It implies a nationalistic determination to liberate her colonized motherland. _______
3. It was believed that there was a distinctive and noble language suitable for poetry. _______
4. His ideas were radical compared to conventional poetry found in literary circles of the time. _______
5. He tried to revive their inner peace, which had been lost in the grind of their daily lives. _______
6. All we need is the conviction that these new thoughts aid in the realization of a better world. _______

A. (n) a strong belief or firm opinion about something
B. (n) hard, repetitive, and boring work or routine
C. (n) a condition where there is too much to handle; an overwhelming burden
D. (a) easy to recognize because it is different from others; special
E. (a) very different from the usual, especially in political or social views
F. (v) to set someone or something free

William Wordsworth, born in 1770, was one of the first poets to establish Romanticism in England. We often describe an emotional overload as romantic. However, Romanticism is a much broader concept than that. It originally began with the French Revolution whose spirit was liberty, equality, and fraternity. Therefore, romanticism stood against everything that oppressed equality and freedom.

William Wordsworth

For example, the heroine of a popular Korean drama *Mr. Sunshine* said, "My romance is only in the German-made muzzle."[12] What does her romance mean here? It is not simply an expression of personal affection but rather implies a nationalistic determination to liberate her colonized motherland. In fact, "It is difficult to study either nineteenth-century literature or nineteenth-century history without being struck by the Romantic element in Nationalism."[13] That is, Romanticism is often associated with nationalism. In this light, her romantic feeling expressed in the line above appears to be a reasonable embrace and expression of her nationalistic inclination. As such, it is difficult to properly define Romanticism because its meaning encompasses a wide range of ideas. However, what is clear is that the ideal of romanticism contains a certain energy—one that departs from weary reality and strives toward a new and better one.

As a poet, what was Wordsworth eager to change? His inspiration for poetic reform came from the noble spirit of the French Revolution. It was a great shock to him that common people had opened a new era both for themselves and by themselves. As a poet, he questioned why poetry was not enjoyed by ordinary people. Around that time, it was believed that there was a distinctive and noble language suitable for poetry, and it was considered good only when the rules were followed strictly. So, poetry was the exclusive property of intellectuals and nobles. Wordsworth wished to write poetry that could reach not only aristocrats but also ordinary people. His ideas were radical when compared with conventional poetry found in literary circles of the time. As stated in the "Preface" to *Lyrical Ballads* (1798), he used the everyday language of ordinary people in his poetry. He wrote poems employing grammar and expressions commonly used in spoken language. He tried to show that the essence of poetry was to lie in emotions that naturally overflow, and not to simply follow established rules.

Wordsworth chose nature, enriched with his creative imagination, as the central theme of his poems. He aimed to comfort those exhausted by the rapid social changes brought by the Industrial Revolution. Many have long believed that true peace could be found in the solitude of nature, away from the pressures and fatigue of daily life. However, his view was new in that he saw nature as possessing a special energy capable of connecting with the human mind. According to his philosophy, when we truly communicate with nature by using our imagination, it comforts us and helps restore the inner peace and innocence lost in the grind of daily life. He was convinced that his new poetry could capture and express this process — the human mind gaining its spiritual richness. Perhaps he hoped to create a world where life and art mirror each other.

This is true creativity: rejecting the old and seeking the new. We don't have to cling to the first thought that comes to mind. Creative thinking must be constantly revised and improved, as in the story of Edison, who failed almost ten thousand times before perfecting the light bulb. Like this, creativity grows when we boldly let go of past ideas and pursue even the smallest glimmer of new ideas. All we need is the conviction that these new thoughts contribute to realizing a better world. This is exactly what Wordsworth did. Although it could already be called a work of genius, he continued to refine his work, *The Prelude; or, Growth of a Poet's Mind.* He began it at the age of 28 and completed the first version in 1805 as a 13-book poem. Over the next 50 years, he kept revising it, and after his death in 1850, it was published in an expanded 14-book edition. This work had a great influence on his contemporaries. In recognition of his outstanding achievement, he was appointed Poet Laureate in 1843. Today, he is considered not only one of the greatest Romantic poets but one of the most beloved poets of all time.

Liberty Leading the People by Ferdinand Victor Eugène Delacroix, 1830

Wordsworth's Poem:

Ode: On Intimations of Immortality from Recollections of Early Childhood

The child is father of the man;
And I could wish my days to be
Bound each to each by natural piety.

……

Then sing, ye birds! sing, sing a joyous song!
And let the young lambs bound
As to the tabor's sound!
We, in thought, will join your throng.
Ye that pipe and ye that play.
Ye that through your hearts to-day
Feel the gladness of the May!
What though the radiance which was once so bright
Be now forever taken from my sight,
Though nothing can bring back the hour
Of splendour in the grass, of glory in the flower?
We will grieve not, rather find
Strength in what remains behind
In the primal sympathy
Which, having been, must ever be.
In the soothing thoughts that spring
Out of human suffering,
In the faith that looks through death,
In years that bring the philosophic mind.

Alfoxden House, Somerset, once the home of William Wordsworth

- "Ode: On Intimations of Immortality from Recollections of Early Childhood" is a 206-line poem that consists of eleven stanzas. The quoted part is from the 9th stanza. The well-known three-line epigraph later became part of his other poem, "My Heart Leaps Up."
- ode: a song or poem that honors the merits of a particular person, thing, or event.
- ye: (archaic, poetic) you
- splendour: splendor; great beauty or magnificence
- piety: deep respect or reverence, often religious

Post-Reading 1. Review

1. Define Romanticism based on the reading.
2. Why did Wordsworth think a new type of poem was needed?
3. What effect did Wordsworth want his poetry to have on his readers?
4. How long did it take for Wordsworth to complete *The Prelude; or, Growth of Poet's Mind*?

Post-Reading 2. Paraphrasing

Rewrite Wordsworth's idea as seen in the lines below in simpler, everyday English.

> We will grieve not, rather find
> Strength in what remains behind
> In the primal sympathy
> Which, having been, must ever be.

Post-Reading 3. Discussion

1. What did Wordsworth focus on when writing poetry for ordinary people?
2. Discuss why Wordsworth's poetry emphasizes nature.

Post-Reading 4. Critical Thinking

1. Talk about the significant influence of the ideals of the French Revolution on people's minds.
2. Do you think returning to nature is necessary in today's fast-changing world? How can this idea help people's happiness today?
3. Wordsworth repeatedly revised his work *The Prelude; or, Growth of a Poet's Mind.* Do you think this process reflects true creativity? Why or why not?
4. To create something, you need inspiration and dedication. Which do you think is more important for development?

Further Reading 1

Excerpt from "I Have a Dream"*

Martin Luther King Jr.

Five score years ago, a great American, in whose symbolic shadow we stand today, signed the Emancipation Proclamation. [...]

We refuse to believe that there are insufficient funds in the great vaults of opportunity of this nation. And so we've come to cash this check, a check that will give us upon demand the riches of freedom and the security of justice. [...]

We cannot be satisfied as long as the Negro's basic mobility is from a smaller ghetto to a larger one. [...] No, no, we are not satisfied, and we will not be satisfied until justice rolls down like waters, and righteousness like a mighty stream. [...]

I have a dream that one day on the red hills of Georgia.
I have a dream that my four little children will one day live in a nation where they will not be judged by the color of their skin but by the content of their character. [...]

I have a dream that one day every valley shall be exalted... and the glory of the Lord shall be revealed, and all flesh shall see it together. [...]

Discussion Questions

1. What does King mean by "we've come to cash this check"?
2. Why do you think King repeats "We cannot be satisfied"? What effect does this have?
3. In the "dream" section, what kind of future is King describing?
4. How do these ideas still relate to issues of justice and equality today?

* Martin Luther King Jr.'s "I Have a Dream" speech, delivered in 1963 at the Lincoln Memorial, emphasizes America's broken promise to its Black citizens, the urgent call for justice captured in the refrain "We cannot be satisfied," and the hopeful vision expressed in the repeated words "I have a dream." Through vivid imagery and powerful repetition, King blends legal, emotional, and spiritual appeals to expose injustice while inspiring hope for a more inclusive America.

Further Reading 2

Excerpt from "Pale Blue Dot"*

Carl Sagan

[...] Science is merely an extremely powerful method of winnowing what's true from what feels good. Without the error correcting machinery of science, we are lost to our subjectivity, to our chauvinism, to our longing to be central to the purpose of the universe. [...]

The Earth is a very small stage in a vast cosmic arena. Think of the rivers of blood spilled by all those generals and emperors so that in glory and triumph they could become the momentary masters of a fraction of a dot. Think of the endless cruelties visited by the inhabitants of one corner of the dot on the scarcely distinguishable inhabitants of some other corner. How frequent their misunderstandings, how eager they are to kill one another, how fervent their hatreds. [...]

Our posturings, our imagined self-importance, the delusion that we have some privileged position in the universe, are challenged by this point of pale light. Our planet is a lonely speck in a great enveloping cosmic dark. [...]

In our obscurity, in all this vastness, there is no hint that help will come from elsewhere to save us from ourselves. It is up to us. [...]

Discussion Questions

1. What does Carl Sagan mean by "Our planet is a lonely speck in a great enveloping cosmic dark"?
2. How does the image of Earth as a "pale blue dot" challenge the idea that humans are the center of the universe? Do you find this idea comforting or unsettling?
3. What message do you think Sagan wants future generations to remember from this reflection?

* This excerpt is adapted from Carl Sagan's *Pale Blue Dot: A Vision of the Human Future in Space* (1994), later echoed in his 1995 speech delivered at the United Nations' 50th anniversary celebration, held at the Cathedral of St. John the Divine in New York City. Sagan's reflections remind us that, despite being a tiny presence in the vast universe, humanity has always dared to dream. From stone tools to space probes, we have shaped the world through imagination and inquiry. In Sagan's vision, dreaming is not passive hope but a responsibility: we must understand our science, our place in the cosmos, and each other. The "pale blue dot" is more than home—it is a shared promise to use knowledge wisely, act responsibly, and never stop seeking.

Chapter 2

Empathy and Love

Warm-Up!

Talk about the following questions with your partners.

1. What is empathy? How do you define it in your own words?
2. Can you explain the difference between empathy, altruism, and love?
3. What are the different kinds of love? Can you give examples of each?

Empathy is the ability to understand and share the feelings of others. It is an emotional skill that shapes the way we build relationships and social networks. In today's rapidly changing world, developing social and emotional skills has become more important than ever. As individuals, we benefit from empathy because it strengthens social bonds and helps us connect meaningfully with others.

Empathy plays a larger role in our lives than we might realize. People with a strong sense of empathy often experience greater satisfaction in life. They tend to be healthier both physically and mentally, more creative, and more passionate in their work. Empathy also provides resilience, helping people overcome difficulties without easily giving up. However, empathy is sometimes misunderstood as a sign of weakness. In truth, it is a powerful force for change: it helps us resolve conflicts and build stronger relationships. It also allows us to see problems from multiple perspectives, broadening our awareness beyond individuals to entire communities—and even to the planet we share.

To meet the challenges of rapid social and technological change, we need to act with empathy while holding on to our own identities. Altruism begins with empathy: by putting ourselves in others' shoes, we can understand their thoughts, feelings, and experiences more deeply. Love, too, grows and matures through empathy. There are many forms of love, but all become richer when we learn to see the world from another person's perspective. As John Locke said, "No man's knowledge here can go beyond his experience."[14] In the same way, our ability to empathize depends on broadening our understanding of the lives and experiences of others.

What We Will Read

Unit 4: Joy of Love
Unit 5: Pain of Love
Unit 6: Various Forms of Love Ⅰ: Parents and Children
Unit 7: Various Forms of Love Ⅱ: Friendship
Unit 8: Various Forms of Love Ⅲ: Beyond Boundaries

Further Reading 1: Excerpts from "President Gerald R. Ford's Tribute to President Jimmy Carter"
Further Reading 2: Excerpts from "Farewell Speech"

Unit 4
Joy of Love

Only a life lived for others is worth living.

—Albert Einstein

Preview 1. Main Ideas

1. Love remains difficult to define precisely.
2. Love allows us to find beauty in the world that would otherwise go unnoticed.
3. Mature love is a union that preserves one's individuality.

Preview 2. Keywords

Define the words below in your own words. Then, search online for example sentences that show how each word is used. Share your definitions and sentences with your partner.

1. unrequited love:

   ____

2. multifaceted nature:

   ____

3. star-crossed lovers:

   ____

4. integrity:

   ____

5. mature love:

   ____

Preview 3. Talk About

Look at the following questions and discuss your ideas with a partner.

1. Do you agree that love enables us to overcome challenges or barriers in life?
2. In what ways do you think love can make someone a better person?

Preview 4. Further Discussion

1. Describe a love story you are familiar with other than *Romeo and Juliet*.
2. What lessons or benefits can people gain from experiencing love?
3. Is there an alternative to love? If so, what might it be?
4. Why do you think being in love might challenge a person's sense of identity?
5. How can someone love another deeply while still keeping their own identity and values?

Sometimes described as noble and sometimes as beautiful, love takes many forms: puppy love, first love, unrequited love, or eternal love. Yet, despite its many faces, it remains difficult to define precisely. Because of this multifaceted nature, love has inspired art and literature for thousands of years.

Perhaps the most famous love story of all time is Shakespeare's *Romeo and Juliet*. The two star-crossed lovers meet at a ball and fall in love at first sight. Even though their families are bitter enemies, their love grows quickly and deeply. Romeo risks everything for Juliet, and Juliet gives up everything for Romeo. Love can make us feel as if we are walking on clouds, experiencing emotions we have never known before. It can shake the foundations of our lives or give them deeper meaning.

The psychologist Erich Fromm, author of *The Art of Loving* (1956), explained that mature love is a profound union that still preserves one's integrity and individuality.[15] He suggested that when two people love each other, they feel closely connected but remain independent as individuals. Through this experience, people often come to understand themselves better, learning how to share their feelings while respecting each other's differences. In this way, love helps us grow as individuals while building a strong and positive relationship.

Such love cannot truly be learned in a classroom. Even if it could, we would still miss the true joy of experiencing it. Love teaches us not only about ourselves but also how to form deep connections with others without losing our integrity or individuality. These emotional experiences last much longer than the knowledge we gain through reason or study, remaining with us as powerful memories. As we will see in the poems in these units, exploring love through literature can be even more rewarding than we first imagine.

4A: D. H. Lawrence

Pre-Reading 1. General Questions

1. Search for information about D. H. Lawrence online.
2. What is the plot of his novel, *Lady Chatterley's Lover* (1928)?
3. How can we tell whether a love scene depicted in the work is artistic or beautiful?
4. How many poems did he write, and which ones are especially well-known?

Pre-Reading 2. Vocabulary

Guess the meaning of each underlined word and choose its definition from the list below.

1. The working class in the U.K. was <u>confronted</u> with a major social problem: alcoholism. ________
2. His parents experienced a lot of <u>discord</u> over his father's drinking habits. ________
3. His book reflects a mother's <u>excessive</u> affection. ________
4. The popularity of Lawrence's novels often <u>eclipses</u> the fact that he was also an accomplished poet. ________
5. The essence of his message is that we should <u>restore</u> the powerful energy of life. ________

A. (a) beyond the ordinary, normal, reasonable; immoderate
B. (v) to make (something) less important or popular
C. (v) to return someone or something to the original condition or position
D. (v) to face the challenge
E. (n) disagreement between people, ideas, etc.

D. H. Lawrence

David Herbert Lawrence was born in 1885 in Eastwood, a small coal-mining village in Nottinghamshire, England. His father, a miner, was of the uneducated working class while his mother was a former teacher of middle-class background. At the time, the working class in the U.K. was confronted with a major problem—alcoholism—which caused serious social and economic consequences. From a national perspective, alcohol addiction was the major obstacle to economic productivity, leading to a decline in labor quality and early workforce loss. On a micro level, each family affected by alcohol-related issues suffered from poor health, heavy spending, and domestic violence.

Lawrence's family was no exception. His parents experienced much discord over his father's drinking habits, and his mother, who had a background in education, deeply resented him. This situation led his mother to devote her affection to her children, and after the death of her eldest son, that affection was fully concentrated on Lawrence. Lawrence's first novel *Sons and Lovers* (1913) was based on his own experiences, showing a mother's excessive affection and her son's sense of being pressured by it.

Though his novels are now listed among the great classics, at the time of their publication, they caused considerable controversy. For example, when his novel *Sons and Lovers* was first published, the editor replaced certain words with what were considered more "decent" alternatives at the time. Words like hips were changed to body and thighs to limbs, and several scenes were omitted because they were considered too erotic or overly sensational.[16] Another of his famous novels, *Lady Chatterley's Lover,* was published in Italy in 1928 and France in 1929 but was banned in Britain for obscenity. It was not until around 30 years later that the complete version was officially printed for the first time in the UK by Penguin Books in 1960. A famous story tells that the typist who first typed this novel refused to continue working because it was too explicit. With such a background, his novels often became the subject of unfair and prejudiced opinions, with critics claiming that his works could arouse inappropriate feelings in readers.

However, his aim was not to dwell on the surface-level relationships among the characters; he set out to criticize the mechanized civilization and capitalist order that he saw as the chronic illness of modern society. He portrayed people as worn down by this system, yet maintained that human beings are filled with vitality and innately seeking freedom. The essence of his message is that we should restore the powerful energy of life and return to our free nature.

Allen Lane, founder of Penguin Books and co-defendant in the 1960 trial under the Obscene Publications Act for publishing *Lady Chatterley's Lover*

The popularity of Lawrence's novels often eclipses the fact that he was also an accomplished poet. His poems are as highly regarded as his novels, and many consider them to have enriched the history of literature. The themes of his poems are similar to those of his novels, praising the primal energy and innate freedom of humans. His poems are simple yet free-spirited. Critics have described his poetry as energetic, direct, and emotionally engaging. In his poetry, nature is full of vitality, and humans wholeheartedly embrace this vitality as their own.

"First Morning," his poem included in this unit, describes humans as being most alive when in nature with a beloved one. The lovers are transformed into beings filled with primordial energy. When they spend the night indoors, separated from nature, their time is filled with skepticism, doubt, and anxiety. On the contrary, the morning bursts with freedom and vitality when they are together. If you were to spend a morning with your lover for the first time, would it be the kind of morning Lawrence described? Regrettably, Lawrence passed away too soon. In 1930, at the age of 45, he died from complications of tuberculosis. He never saw his most famous novel, *Lady Chatterley's Lover,* published in his homeland. Had he lived longer, our literary history would have been even richer.

Lawrence's Poem:

D. H. Lawrence with his wife Frieda, 1914

First Morning

The night was a failure
    but why not—?

In the darkness
    with the pale dawn seething at the window
    through the black frame
    I could not be free,
    not free myself from the past, those others-
    and our love was a confusion,
    there was a horror,
    you recoiled away from me.

Now, in the morning
As we sit in the sunshine on the seat by the little shrine,
And look at the mountain-walls,
Walls of blue shadow,
And see so near at our feet in the meadow
Myriads of dandelion pappus
Bubbles ravelled in the dark green grass
Held still beneath the sunshine—

It is enough, you are near—
The mountains are balanced,
The dandelion seeds stay half-submerged in the grass;
You and I together
We hold them proud and blithe
On our love.
They stand upright on our love,
Everything starts from us,
We are the source.

- seething: moving like boiling; full of intense activity or emotion
- dandelion: a common wild plant with bright yellow flowers and fluffy white seed heads (Korean: 민들레)
- Pappus: fine hairs on a dandelion seed that help it float in the wind

Post-Reading 1. Review

1. What was Lawrence's home environment like when he was a child?
2. Why did the editor replace some words in *Sons and Lovers* when it was first published?
3. What message did Lawrence aim to convey about human relationships in his novel?

Post-Reading 2. Paraphrasing

Rewrite Lawrence's idea as seen in the lines below in simpler, everyday English.

It is enough, you are near—
The mountains are balanced,
The dandelion seeds stay half-submerged in the grass;
You and I together
We hold them proud and blithe
On our love.
They stand upright on our love,
Everything starts from us,
We are the source.

Post-Reading 3. Discussion

1. Discuss what you think is the difference between obscenity and art.
2. The editor replaced some words in Lawrence's work *Sons and Lovers*. How might these changes affect the artistic integrity of the work and the writer's original intent?
3. Does this poem depict mature love? Find the lines that support your answer and discuss it.

Post-Reading 4. Critical Thinking

1. How can spending time with a loved one change the way you see the world or understand things?
2. In his poem, what does this line "Everything starts from us / We are the source" mean?
3. Do you agree with the idea that love restores human vitality? If so, how?
4. Discuss social issues that affect relationships between people today.

4B: Elizabeth Barrett Browning

Pre-Reading 1. General Questions

1. Search for information about Elizabeth Barrett Browning.
2. Talk about a love relationship that begins without the two people meeting in person.
3. Find a song that expresses the feeling when love first begins.

Pre-Reading 2. Vocabulary

Guess the meaning of each underlined word and choose its definition from the list below.

1. Her parents recognized her literary talent and paid the greatest attention to her.

   ____

2. She began having health problems causing severe headaches and back pain.

   ____

3. She published a new collection of poetry, which led to one of the most famous love stories in the history of English literature. ________

4. Robert became captivated by them and sent her a letter full of praise. ________

5. It is probable that Elizabeth did not want to show her feelings to others. ________

A. (a) very bad, serious, or unpleasant; causing pain or suffering
B. (a) likely to happen; expected
C. (a) strongly attracted to or fascinated by someone or something
D. (v) to cause or bring about a particular result
E. (n) the ability of a person to be naturally good at something

Elizabeth Barrett Browning is always referred to by her full name so as not to confuse her with her husband, Robert Browning, who was also a notable poet of the 19th century. Elizabeth was born in 1806 and wrote her first poem at the age of eleven. She originally had twelve siblings, but one died in infancy. Her parents recognized her literary talent and paid particular attention to her. Her father was very proud of her poetic gift, and her mother collected all of her early poems. In the early 19th century, there was a general lack of interest in developing women's intellectual abilities. It appears that her parents stood out compared to most families of those days.

Elizabeth Barrett Browning by Károly Brocky, c. 1839–1844

Given that her father, a successful entrepreneur, and her mother, who came from a family with a strong financial base, one could expect that Elizabeth's life would have been comfortable and smooth in every way. Contrary to expectations, her life was far from it. After falling off a horse at the age of nine and sustaining a severe injury, she began experiencing health problems, including chronic headaches and back pain that left her physically inactive. Historical records reveal that her condition was so serious that doctors prescribed opiates, and she continued to live with persistent pain even after regaining partial health as an adult. As a result, she could neither make her debut nor attend social gatherings, as ordinary middle- and upper-class young ladies could. Instead, she spent most of her time reading books and writing poems. By reflecting on the nature of life and existence, her poetic world grew more profound.

Due to her health problems and isolation, she might have remained single all her life if she hadn't met Robert Browning. After publishing her first collection of poetry in 1838, her fame as a poet soon rose because of her outstanding talent and the deep emotions expressed in her works. In 1844, she published another collection of poetry, which led to one of the most famous love stories in the history of English literature. Robert was six years younger than Elizabeth and, at that time, had a less established career as a poet. After reading Elizabeth's poems, Robert sent her a letter full of praise, which could be described as a *fan letter*: he confessed that, ever since reading her poems, he had been completely captivated and loved her verses with all his heart, and that his praise was entirely sincere.*

Through their correspondence of over 570 letters, they eventually developed a relationship based on mutual love and respect. Robert wanted to save Elizabeth from her illness and isolation and decided to take her to Italy. The two secretly married despite opposition from Elizabeth's parents. In Italy, they happily supported each other, and Elizabeth became much healthier thanks to Robert's care. Although they spent much of their time abroad, her literary reputation in Britain continued to grow. After fifteen years of a happy marriage, Elizabeth passed away. Robert never remarried.

Elizabeth's love for Robert is clearly expressed in her 44 sonnets, written within two years beginning in 1845, when she first met Robert. They were given the title *Sonnets from the Portuguese* (1850), which made them appear as if translated from Portuguese poetry. Probably, Elizabeth did not want to reveal her feelings openly. The poems in this collection have been well-loved by readers ever since they were published and are regarded as among the most beautiful expressions of the emotions inspired by love.

Portraits of Elizabeth Barrett and Robert Browning by Thomas Buchanan Read

* The original letter reads, "I love your verses with all my heart, dear Miss Barrett,—and this is no off-hand complimentary letter that I shall write,—whatever else, no prompt matter-of-course recognition of your genius, and there a graceful and natural end of the thing. Since the day last week when I first read your poems, I quite laugh to remember how I have been turning and turning again in my mind what I should be able to tell you of their effect upon me, for in the first flush of delight I thought I would this once get out of my habit of purely passive enjoyment, when I do really enjoy, and thoroughly justify my admiration..."[17]

Browning's Poem:

How do I love thee?*

How do I love thee? Let me count the ways.
I love thee to the depth and breadth and height
My soul can reach, when feeling out of sight
For the ends of being and ideal grace.
I love thee to the level of every day's
Most quiet need, by sun and candle-light.
I love thee freely, as men strive for right.
I love thee purely, as they turn from praise.
I love thee with the passion put to use
In my old griefs, and with my childhood's faith.
I love thee with a love I seemed to lose
With my lost saints. I love thee with the breath,
Smiles, tears, of all my life; and, if God choose,
I shall but love thee better after death.

Clasped Hands of Robert Browning and Elizabeth Barrett Browning, cast from a plaster life-cast made in Rome in 1853 by Harriet Goodhue Hosmer

- thee: you
- sun and candle-light: day and night
- right: a sense of justice; what is morally right
- they turn from praise: to turn away from seeking praise, showing humility and purity valued in 19th-century Christian life

* This poem is the 43rd sonnet in *Sonnets from the Portuguese* (1850). A sonnet is a poetic form consisting of 14 lines and follows very strict rules of rhyme. Browning's sonnet follows the Italian (Petrarchan) form, which is usually divided into two parts. The first eight lines, called the octave, follow an *abba abba* rhyme scheme, while the last six lines, called the sestet, follow a *cdc cdc* pattern. In contrast, Shakespeare's sonnets also have 14 lines but use a different rhyme structure: *abab cdcd efef gg*. Although the sonnet form originally came from Italy, it has developed significantly in English poetry. British poets worked hard to express deep human emotions within this fixed structure, and their efforts greatly contributed to the growth of both English poetry and the English language.

Post-Reading 1. Review

1. Who was Elizabeth Barrett Browning?
2. What was the major challenge in her life?
3. How did Elizabeth first meet her husband, Robert Browning?

Post-Reading 2. Paraphrasing

Rewrite Elizabeth's idea as seen in the lines below in simpler, everyday English.

> How do I love thee? Let me count the ways.
> I love thee to the depth and breadth and height
> My soul can reach, when feeling out of sight
> For the ends of being and ideal grace.

Post-Reading 3. Discussion

1. What gave Elizabeth the strength to overcome challenges in her life?
2. Robert Browning first fell in love with Elizabeth's poetry and then fell in love with her. How could this happen?
3. How did love affect Elizabeth? Refer to the poem you read.

Post-Reading 4. Critical Thinking

1. Which do you think is better: being in love with someone with a similar personality, or with someone with a different personality?
2. Discuss the pros and cons of meeting your loved one in a virtual ("contactless") setting.
3. How can love inspire creativity and imagination in people?
4. What is the best way to love someone so that they can grow and mature?

Unit 5

Pain of Love

The most painful thing is losing yourself in the process of loving someone too much, and forgetting that you are special too.

—Ernest Hemingway

Preview 1. Main Ideas

1. People want their love to last forever, but this often turns out not to be the case.
2. The eternal and romantic love depicted in movies and novels is often a kind of false or idealized love.
3. The sorrow of love can make a person's soul as mature as the joy of love can.

Preview 2. Search the Meaning of the Keywords Online

Define the words below in your own words. Then, search online for example sentences that show how each word is used. Share your definitions and sentences with your partner.

1. *Eternal Sunshine of the Spotless Mind* (2004): ____________________

2. Eros and Psyche: ____________________

3. eternal love: ____________________

4. knights and noble ladies: ____________________

5. heartbreak and loneliness: ____________________

6. reflection: ____________________

Preview 3. Talk About

Look at the following questions and discuss your ideas with a partner.

1. Provide some examples of eternal love shown in movies or novels.
2. Do you believe eternal love truly exists or is possible in the real world?
3. Share what you know about the gods of love, Venus and Eros.

Preview 4. Further Discussion

1. Do you agree with the idea that the pain of love can help you become more mature?
2. What benefits can experiencing the pain of love bring?
3. Can going through heartbreak help make future relationships healthier? Why or why not?

People have always longed for a love that lasts forever. *Eternal Sunshine of the Spotless Mind* (2004), an acclaimed romantic science-fiction film, captures this desire beautifully. In the story, two lovers fall deeply in love, separate soon after, and choose to erase all memories of their relationship. Yet, by fate, they meet again and fall in love once more. Audiences are deeply touched by the idea that love can endure under any circumstances. Where did this powerful notion of eternal love begin?

In ancient Greek and Roman mythology, love was rarely seen as something worth risking one's life for. Venus, the goddess of love, was known for her many affairs, while Eros mischievously interfered with human relationships by shooting his arrows. Among these myths, the story of Eros and Psyche—where the two fall in love and remain together for life—stands out as an exception.

The notion of eternal and romantic love began to take clearer shape during the Middle Ages. Medieval literature is filled with romanticized tales of knights and noble ladies. In these stories, love was expressed more emotionally and spiritually than physically. Since physical relationships between high-born women and knights were considered morally inappropriate, affection was shown through admiration, loyalty, and acts of bravery. Knights—who proved their devotion on the battlefield—were praised by noble ladies for their courage. In this way, ideas of love in medieval times helped support and reinforce the structure of the feudal system.

Over time, however, the ideal of eternal love has gradually faded into myth. Today, some scientists describe love as a hormonal process with a natural time limit. The social psychologist Erich Fromm argued that the kind of love often portrayed in movies and novels is more of an idealized fantasy than a reflection of everyday reality.[18] Still, people continue to dream of such enduring love. They do their best to make it last by listening carefully, making compromises, and solving problems together. Yet, despite these efforts, many relationships come to an end, leaving people to face heartbreak and loneliness—feelings that are often captured in the poems we will read in this unit.

In times of sadness, it helps to look inward and reflect quietly. Through reflection, we may better understand how deeply we wish to connect with others and how much patience and tolerance we bring to our relationships. The sorrow of love can mature the soul just as much as the joy of love can. If you ever experience the grief of love, you may also come to value the personal growth and strength it can bring.

5A: Edgar Allan Poe

Pre-Reading 1. General Questions

1. Search for information about Edgar Allan Poe online.
2. Have you heard of the movie *The Pale Blue Eye* (2023)? If you have, what is the story about, and how is Poe portrayed in it?
3. Can you name any mystery stories or poems that Poe wrote?
4. Think about how an author's life can influence the themes in their works.

Pre-Reading 2. Vocabulary

Guess the meaning of each underlined word and choose its definition from the list below.

1. Poe's life was filled with unhappiness and <u>oddities</u> that are difficult for ordinary people to understand. ________
2. His foster mother's <u>excessive</u> love seems to stoke his stepfather's jealousy. ________
3. He created gloomy and <u>eerie</u> atmospheres in his novels. ________
4. Pulmonary tuberculosis was incurable and <u>fatal</u> at the time. ________
5. His drinking habit <u>spiraled</u> out of control. ________

A. (a) going beyond what is necessary, ordinary, or desirable
B. (n) the quality or condition being strange or unusual
C. (a) leading to death
D. (v) to move in a twisting, circular pattern; to increase or decrease continuously and often uncontrollably
E. (a) strange, mysterious, and scary

Poe was born in Boston, Massachusetts in 1809. Poe's life was filled with unhappiness and oddities that were difficult for ordinary people to relate to. His mother died when he was just two years old, and his father disappeared before her death, leaving Poe to be adopted by the childless John Allan. Unfortunately, Poe did not have a good relationship with his foster father, as his foster mother's excessive love seemed to fuel Allan's jealousy. Poe quit the University of Virginia and left home after his discord with Allan grew unbearable.

Edgar Allan Poe

Under pressure from Allan, who wanted to discipline him and threatened to cut off financial support, Poe was driven to join the U.S. Army in 1827. For him, military life was full of discipline and rules that were too strict for his active imagination. After two years of service, he left the army and later entered the U.S. Military Academy at West Point, but he was expelled for neglecting his duties. To make matters worse, Allan died without leaving him a penny. Abject poverty remained Poe's lifelong companion.

Poe's literary works include poetry and short stories, especially in the mystery and horror genres. His name should be remembered by those who appreciate these genres because he is widely acknowledged as a pioneer. His short stories "The Black Cat" and "The Murders in the Rue Morgue" are still widely read. "The Fall of the House of Usher" is regarded as a classic example of psychological horror-mystery fiction. He had an unparalleled talent for captivating readers with the gloomy and eerie atmosphere that filled his works.

His poems are, in this sense, much the same as his stories. "The Raven," one of his most famous poems, is renowned for its ominous and mysterious atmosphere. During Poe's time, most people believed that poetry should be lyrical, beautiful, and genuinely touching. No one at the time could have imagined choosing a raven as the topic of a poem and writing poems about fear, horror, doubt, and death. Even today, curiosity about what the raven stands for and what it is trying to say often leads readers to end up reading all 108 lines of this poem. The literary world of Europe was immediately fascinated by the unique atmosphere and new aesthetics in Poe's works. In contrast, American literary circles, dominated by a rigorous Puritan culture, could not readily accept the new literary world created by Poe. Charles Pierre Baudelaire, a French poet and critic, declared that the United States was nothing more than a huge prison for Edgar Allan Poe.[19] Poe was a great poet whose imagination was either too vast or too free to be confined by America.

Poe didn't live long. Since childhood, he had been used to unhappiness and poverty, which led him to drink heavily. His strange and heartbreaking love also damaged his health. When he was 26 years old, Poe fell in love with his cousin Virginia, who was only 13. As anyone could predict, her family was strongly opposed to the marriage. Yet Poe eventually married the 14-year-old Virginia the following year. This further cemented Poe's reputation as an eccentric. Despite their poverty, Poe and Virginia were happy, but their happiness didn't last long. In 1842, Virginia, who was only 20 years old, contracted pulmonary tuberculosis, which was fatal at the time. Poe wasted away in agony watching death's shadow slowly creep over his beloved wife, Virginia. His literary world grew still darker and more desolate, reflecting the deep sorrow and tragic aspects that filled his life.

Virginia Clemm Poe

While waiting for his wife's fate, his drinking spiraled out of control, and his health deteriorated. Virginia died in 1847 at the age of twenty-five. Two years later, Poe was found collapsed on the streets of Baltimore, drunk and never to wake again. Another famous poem by Poe, "Annabel Lee," was his last work. Everyone can guess who Annabel Lee was even without being told. The bitterness of losing his love made it difficult for him to find the strength to go on living.

Poe's Poem:

Annabel Lee

It was many and many a year ago,
  In a kingdom by the sea,
That a maiden there lived whom you may know
  By the name of Annabel Lee;
And this maiden she lived with no other thought
  Than to love and be loved by me.

I was a child and she was a child,
  In this kingdom by the sea,
But we loved with a love that was more than love—
  I and my Annabel Lee—
With a love that the wingèd seraphs of Heaven
  Coveted her and me.

And this was the reason that, long ago,
  In this kingdom by the sea,
A wind blew out of a cloud, chilling
  My beautiful Annabel Lee;
So that her highborn kinsmen came
  And bore her away from me,
To shut her up in a sepulchre
  In this kingdom by the sea.

The angels, not half so happy in Heaven,
  Went envying her and me—
Yes!—that was the reason (as all men know,
  In this kingdom by the sea)
That the wind came out of the cloud by night,
  Chilling and killing my Annabel Lee.

But our love it was stronger by far than the love
  Of those who were older than we—
  Of many far wiser than we—
And neither the angels in Heaven above
  Nor the demons down under the sea
Can ever dissever my soul from the soul
  Of the beautiful Annabel Lee;

For the moon never beams, without bringing me dreams
  Of the beautiful Annabel Lee;
And the stars never rise, but I feel the bright eyes
  Of the beautiful Annabel Lee;
And so, all the night-tide, I lie down by the side
  Of my darling—my darling—my life and my bride,
In her sepulchre there by the sea—
In her tomb by the sounding sea.

Illustration by Harry Clarke for Edgar Allan Poe's *Tales of Mystery and Imagination* (1919 edition)

Post-Reading 1. Review

1. Why did he drop out of the University of Virginia?
2. Why were Poe's works not well received by American literary circles?
3. Talk about the relationship between Poe and Virginia.

Post-Reading 2. Paraphrasing

Rewrite Poe's idea as seen in the lines below in simpler, everyday English.

> The angels, not half so happy in Heaven,
> Went envying her and me—
> Yes!—that was the reason (as all men know,
> In this kingdom by the sea)
> That the wind came out of the cloud by night,
> Chilling and killing my Annabel Lee.

Post-Reading 3. Discussion

1. Can you understand Poe's love for Virginia?
2. What parts of Poe's life story do you see reflected in his poems or stories? Give specific examples.
3. How do Poe's poems show his feelings for Virginia?

Post-Reading 4. Critical Thinking

1. Do you think love should have limits or boundaries, considering Poe's relationship with Virginia?
2. What qualities are most important for genuine love?
3. How does the pain of love affect ordinary people? Discuss both the positive and negative aspects.
4. What can be done to overcome the pain of love?

5B: Thomas Hardy

Pre-Reading 1. General Questions

1. Search for information about Thomas Hardy online.
2. Find and briefly summarize a story (from literature, film, or history) that shows the sorrow of love.
3. Share your ideas about possible reasons why romantic relationships may fail.

Pre-Reading 2. Vocabulary

Guess the meaning of each underlined word and choose its definition from the list below.

1. Hardy's career began in the field of <u>architecture</u>. ________
2. He was trained as an <u>apprentice</u> to a church-building expert. ________
3. Emma had the <u>sensibility</u> to recognize Hardy's potential as a novelist. ________
4. His thoughts <u>clashed</u> with the Victorian concept of pursuing strict moral rules. ________
5. He <u>preferred</u> to be called a poet rather than a novelist. ________
6. Hardy's physical body was <u>enshrined</u> at Westminster Abbey in London. ________

A. (n) fighting or creating conflicts on opposing issues
B. (v) to like something more than other things
C. (n) inner ability to understand and feel emotions and the outside world
D. (v) to protect a person or thing in a special place so it will be remembered
E. (n) a beginner who works under a skilled person to learn a trade
F. (n) designing and making buildings

Thomas Hardy was born in 1840 in a small rural village in Dorset, England. His father was a self-taught mason. Skilled masons were highly valued because their craft required lengthy, intensive training, along with aesthetic sensitivities. Although they still belonged to the lower class, they enjoyed a somewhat better financial status than the average working-class individual. Following in his father's footsteps, Hardy also began his career in the field of architecture. At the age of 16, he was trained as an apprentice to a church-building expert. At 22, he moved to London and worked as an assistant in an architect's office.

Thomas Hardy

Emma Gifford, an aspiring writer whom he met at the age of 30, had the sensibility to recognize Hardy's potential as a novelist and encouraged him to write novels. Hardy wrote several novels in succession and quickly attracted the public's interest. He had written poetry before, but it gained little attention and brought him little financial reward. His novels, on the other hand, gained popularity and afforded him economic stability as well as fame. Hardy and Emma married, fully expecting a happy life together. However, this contentment was sadly short-lived, as their marriage soon began to fall apart. Some say it was because Emma, a self-struggling writer, was jealous of Hardy's success. Others say that Hardy emotionally neglected Emma. Regardless of the reasons, by the end of the marriage, Emma was said to have suffered from various mental and emotional problems.

The two most popular novels by Hardy are *Tess of the d'Urbervilles* (1889) and *Jude the Obscure* (1896). Although both novels gained tremendous popularity, they also received fierce criticism. Hardy described Tess, in *Tess of the d'Urbervilles*, an unmarried mother, as a pure woman, suggesting that purity of the soul is more important than physical chastity. His thoughts clashed with the Victorian pursuit of strict moral codes based on Christian ethics.

Jude the Obscure caused even greater controversy. The life of Jude, the protagonist, is marked by a series of failures. The mood is so gloomy that it is hard to tell whether his gloomy attitude is the cause or the effect of his tragic fate. Jude's forbidden love and secret marriage to his cousin, Sue, further deepens his suffering. Nevertheless, Jude is not dissuaded. He persists in trying to live life on his own terms, despite his contemporaries' attempts to suppress his human nature. *Jude the Obscure* generated enormous sales but also endless criticism at the same time. It is said that a bishop openly burned the copies of the book. Although the novel is now included in the list of the 100 greatest books, it was once discarded as trash by the stubborn moralists of its time. Moreover, the novel's stirring portrayal of Hardy's first love, his cousin Tryphena Sparks, permanently damaged the relationship between Hardy and his wife Emma. From then on, Hardy never wrote novels.

Emma Lavinia Gifford

Instead, Hardy returned to writing poems. Having published around 950 poems, he preferred to be called a poet rather than a novelist. The characteristics of his poems are similar to those of his novels. In both, he explored the idea that human destiny is shaped by mere chance rather than by any divine plan. This theme appears vividly in his novel *Tess of the d'Urbervilles*, when the letter in which Tess confesses her past—written on the eve of her marriage—*accidentally* slips under the carpet, leading to further misfortune. His poems similarly reflect this view of life. His well-known poem "The Convergence of the Twain" describes how the tragic collision of two great forces—the *Titanic* and the iceberg—symbolizes the blind workings of chance, indifferent to human fate. While this poem deals with human destiny in general, other poems of his speak more personally of love and loss, like the one we will read in this unit.

Fortunately, his works were reevaluated in the early 20th century, and he received the Order of Merit in recognition of his literary achievements. His novels are now regarded as a turning point in modern literature because they challenged the social systems and conventions of the 19th century. After his wife's death in 1912, his regret and deep sorrow for not having done the best for her were clearly reflected in his later, much-loved poems. When he died in 1928, Hardy's body was enshrined at Westminster Abbey in London in recognition of his contribution to the literary world, but his heart was buried next to his wife's grave in his hometown. His soul was finally reunited with his wife, Emma.

Hardy's Poem:

A Broken Appointment

You did not come,
And marching Time drew on, and wore me numb,—
Yet less for loss of your dear presence there
Than that I thus found lacking in your make
That high compassion which can overbear
Reluctance for pure lovingkindness' sake
Grieved I, when, as the hope-hour stroked its sum,
You did not come.

You love not me,
And love alone can lend you loyalty;
–I know and knew it. But, unto the store
Of human deeds divine in all but name,
Was it not worth a little hour or more
To add yet this: Once you, a woman, came
To soothe a time-torn man; even though it be
You love not me?

The graves of Thomas Hardy's heart (foreground) and his first wife, Emma Hardy (background), in Stinsford Churchyard, Dorset. Photo by Becky Williamson, licensed under CC BY-SA 2.0 via Wikimedia Commons

- make: a person's character or his nature
- the hope-hour: an appointment time

Post-Reading 1. Review

1. Who is Thomas Hardy?
2. Why did Hardy first choose architecture as a career?
3. What inspired Hardy to pursue novel writing seriously?

Post-Reading 2. Paraphrasing

Rewrite Hardy's idea as seen in the lines below in simpler, everyday English.

Grieved I, when, as the hope-hour stroked its sum,
You did not come.

Post-Reading 3. Discussion

1. Who or what do you think was most responsible for the unhappy relationship between Hardy and Emma?
2. Why do you think Hardy's novels were criticized during his time?
3. Was it the right decision to have Hardy's heart buried beside his first wife, Emma?
4. How does Hardy describe a person who does not keep promises in his poem, "A Broken Appointment"? Do you agree with his perspective?

Post-Reading 4. Critical Thinking

1. Is Emma's jealousy understandable as a natural human emotion? How could jealousy be turned into something positive?
2. Reflecting on Hardy and Emma's love story, what efforts could help keep a relationship alive?
3. After Emma's death, Hardy wrote poems filled with regret and pain, which became widely loved. Yet some criticize him for expressing deep sorrow after her death while being unfaithful during her life. What is your opinion of this criticism?
4. Psychological wounds after a breakup sometimes lead to serious social problems. What efforts can be made to prevent or overcome these issues?

Unit 6

Various Forms of Love Ⅰ: Parents and Children

Children begin by loving their parents; as they grow older they judge them; sometimes they forgive them.

—Oscar Wilde

Preview 1. Main Ideas

1. A parent's love for their children is often seen as unconditional.
2. A child's filial piety is regarded as one of the most important virtues.
3. As the world changes, so do our notions of family and responsibility.

Preview 2. Keywords

Define the words below in your own words. Then, search online for example sentences that show how each word is used. Share your definitions and sentences with your partner.

1. parental love: ________________________________

2. infanticide: ________________________________

3. *Brave New World* (1932): ________________________________

4. filial piety: ________________________________

5. essential relationship: ________________________________

Preview 3. Talk About

Look at the following questions and discuss your ideas with a partner.

1. Do you agree with the idea that parental love is unconditional? Why or why not?
2. How important do you think filial piety is in today's society?

Preview 4. Further Discussion

1. Find a story online that describes a parent-child relationship and share why it stood out to you.
2. Talk about aspects of family relationships that are markedly different today compared to the past.
3. What quality do you think is most important for being a good parent?

A parent's love for a child is often viewed as unconditional. However, throughout history, there have been cases where parental love seemed conditional, sometimes putting children's lives at risk. One example is infanticide, the killing of unwanted infants, which was common in ancient Greece and Rome. Even in the last century, a preference for boys led to the tragic loss of many female infants in countries such as China and India. Although such practices are now illegal, they remind us of the dangers that conditional love can bring.

In Aldous Huxley's *Brave New World* (1932), children are born in a scientifically controlled factory, yet the protagonist, Bernard Marx, develops differently from the pre-set expectations. If such attempts to control human traits cannot succeed even in science fiction, they are all the more impossible in the real world. Every human being is born with unique qualities and a sense of autonomy. Consequently, children naturally grow up making their own choices instead of simply following what their parents or society want for them.

On the other hand, cultural traditions and moral codes generally emphasize the duty of children to honor and respect their parents. This emphasis is often reinforced through formal teachings or moral lessons. In the Bible, the fifth commandment is, "Honor your father and your mother, so that you may live long in the land the LORD your God is giving you."[*] In Eastern philosophies, there are more detailed guidelines for honoring one's parents, such as taking care of one's body, respecting their feelings, and bringing honor to the family.[**] *Hyo*, a traditional term for filial piety, has long been regarded as one of the most important virtues for children.

As society evolves, human ideas of family and responsibility also change. Blended families, adoptive families, and individuals who choose not to become parents are becoming more common. The different types of families and relationships are too numerous to describe, but one thing is certain: as long as humanity exists, the parent-child bond will endure in one form or another. Let's explore this essential relationship in greater detail.

* This verse is from the Bible, specifically Exodus 20:12 (New International Version).

** This sentence summarizes teachings from the *Classic of Filial Duty* (효경), a Confucian text attributed to Zengzi(증자), a disciple of Confucius.

6A: Joanna Baillie

Pre-Reading 1. General Questions

1. Search for information about Joanna Baillie online.
2. Talk about what parental love means to you.
3. Consider how parental love can affect a person's growth.

Pre-Reading 2. Vocabulary

Guess the meaning of each underlined word and choose its definition from the list below.

1. In her dramas, the protagonist has strong passions. ________

2. Her father was her first teacher and laid a strong ethical foundation for her. ________

3. Her ideas anticipated the rise of Freudian psychology. ________

4. Her father governed the family with strict religious discipline. ________

5. Her childhood deficiency persisted into her adulthood. ________

A. (a) morally right or wrong according to accepted rules or principles
B. (v) to control and direct (a group of people)
C. (n) the main character in a story
D. (n) the state of not having enough of what is needed
E. (v) to expect or predict something before it happens

Joanna Baillie by Mary Ann Knight

Joanna Baillie was born in Bothwell, Scotland, in 1762. Her father was a Presbyterian pastor and, for the last two years of his life, served as a Professor of Divinity at the University of Glasgow. Glasgow was once the largest industrial city in Scotland and is now the third largest city in the UK. Given her father's social status, Joanna could have benefited from an early education, but records show that she did not attend a school until she was 10 years old.

Baillie was not extensively educated in literature, but, thanks to her intellectual abilities and literary talent, her first collection of poetry was published in 1790, the year she turned 28. Her literary career, which lasted until she died in 1851, focused more on drama than on poetry. She wrote a total of 26 dramas. Unfortunately, her works were not widely appreciated during her lifetime. During the Romantic and Victorian eras,* when Baillie was active, plays were not as popular as they had been in Shakespeare's era in the sixteenth century. In addition, the moral norms of the period often conflicted with the intense emotions and unrestrained passions depicted in her characters.

Today, many scholars of English literature call her the most talented female playwright of the Romantic period and regard her as one of the important writers who filled the gap between Shakespeare and Oscar Wilde. This high praise is probably because her dramas introduced a new idea: a person's fate can be influenced by dark passions within themselves that they cannot control. Some scholars even believe that her ideas anticipated the rise of Freudian psychology at the end of the 19th century. In her works, however, she tried to balance her new ideas with the old moral values of her time. Through her dramas, she encouraged people to become desirable and worthy members of society, by helping them realize how dangerous life can be when they are dominated or swayed by passion.

She is said to have been something of a tomboy in her youth, spending much of her time playing and running around the fields of her small town rather than focusing on her studies. Her father, who was her first teacher, laid a strong ethical foundation for her and governed the family with strict religious discipline, emphasizing emotional control and a modest lifestyle. Her mother, meanwhile, often scolded her for not being feminine enough. Even though her parents tried to raise her to be a "lady" who behaved appropriately in society, their efforts were unsuccessful. Under her parents' strict and conservative attitude toward her education, she had a childhood lacking in warm and loving attention. She spent several years at a school notorious

* The Victorian era refers to the reign of Queen Victoria of Britain (1837–1901). It was a transitional period between the Romantic era and Modernism. Although it is difficult to describe the period with a single defining characteristic due to its ongoing changes, values such as morality, modesty, and temperance were especially emphasized.

for training girls to conform to the standards of a "lady" of the time. As a result, she was later depicted as an educated, mature, and well-mannered lady. Even the poet Wordsworth described her as "a model of an English Gentlewoman."[20] One reason she earned such a good reputation was her deep devotion to her mother, who was left alone after her father's death. She cared for her mother day and night, especially as her mother became blind in old age.

Although she appeared calm and graceful like a lady, her inner energy and passion were fully expressed in her literary works. Many of these writings reflect her longing for the affection she lacked during childhood. Such emotional deficiency seems to have continued to influence her adult life, supporting Freud's theory that childhood experiences have a lasting impact on a person's emotional development. Her poem in this unit, which celebrates warm maternal love, portrays both the affection she felt for her parents and the lack of warmth she received from them. She never married.

Joanna Baillie House. Photo by Megalit, licensed under CC BY-SA 4.0 via Wikimedia Commons

Baillie's Poem:

A mother to her waking infant

Now in thy dazzling half-oped eye,
Thy curled nose and lip awry,
Uphoisted arms and noddling head,
And little chin with crystal spread,
Poor helpless thing! what do I see,
That I should sing of thee?

From thy poor tongue no accents come,
Which can but rub thy toothless gum:
Small understanding boasts thy face,
Thy shapeless limbs nor step nor grace:
A few short words thy feats may tell,
And yet I love thee well.

......

Mother and Child by Jean-Baptiste-Camille Corot, c. 1860s

- oped: opened
- uphoisted: archaic; to lift or raise something up
- shapeless: having no clear or definite shape or form

Post-Reading 1. Review

1. Who was Joanna Baillie? Briefly describe her life and achievements.
2. What were her parents like when she was a child?
3. In what genre did she write most of her works? How are her works evaluated today?

Post-Reading 2. Paraphrasing

Rewrite Baillie's idea as seen in the lines below in simpler, everyday English.

> Thy shapeless limbs nor step nor grace:
> A few short words thy feats may tell,
> And yet I love thee well.

Post-Reading 3. Discussion

1. How do you think her parents' strict religious discipline shaped her upbringing?
2. Baillie believed that a person's destiny is affected by dark passions within themselves that they cannot control. Do you agree with her idea?

Post-Reading 4. Critical Thinking

1. How can young people maintain a good relationship with their parents?
2. What roles do children play in modern society?
3. How can we maintain balance between emotion and reason?

6B: William Shakespeare

Pre-Reading 1. General Questions

1. Search for information about William Shakespeare online.
2. Learn the story of Shakespeare's tragedy, *King Lear*.
3. Think about how to show your love for your parents or children appropriately.

Pre-Reading 2. Vocabulary

Guess the meaning of each underlined word and choose its definition from the list below.

1. His distinctive poetry is <u>unparalleled</u> in beauty. ________
2. His dramas are still being <u>adapted</u> and replayed for film and theater. ________
3. Shakespeare's works may have been the result of <u>collaboration</u> among several authors. ________
4. Shakespeare became both the agent and the <u>subject</u> of the imagination. ________
5. *King Lear* questions the love that everyone takes for <u>granted</u>. ________

A. (n) a topic or theme that is discussed or studied in detail
B. (a) considered to be deserved or expected without appreciation
C. (n) working together
D. (v) to change something so it fits a new situation or purpose
E. (a) being without equal or match; incomparable in quality or extent.

William Shakespeare by John Taylor

Almost everyone knows the name Shakespeare. From his birth in 1564 until his death in 1616 at the age of 52, he wrote 154 sonnets and many plays, too many to enumerate. The distinctive poetic form he developed, called the Shakespearean sonnet, is unparalleled in beauty and has made him a great pioneer of English sonnets. However, it is his dramas that made him truly world-famous. *Hamlet, King Lear, Othello,* and *Macbeth* are called his Four Tragedies, and *A Midsummer Night's Dream, The Merchant of Venice, Twelfth Night, As You Like It,* and *The Taming of the Shrew* are known as his Five Comedies. Loved all over the world, *Romeo and Juliet* and *The Merchant of Venice* are classified as tragicomedies, in that they include many comedic plot points but end tragically. Shakespeare also wrote several historical plays. His plays are still being adapted, performed, and loved for film and theater because they have solid plots and reflect timeless issues of universal human nature.

Though he is one of the most well-known English playwrights, there are still some mysteries about the life of Shakespeare. It seems hard to believe that so many excellent works were written in such a relatively short period by himself, even if it is true that he did have great talent. Some theories suggest that Shakespeare's works may have been the result of collaboration among several authors or that they were written by a politician using "Shakespeare" as a pseudonym. However, most scholars agree that all of Shakespeare's works were indeed written by him. Yet, aside from the fact that in 1582, while still a teenager, he married a woman who was eight years older than him, and had three children with her, much of his life is still unknown.

Given the circumstances, it is natural to have questions about his works and his life. Shakespeare was not wealthy enough to travel abroad, so how did he portray foreign landscapes with such exquisite detail? Although Shakespeare never attended college, it is remarkable how skillfully he used words derived from Old English, Norman French, Latin, and other languages. He also had a deep knowledge of court manners and the lives of the upper class, which makes his works even more impressive. The answers to these mysteries have remained—and will likely continue to remain—elusive. Putting aside all the riddles, Shakespeare contributed greatly to the refinement of the English language. He coined more than 1,700 English words that are commonly used today, such as *gossip* and *kissing*.[21]

The more we learn about him, the more the story of his life becomes an object of our imagination. The movie *Shakespeare in Love* (1998) depicts an imagined story of Shakespeare's life, where he falls in love like Romeo and grows into a great playwright. The film swept several awards at the Academy Awards (Oscars) and at major international film festivals the following year. Rave reviews said that Shakespeare became both the agent and the subject of the imagination. Because his life remains shrouded in mystery, it continues to inspire people to imagine and create fictional stories about him.

Why does Shakespeare continue to fascinate people? His greatest strength lies in a body of work that probes human nature. One example is *King Lear*. Although many other masterpieces have been written since, *King Lear* is still widely regarded as one of the greatest tragedies in world literature. What makes it so special? The play questions the love between parents and children that many take for granted. It shows how human folly and greed can cause relationships to deteriorate, with catastrophic results. As they watch the play, audiences often empathize with Lear's sadness and fear. Like Lear, they may at times have wanted—or even asked—their loved ones to prove their affection. They may also imagine the sacrifices they would be willing to make in return for such love. How can we prove the extent of love? Can love be proved or measured at all?

The Globe Theatre (right), where many of Shakespeare's plays were performed, and the Bear Garden (left), a popular site for bear-baiting in Elizabethan London

Shakespeare's Poem:

*King Lear** (From Scene I, Act I)

GONERIL.

Sir, I love you more than word can wield the matter;
Dearer than eyesight, space, and liberty;
Beyond what can be valued, rich or rare;
No less than life, with grace, health, beauty, honour;
As much as child e'er loved, or father found;
A love that makes breath poor and speech unable;
Beyond all manner of so much I love you.

REGAN.

Sir, I am made of the self mettle as my sister,
And prize me at her worth. In my true heart
I find she names my very deed of love;
Only she comes too short, that I profess
Myself an enemy to all other joys
Which the most precious square of sense possesses,
And find I am alone felicitate
In your dear highness' love.

CORDELIA.

Unhappy that I am, I cannot heave
My heart into my mouth: I love your majesty
According to my bond; no more nor less.

……

Good my lord,
You have begot me, bred me, loved me: I
Return those duties back as are right fit,
Obey you, love you, and most honour you.

King Lear and Cordelia by Benjamin West, 1793

* *King Lear,* as all of Shakespeare's plays, is a grand poetic work, written especially in blank verse without an end rhyme scheme. It is composed in iambic pentameter, consisting of five feet per line with ten syllables alternating between unstressed and stressed sounds. As a result, the characters' lines emphasize the natural rhythm of English, and the emotions are richly conveyed. Goneril, Regan, and Cordelia are the three daughters of King Lear.

Post-Reading 1. Review

1. What new things did you learn about Shakespeare?
2. What is the best-known historical fact from Shakespeare's life?
3. Why did some people assume that someone else wrote Shakespeare's works?

Post-Reading 2. Paraphrasing

Rewrite Shakespeare's idea as seen in the lines below in simpler, everyday English.

> Unhappy that I am, I cannot heave
> My heart into my mouth: I love your majesty
> According to my bond; no more nor less.

Post-Reading 3. Discussion

1. Shakespeare was neither well-educated nor aristocratic. How was he able to incorporate such a wealth of knowledge into his works?
2. In *King Lear*, Cordelia upsets her father Lear with her words of love. Describe the logic behind her actions and the actions of Lear.
3. Lear believed that love could be expressed in words. This belief led to the ruin of both him and his daughters. Let's talk about what went wrong with Lear's understanding of love.

Post-Reading 4. Critical Thinking

1. What types of communication and behavior are essential for maintaining relationships with loved ones? How do they help those relationships last?
2. Why do people often seek proof of love in a relationship?
3. What is the ideal role of parents in modern society? How can they fulfill this role effectively?

Unit 7

Various Forms of Love Ⅱ: Friendship

Some people go to priests. Others to poetry. I to my friends.

—Virginia Woolf

Preview 1. Main Ideas

1. Friendship is a bond based on mutual consideration and respect.
2. Friendship involves deep emotions.
3. Friendship allows us to share our feelings and respect each other's dignity as human beings.

Preview 2. Keywords

Define the words below in your own words. Then, search online for example sentences that show how each word is used. Share your definitions and sentences with your partner.

1. *The Intouchables* (2011): ______________________

2. empathy: ______________________

3. mutual understanding: ______________________

4. brotherhood: ______________________

5. shared humanity: ______________________

Preview 3. Talk About

Look at the following questions and discuss your ideas with a partner.

1. How do you define friendship?
2. What are some similarities and differences between friendship and love? Can you give examples from stories or personal experiences?
3. Think of a few of your close friends. Describe the emotions and thoughts that come to mind when you think about them.
4. What do you do to build and keep good friendships?

Preview 4. Further Discussion

1. Can you name a movie that depicts friendship? How did the characters in the movie develop their relationships?
2. Reflect on a friendship you consider deeply meaningful. What experiences or moments made it stronger?

Many stories have explored the power of friendship. In the movie *The Intouchables* (2011) by Olivier Nakache and Éric Toledano, we meet two people from very different backgrounds. Philippe is a wealthy man who became paralyzed from the neck down after a paragliding accident, while Driss is healthy but unemployed, with little education and a minor criminal record. At first, they seem to have nothing in common, but over time, Driss comes to understand Philippe's pain, and Philippe, in turn, learns to see Driss's true nature. The barrier between them disappears, and they grow close through empathy and shared experiences. In the final scene, the two real people on whom the movie is based stand side by side, smiling at each other by the sea. It reminds us that this bond can be built despite differences.

Friendship is based on mutual understanding and respect. When you are with close friends—laughing, talking, and sharing good food—you feel genuinely happy. Unlike romantic love, which often involves strong passion, friendship is generally more stable and balanced. It can even help us make more thoughtful and reasonable decisions. However, this bond is not always easy. Sometimes we face struggles and conflicts even with close friends, and these moments can bring feelings of loneliness or heartache. Yet, through these relationships, we learn an important lesson: while people share many similarities, each person has a unique personality and perspective.

In this way, friendship can be seen as the starting point of a broader sense of connection—a kind of brotherhood that celebrates our shared humanity. Through empathy and mutual respect, friendship can expand beyond personal circles to include larger communities and even humanity as a whole. Muhammad Ali once said, "Friendship is the hardest thing in the world to explain. It's not something you learn in school. But if you haven't learned the meaning of friendship, you really haven't learned anything."[22] Now, let's explore the meaning of this connection together.

7A: Alfred, Lord Tennyson

Pre-Reading 1. General Questions

1. Search for information about Tennyson and Hallam online.
2. How do friendships usually begin?
3. Have you ever lost a close friend? How did that make you feel?

Pre-Reading 2. Vocabulary

Guess the meaning of each underlined word and choose its definition from the list below.

1. His excessive drinking habits had a detrimental effect on his mental health and family's finances. ________

2. Hallam became an invaluable friend to Tennyson. ________

3. He was devastated by the loss. ________

4. He had to suppress his sadness for a long time. ________

5. He began to feel skeptical about science. ________

   A. (a) doubtful or having distrust
   B. (a) extremely valuable; too valuable to measure
   C. (a) too much; more than is reasonable or necessary
   D. (a) completely shocked or destroyed
   E. (v) to hold back (emotion or emotional expression)

Alfred, Lord Tennyson

Alfred, Lord Tennyson, was born in 1809, the fourth of twelve children. His father, George, was the parish priest of Somersby but had a negative influence on Tennyson. George's strict enforcement of religious doctrine, coupled with his depression and frequent outbursts of anger, created a tense family environment. Additionally, his excessive drinking, a habit he also passed to Alfred's older brother Arthur, severely impacted the family's mental health and finances. Several family members exhibited symptoms of mild epilepsy. Tennyson suffered from anxiety stemming from the fear that he might be mentally ill like his family members. This troubled him all his life and had a major impact on Tennyson's poetry.

Tennyson began his literary career in 1827 by publishing an anonymous collection of poems *Poems, by Two Brothers* with his brother Charles. The following year, he enrolled at Trinity College, Cambridge, but dropped out after his father's death in 1831. However, while there, he met Arthur Hallam, who comforted him during his time of mourning. Hallam even traveled to Europe to support his grieving friend, Tennyson, and wrote an article for a newspaper introducing Tennyson's poetry. He even became the fiancé of Tennyson's sister, Emily. Hallam's empathy and integrity made him an irreplaceable part in Tennyson's life.

Unfortunately, Hallam died of a fever at only 22. Tennyson was devastated by the loss but also had to care for his younger sister, Emily, who was mourning the sudden death of her fiancé. Hallam is perhaps one of the most frequently mentioned figures in literary history—famous not for his own achievements, but because his name is inseparable from Tennyson's.

Tennyson had to suppress his sadness for a long time. Being unable to contain his grief any longer, he poured his emotions into poetry. In 1850, he published *In Memoriam*, a collection of poems with a total of 2,916 lines that captures his grief over the previous 17 years. This work not only expresses sorrow and mourning for the death of a friend but also explores questions about human existence and the universe itself. At that time, people believed that they were living in an age of science that was advancing by leaps and bounds. They anticipated that such progress would open up a new paradise for humanity. Tennyson, however, questioned why his friend had to die in vain without receiving proper treatment in such a developed era. He reached the conclusion that life and death lie beyond the boundaries of science. He grew skeptical of science—a doubt often regarded as characteristic of the modern age.

In *In Memoriam*, Tennyson begins by expressing his deep mourning for his dear lost friend. This grief soon becomes linked to his rejection of the rapidly changing society. As the work progresses, however, his poetry gradually moves beyond skepticism and develops into a message of hope and positivity. He dreams of a new era characterized by moral progress and spiritual renewal, where faith and reason can coexist in harmony. Eventually, he proposes the idea that the human soul does not end meaninglessly but has a place to return to.

As soon as *In Memoriam* was published, it began to gain immense popularity. The story of a man growing spiritually after the loss of a dear young friend was touching. In addition, every poem in *In Memoriam* was admired for its deep and thoughtful ideas, and each was considered an independent piece reflecting the concerns of the time. Tennyson's fame grew quickly and he was soon appointed Poet Laureate. At last, his marriage which had been delayed for 13 years because of poverty could become a reality. Queen Victoria admired *In Memoriam* so much that she gave Tennyson the title of Baron. The work became one of the best-selling books of poetry published throughout the Victorian era. Since its publication, it has been regarded as one of the best works on friendship. Just because a book sells well does not necessarily mean that it is good. In this case, however, this certainly seems to be true.

Tennyson's Poem:

In Memoriam (Canto 7)

Dark house, by which once more I stand
　　Here in the long unlovely street,
　　Doors, where my heart was used to beat
So quickly, waiting for a hand,

A hand that can be clasp'd no more—
　　Behold me, for I cannot sleep,
　　And like a guilty thing I creep
At earliest morning to the door.

He is not here; but far away
　　The noise of life begins again,
　　And ghastly thro' the drizzling rain
On the bald street breaks the blank day.

Tennyson Monument, Tennyson Down, Isle of Wight, England, Photo by ITookSomePhotos, licensed under CC BY-SA 4.0 via Wikimedia Commons

- Canto: a part of a long poem
- dark house: Hallam's house in London
- clasp'd: clasped, hold something tightly in your hands

Post-Reading 1. Review

1. How did Tennyson and Hallam become such close friends?
2. What is *In Memoriam* about?
3. How did the immense popularity of his book affect his life?

Post-Reading 2. Paraphrasing

Rewrite Tennyson's idea as seen in the lines below in simpler, everyday English.

> Dark house, by which once more I stand
>   Here in the long unlovely street,
>   Doors, where my heart was used to beat
> So quickly, waiting for a hand,

Post-Reading 3. Discussion

1. What does it mean to be a Poet Laureate?
2. Why were people enthusiastic about Tennyson's poetry?
3. How are Tennyson's feelings shown in *In Memoriam* (Canto. 7)? Could writing this poem helped him heal from his loss?
4. Can you think of someone like Hallam, known not for their own work but for being connected to a famous person? Describe the person and the background story.

Post-Reading 4. Critical Thinking

1. What kind of experiences might have deepened Tennyson and Hallam's bond as friends?
2. Think of your friends and discuss what you can do for a friend who needs you.
3. Do you think a friendship like Tennyson and Hallam's is possible in today's world?

7B: George Gordon, Lord Byron

Pre-Reading 1. General Questions

1. Search for information about Lord Byron online.
2. Find out about the Greek War of Independence (1820s).
3. Share a story about a famous person's friendship.

Pre-Reading 2. Vocabulary

Guess the meaning of each underlined word and choose its definition from the list below.

1. The poets would not have represented Britain and their time as much as Byron did. ________
2. Many of his problems stemmed from the indifference and contempt of his parents. ________
3. The charm of the rebellious and gloomy protagonist fascinated readers. ________
4. They could no longer overlook his misbehavior. ________
5. He entrusted all unpublished handwritten manuscripts to his close friend. ________

A. (v) to give someone responsibility for something because you fully trust them
B. (a) refusing to obey the authority of existing social norms and fighting against them
C. (n) a lack of interest, concern, or sympathy
D. (n) improper or unacceptable conduct by social or moral standards
E. (v) to serve as a symbol or example of something, especially in art or literature

Byron was a star. Many Romantic poets have been acclaimed by the public, but none has been celebrated so enthusiastically or so quickly as Byron. In the 1850s, a French critic said that Byron had been one of the greatest poets of his time and best represented the spirit of his age.[23] He believed that no other poets of the period could express the nation as powerfully as Byron did. That was high praise for Byron as a poet. His life, however, was equally marked by darkness.

Portrait of Byron by Thomas Phillips, c.1813

He was born in 1788 to a distinguished noble family; even so, his father and mother were far from good parents. His father squandered his family's fortunes through his irresponsible first marriage and extravagant lifestyle, and he remarried Byron's mother purely for her wealth. Byron was born with a clubfoot on his right leg. For this reason, his mother treated him with coldness for most of her life. Many of the problems Byron had as an adult may have come from the indifference and contempt he received at a time when he should have been loved and cared for.

It was in 1812 that Byron published his first poem. Before then, he had spent three years living a reckless, pleasure-seeking life after being accepted into Trinity College, Cambridge. After leaving the university, Byron joined the wave of the *Grand Tour*. It was a long-standing custom in Britain, serving as a major channel for young British aristocrats to establish political and diplomatic connections with nobles from various European countries. However, not all aristocrats who participated in the *Grand Tour* achieved positive results; for some, it became an opportunity to adopt a more unrestrained lifestyle. Byron's tour was more about enjoying a freer way of life.

After returning from a two-year trip to Europe and the East, he put together his memories of wild living and remarkable adventure in a long epic poem, *Childe Harold's Pilgrimage*. The charm of the rebellious and gloomy protagonist and his romantic longing for a new world fascinated readers. On his sudden popularity, he is quoted as saying, "I awoke one morning and found myself famous."[24] He succeeded with every collection of poems he published and was praised as the greatest poet of his time.

Meanwhile, his numerous romances earned him a reputation

as a Casanova. British society was more concerned about his talents and tolerated most of his indiscretions with surprising generosity. Yet, when one of Byron's scandals involved his stepsister, society could no longer ignore his misbehavior. Byron had to leave Britain as if he were a man on the run.

Arriving in Italy, he spent six years gradually growing weary of pursuing love and physical pleasures. Then, after entrusting all his unpublished handwritten manuscripts to his friend Thomas Moore, he redirected his devotion and energy to political issues. He supported the Greek independence movement, which he found similar in spirit to Romantic ideals. He was convinced that Greece must be liberated from Ottoman oppression, just as a man must preserve his freedom, will, and humanity. He even took part in the war between the Greek forces and the Ottoman Empire, leading troops into the battle himself. He worked so passionately that he even sold his property in Britain to support the movement. However, before long, he contracted a fever and died in 1824. He was only 36 years old. The Greeks honored and mourned him as a revolutionary hero.

Portrait of Thomas Moore
by Thomas Lawrence

Soon after Byron's death, his friend Moore burned the manuscripts that had been entrusted to him. Why did Moore decide to betray Byron's trust? Moore might have thought that it would be difficult to restore Byron's reputation and probably did not want to take the risk of bringing Byron's name back before the public. Byron had left Britain at the height of a notorious scandal and taken part in the Greek Revolution. At the time, the British royal family was extremely cautious about the spread of revolutionary ideas in Britain after the French Revolution. Moreover, Byron's scandalous life and unconventional works were deeply at odds with the moral standards of that society. Indeed, Byron's poetry was so undervalued in Britain throughout the Victorian era that the word 'immorality' was associated with his life and works. As time passed, however, a new era emerged at the end of the 19th century, in which people sought to escape outdated moral codes and glorify a free spirit. Byron's poetry once again returned to the spotlight. Moore's burning of Byron's manuscripts is now regarded as one of the gravest crimes in the history of literature.

Byron's Poem:

To Thomas Moore

My boat is on the shore,
And my bark is on the sea;
But, before I go, Tom Moore,
Here's a double health to thee!

Here's a sigh to those who love me,
And a smile to those who hate;
And, whatever sky's above me,
Here's a heart for every fate.

Though the ocean roar around me,
Yet it still shall bear me on;
Though a desert should surround me,
It hath springs that may be won.

Weren't the last drop in the well,
As I gasp'd upon the brink,
Ere my fainting spirit fell,
'Tis to thee that I would drink.

With that water, as this wine,
The libation I would pour
Should be - peace with thine and mine,
And a health to thee, Tom Moore!

Lord Byron Swears on the Grave of Markos Botsaris by Ludovico Lipparini (1850). Museo Civico Luigi Bailo, Treviso. Image licensed under CC BY-SA 4.0 via Wikimedia Commons

- hath: has
- gasp'd: gasped
- 'Tis: It is
- thine: yours
- thee: you

Post-Reading 1. Review

1. Describe the main events and key aspects of Lord Byron's life.
2. How did Byron's childhood hardships influence his life and work?
3. Why do you think Byron entrusted his handwritten manuscripts to Thomas Moore?

Post-Reading 2. Paraphrasing

Rewrite Lord Byron's idea as seen in the lines below in simpler, everyday English.

> With that water, as this wine,
> The libation I would pour
> Should be - peace with thine and mine,
> And a health to thee, Tom Moore!

Post-Reading 3. Discussion

1. If you were to divide Byron's life into two phases, at which point would you do so, and why?
2. Why do you think Byron's works, which often reflected his controversial thoughts and actions, were appealing to readers of his time?
3. Discuss Byron's relationship with Moore, referring to Byron's poem "To Thomas Moore."
4. Why do you think Byron shifted his lifestyle and devoted himself to the Greek independence movement?

Post-Reading 4. Critical Thinking

1. As an adult, Byron struggled to form healthy relationships with others. Considering that childhood experiences can affect our adult lives, how can we overcome such problems and build healthy relationships?
2. Do you think Moore's burning of Byron's manuscripts was selfish or selfless?
   Discuss both perspectives.
3. Friendship, unlike love, is not an exclusive relationship. What role do you think loyalty plays in friendship, and why?

Unit 8

Various Forms of Love Ⅲ: Beyond Boundaries

Love is not love which alters when it alteration finds.

—William Shakespeare

Preview 1. Main Ideas

1. Love between people of the same sex has become a major topic of discussion in academic and cultural fields in recent decades.
2. There were many influential figures in history who supported homosexuality.
3. Some countries use homosexuality as a political tool to manipulate public opinion.

Preview 2. Keywords

Define the words below in your own words. Then, search online for example sentences that show how each word is used. Share your definitions and sentences with your partner.

1. diversity: ____________________
2. taboo: ____________________
3. Alan Turing: ____________________
4. multiracial democracy: ____________________
5. cultural values: ____________________

Preview 3. Talk About

Look at the following questions and discuss your ideas with a partner.

1. Talk about pop culture such as movies, plays, or shows that explore human relationships, diversity, or inclusion.
2. In the example you chose, discuss how the characters show understanding, kindness, or empathy toward others with different backgrounds or identities.

Preview 4. Further Discussion

1. Share examples of how characters in books or films overcome challenges in their relationships or identity.
2. How can communities create a respectful and inclusive environment for everyone?

In the 1980s, the postmodern era brought new ideas of diversity and individuality. The topic of same-sex relationships, once heavily stigmatized or considered taboo, began to receive more attention in academic and cultural discussions. Historical evidence shows that such relationships have existed for thousands of years. In ancient Greece, they were part of cultural and social customs, and they are still accepted in some ethnic groups today. For example, some African tribes reportedly regarded such relationships as a common practice until the early 20th century.

Throughout history, many influential people have supported same-sex relationships. The English philosopher Jeremy Bentham, famous for his idea of utilitarianism, argued that fear of such relationships often came from religious beliefs and the wish to keep social order. Moreover, he suggested that same-sex relationships might help reduce problems such as overpopulation. Ironically, in Bentham's home country, Britain, they were illegal at the time. One of the first famous people punished under these laws was Oscar Wilde, a well-known playwright and poet. Later, Alan Turing, a brilliant mathematician who helped create the first computer algorithm and whose life was portrayed in *The Imitation Game* (2014), was also persecuted for his sexual orientation. In most modern Western countries, however, these relationships are no longer punished by law.

In many parts of the world, however, same-sex relationships remain illegal and can lead to severe punishment, or even the death penalty. Some African leaders have used this issue to gain political support. In the 1990s, Robert Mugabe, president of Zimbabwe, and Sam Nujoma, president of Namibia, strongly opposed sexual diversity, calling it a corrupt influence brought from the West.[25] In contrast, Nelson Mandela, the founding father of South Africa's multiracial democracy, rejected the claim that same-sex relationships were un-African.[26] He viewed them as a natural form of diversity that had long been suppressed and deserved recognition within African societies.

Despite Mandela's progressive views, opposition to these identities remains strong in many African countries. Some people regard such relationships as immoral or even evil, which raises serious questions about human rights and cultural values. A Ugandan woman once asked: "What kind of human rights are we talking about when people are turning away from reasonable human beings to evil?"[27]

This question invites us to think more deeply. How should we balance cultural traditions with the principle of equality? How far should human rights extend when values conflict? As we read the following texts, let's explore these difficult yet important issues together.

8A: Oscar Wilde

Pre-Reading 1. General Questions

1. Search for information about Oscar Wilde online.
2. Talk about any of Oscar Wilde's works that you are familiar with.
3. Search for what the Decadent Movement was.
4. Research the history of same-sex relationships and their social impact.

Pre-Reading 2. Vocabulary

Guess the meaning of each underlined word and choose its definition from the list below.

1. The movement opposed the seriousness of life and emphasized aesthetics and pleasure. ________
2. This work marked the pinnacle of his aesthetics and earned him national fame. ________
3. He destroys his portrait, which has become something hideous. ________
4. It was criticized by conservatives as a story that encourages moral corruption. ________
5. Wilde's last days were not blissful. ________
6. Their hostility toward it gradually increased. ________

A. (a) characterized by or experiencing extreme happiness, joy, and contentment
B. (n) intense opposition, dislike, or unfriendliness
C. (n) bad or dishonest behavior, or losing a sense of what is right and wrong
D. (a) extremely ugly or disgusting to see
E. (n) the highest or best point of something; the peak
F. (n) the study or appreciation of beauty, especially in art and design

Oscar Wilde was born in Dublin in 1854. His parents, of British-Irish descent, were wealthy enough to provide him with a quality education. After graduating from Trinity College in Dublin in 1871, he moved to England to study at Oxford University. Wilde was a modern intellectual who spoke French and German fluently. He was also very fashionable. He became a central figure in cultural society and took the lead in the Decadent Movement. This movement is one of the most prominent art and literary movements that arose in Western Europe in the late 19th century. It rejected the strict seriousness of life and emphasized aesthetics and pleasure.

Oscar Wilde

He was already a celebrity in social circles and published short stories and essays while working as a journalist. However, his first major success, *The Picture of Dorian Gray*, made him nationally famous and marked the peak of his artistic achievement. The main character, Dorian, wants to stay young forever and gives up his soul to keep the youth shown in his portrait. As a result, he stays young while his portrait grows older. After living a life full of wrongdoing, he destroys the portrait, which has become hideous. At that moment, he becomes old and deformed, and the portrait returns to its original beauty. Wilde showed people's secret wish to stay young and free from social rules through the story of Dorian. Although young readers liked its honest picture of human desires and emotions, the novel was criticized by conservatives as a story that encourages moral corruption.

Wilde not only explored the inner darkness within human beings but also encouraged the good qualities that people may have forgotten or overlooked. "The Happy Prince" is one of Wilde's most famous fairy tales, teaching a lesson on the virtues of charity. The Prince in the story is a statue overlooking a city, decorated with beautiful jewels such as bright sapphires for his eyes and a large red ruby on his sword. Although he appears glorious, the Prince feels deep sorrow for the suffering he sees in the city. His heart, made of lead, grows heavy with sadness, and he cannot stop crying for the people. A swallow notices his sadness and, at the Prince's request, takes the jewels from his body one by one to give them to the poor. The Prince loses everything he has, but in the end, he feels true happiness.

In contrast to his enchanting stories, Wilde's last days were far from blissful. Although Britain had enforced laws against same-sex relationships since the 1840s, Wilde became the most famous person to be punished under these laws. In 1895, he was sentenced to two years of hard labor in prison for "gross indecency." The word "homosexuality," created by an American doctor in 1892, was not yet commonly used in the UK. Most British people at that time did not see same-sex relationships as natural but as wrong. Media coverage of the topic often increased public hostility.

In fact, Wilde's sexuality had already been known among people in literary and artistic circles long before his trial. His gentle and feminine manner matched "the Victorian stereotype of the homosexual."[28] When the father of his lover, Alfred Douglas, accused him of corrupting his son, Wilde sued him for written defamation. During the trial, Wilde's sexual orientation became known across the country, and the press turned the case into a major scandal. Conservative critics fiercely attacked and condemned him. As a result, Wilde was punished to "the fullest extent of the law," even though the evidence was weak, circumstantial, and unreliable.[29]

Wilde and Lord Alfred Douglas, 1893

Prison conditions at the time were extremely harsh. Wilde endured hard labor, hunger, cold, daily humiliation, and despair. He suffered from diarrhea and exhaustion caused by poor-quality, unhygienic food and struggled with chronic sleeplessness.[30] After his release, Wilde never recovered his health or reputation. His once free and lively personality also faded. He was only 45 when he died in 1900. Despite his tragic end, Wilde is still celebrated in Ireland as a national treasure and one of their greatest literary figures. His plays are considered the best since Shakespeare, and his fairy tales are still widely loved.

Wilde's Poem:

Apologia

Is it thy will that I should wax and wane,
Barter my cloth of gold for hodden grey,
And at thy pleasure weave that web of pain
Whose brightest threads are each a wasted day?

Is it thy will–Love that I love so well–
That my Soul's House should be a tortured spot
Wherein, like evil paramours, must dwell
The quenchless flame, the worm that dieth not?

Nay, if it be thy will I shall endure,
And sell ambition at the common mart,
And let dull failure be my vestiture,
And sorrow dig its grave within my heart.

Perchance it may be better so—at least
I have not made my heart a heart of stone,
Nor starved my boyhood of its goodly feast,
Nor walked where Beauty is a thing unknown.

……

But surely it is something to have been
The best beloved for a little while,
To have walked hand in hand with Love, and seen
His purple wings flit once across thy smile.

Ay! though the gorged asp of passion feed
On my boy's heart, yet have I burst the bars,
Stood face to face with Beauty, known indeed
The Love which moves the Sun and all the stars!

"The Wilde v. Queensberry Case and how it ended."
Illustration from a police news publication, 1895

- thy: (archaic) your
- paramours: lover
- quenchless: unquenchable; unable to be extinguished or satisfied (e.g., a quenchless thirst or passion)
- dieth: die
- vestiture: clothing
- hath: have

Post-Reading 1. Review

1. Discuss Wilde's first major success, *The Picture of Dorian Gray*. What themes are explored in this novel?
2. Why was *The Picture of Dorian Gray* so well received? How does it differ from novels written before its time?
3. Who are the main characters in the story "The Happy Prince"?

Post-Reading 2. Paraphrasing

Rewrite Wilde's idea as seen in the lines below in simpler, everyday English.

> But surely it is something to have been
> The best beloved for a little while,
> To have walked hand in hand with Love, and seen
> His purple wings flit once across thy smile.

Post-Reading 3. Discussion

1. What kind of world did Wilde try to show through the aesthetics of his works?
2. Dorian, the protagonist *in The Picture of Dorian Gray*, desires eternal youth. If you could stay young forever, would you choose to? Why or why not?
3. What do you think true happiness means in "The Happy Prince"?

Post-Reading 4. Critical Thinking

1. What do you think this reading text tells us about society in Wilde's time?
2. Which do you think was harder for Wilde: going to prison or losing his reputation? Why?
3. If Wilde lived today, how might his life and career be different?

8B: John Addington Symonds

Pre-Reading 1. General Questions

1. Search for information about John Addington Symonds online.
2. Find information about an artist or public figure known for their same-sex relationships or identity.
3. Research a historical figure whose achievements were overlooked or criticized because of social attitudes toward their identity.

Pre-Reading 2. Vocabulary

Guess the meaning of each underlined word and choose its definition from the list below.

1. He had a relatively prosperous and stable period of growth. ________
2. While he was studying at Oxford University, his health deteriorated. ________
3. He devoted himself to the spread of Hellenism and Platonism. ________
4. He left a memoir in which he candidly confessed his love. ________
5. An accusation that someone was in a same-sex relationship could be used as blackmail.
6. He died in Italy and many colleagues mourned his death. ________

A. (v) to feel or show sadness after someone's death
B. (v) to sincerely dedicate your time and effort to something or someone.
C. (n) the act of threatening to reveal secrets to get money or force someone to do something
D. (v) to become worse in condition, quality, or health
E. (a) a written account of someone's personal experiences and memories
F. (a) experiencing success, wealth, or growth in a positive and often financial aspect

Symonds was born in England in 1840. His father was a doctor, and he grew up in a relatively prosperous and stable home. Some say he didn't do well in school as a boy, but these claims turned out to be false. His admission to Balliol College, Oxford, at the age of 18 shows his high academic ability. Balliol was the best college for classics at Oxford University at the time. Symonds encountered ancient Greek books and was completely absorbed in them there.

John Addington Symonds

While studying, his health deteriorated. He went to Italy where the weather was favorable for treatment—a common practice among the British upper class when ill. During his stay for treatment, he studied Renaissance culture in depth and became even more fascinated by ancient Greek philosophy.

From this time on, Symonds' main academic interest was Hellenism. He studied hard and took first place in the Greats—the graduation exam—at the university. Subsequently, his research on the Renaissance was also recognized, and in 1862 he was appointed as a Fellow at Magdalen College, Oxford. He devoted himself to the spread of Platonism within Hellenism, focusing especially on what is often referred to as "the Platonic view of same-sex relationships." This concept emphasized the spiritual love between an adult, *erastes*, and an adolescent boy, *eromenos*. The *erastes* acted as both teacher and lover, taking responsibility for the *eromenos'* intellectual, moral, and physical growth.

Symonds was not the only person studying ancient Greek and Roman philosophy and literature at his university, but his work was unique. In 1873, he wrote an essay titled *A Problem in Greek Ethics*, which examines how love between men was practiced in ancient Greece. The essay also explores the ethical principles surrounding same-sex relationships and explains how these views changed across different historical periods and cultures.

For this reason, he is still an important figure in the study of same-sex relationships in the 19th century. Some scholars say that he developed a deep interest in this topic partly because of his personal experiences. Indeed, his poetry clearly reveals his strong affection for men. Moreover, he left a

Norman Moor, known to be Symonds's close companion

memoir in which he candidly yet discreetly confessed his love for young men. It was published under the title *The Memoirs of John Addington Symonds: The Secret Homosexual Life of a Leading 19th-Century Man of Letters* in 1994. It took almost 100 years to be published and is regarded as the first gay autobiography in history.

Before *The Memoirs* was published, it had long remained unclear whether Symonds had ever been in a same-sex relationship, because everyone who was known as his lover refused to admit the truth. While he was at the university, a report about his alleged same-sex relationship was submitted to the university authorities. The accuser was one of his students who wished to enter Magdalen College, Oxford. When Symonds refused to help him, the student claimed that Symonds violated moral norms. At that time, a mere accusation that someone was in a same-sex relationship could be used as blackmail. In the end, the case turned out to be a conspiracy, and Symonds' innocence was proven. Nevertheless, because of this incident, people continued to question his character and even his marriage.

After getting married in 1864, he and his wife, Janet Catherine North, stayed together for about 30 years and had four daughters. He died in 1893 in Italy after suffering from chronic health problems. His death was deeply mourned by many colleagues. Yet only a few years later, when Wilde was imprisoned for homosexuality in 1895, the study of Greek homosexuality—one of the main subjects of Symonds's research—became taboo. All his academic achievements were forgotten. In recent years, however, his writings have been re-evaluated with the view that "his life is a story about the humanistic study, self-development, and a historian's interest in bringing 'human documents' to light."[31]

Symonds' Poem:

Clifton and a Lad's Love

He was all beautiful: as fair
As summer in the silent trees;
As bright as sunshine on the leas;
As gentle as the evening air.

His voice was swifter than the lark;
Softer than thistle-down his cheek;
His eyes were stars that shyly break
At sundown ere the skies are dark.

I found him in a lowly place:
He sang clear songs that made me weep:
Long nights he ruled my soul in sleep:
Long days I thought upon his face.

……

Organ and choir stalls in Ripon Cathedral. Photo by The Wub, licensed under CC BY-SA 4.0 via Wikimedia Commons

- lea: a field with grass.
- lark: a small singing bird, jong-dal-sae
- thistle: a wild purple flower with prickly leaves

Post-Reading 1. Review

1. Beyond an internet search, what new insights did you gain about John Addington Symonds?
2. What were Symonds' main areas of academic interest?
3. Why were Symonds' academic achievements overlooked or under-appreciated?
4. Discuss characteristics of same-sex relationships in ancient Greek society.

Post-Reading 2. Paraphrasing

Rewrite Symonds's idea as seen in the lines below in simpler, everyday English.

> I found him in a lowly place:
> He sang clear songs that made me weep:
> Long nights he ruled my soul in sleep:
> Long days I thought upon his face.

Post-Reading 3. Discussion

1. Discuss whether it is justifiable to undervalue someone's academic achievements based on their sexual orientation.
2. In the poem you have just read, does the depiction of love clearly indicate a same-sex relationship, or could it be understood in other ways? Explain your viewpoint.
3. Why is empathy important when discussing topics like sexuality and identity?

Post-Reading 4. Critical Thinking

1. Why do people sometimes judge others based on stereotypes or social expectations?
2. How have attitudes toward diversity and inclusion changed over time?
3. When is it appropriate to share personal details about someone's private life? How should privacy be respected?

Further Reading 1

*Excerpts from "President Gerald R. Ford's Tribute to President Jimmy Carter"**

Written by President Gerald R. Ford

By fate of a brief season, Jimmy Carter and I were rivals. But for the many wonderful years that followed, friendship bonded us. [...]

Frankly, I wondered how awkward that long flight might be to Cairo—and it was a long flight, but the return trip was not nearly long enough. For it was somewhere over the Atlantic that Jimmy and I forged a friendship that transcends politics. [...]

For Jimmy Carter, honesty was not an aspirational goal; it was part of his very soul. [...] Inspired by his faith, he pursued brotherhood across boundaries of nationhood, across boundaries of tradition, across boundaries of caste. [...]

Jimmy Carter's legacy of peace and compassion will remain unique as it is timeless. [...]

As for myself, Jimmy, I'm looking forward to our reunion. We have much to catch up on.
Thank you, Mr. President. Welcome home, old friend.

Discussion Questions

1. The tribute says that Carter's honesty "was part of his very soul." Why is honesty important in gaining others' respect and love?
2. What makes it hard for people to practice love and compassion today, and how can we change that?
3. What does true friendship mean in times of conflict or loss?

* This posthumous tribute by Gerald R. Ford, the 38th President of the United States, honored his former political rival, Jimmy Carter, the 39th, with rare warmth and respect. Delivered by Ford's son at the Washington National Cathedral, it celebrates a friendship that rose above politics and endured for decades. Through honesty, mutual respect, and shared faith, Ford and Carter built a bond that lasted beyond politics. Their story reminds us that empathy can lead to unexpected connection, and that true love for others often reveals itself through lasting friendship and quiet acts of kindness.

Further Reading 2

Excerpts from "Farewell Speech" *

Edward VIII, King of the United Kingdom

At long last I am able to say a few words of my own. [...] A few hours ago I discharged my last duty as King and Emperor, and now that I have been succeeded by my brother, the Duke of York, my first words must be to declare my allegiance to him. [...]

I have found it impossible to carry the heavy burden of responsibility and to discharge my duties as King as I would wish to do without the help and support of the woman I love. [...]

I have made this, the most serious decision of my life, only upon the single thought of what would, in the end, be best for all. [...]

I now quit altogether public affairs and I lay down my burden. [...] I wish him and you, his people, happiness and prosperity with all my heart.

God bless you all! God save the King!

Discussion Questions

1. What values or personal beliefs influenced Edward VIII's decision to abdicate?
2. How might this speech reflect the tension between public duty and private life?
3. This choice sparked debates about duty versus personal happiness. If you were in Edward VIII's position, would you give up the throne for love? Why or why not?

* Edward VIII abdicated the throne in 1936 because he chose love over duty. He wished to marry Wallis Simpson, an American divorcée who could not become queen under British law, and the government and Church opposed the marriage. Feeling he could not fulfill his role as King without her support, he renounced the crown in favor of his younger brother George VI (formerly Duke of York). This farewell speech was delivered on December 11, 1936, via a radio broadcast from Windsor Castle to audiences across the United Kingdom and the British Empire. After his abdication, he was granted the title Duke of Windsor and lived mostly abroad. Their love story remains one of the most famous royal romances in history.

Chapter 3

Living in Harmony

Warm-Up!

Talk about the following questions with your partners.

1. What comes to mind when you hear the phrase 'living in harmony'?
2. Imagine it is the year 2050. What three major challenges do you think people might face?
3. What do you think is most important for people to live together harmoniously?
4. Rank the following in order of importance for harmonious living: personal freedom, protecting the environment, supporting vulnerable people, and respecting differences

Traditionally, communities were defined by the spatial and historical bonds among their members. However, today communities transcend time and space and may be formed around hobbies, social or political goals, neighborhoods, or even workplaces. As social life becomes increasingly complex, the forms that communities take become more diverse. Each of them may differ greatly, yet we are all still gathered under the protective umbrella of our home—Earth.

On Earth, every one of us has equal value regardless of gender, age, race, or creed. Sadly throughout history and even today, this honorable truth is often forgotten or denied. It is still common to marginalize, exclude, or provoke conflict with others simply because of perceived differences. We should value those differences because they make us unique and bring diversity to society. American novelist Tom Robbins once said, "Equality is not in regarding different things similarly, equality is in regarding different things differently."[32]

Furthermore, many other living beings share the Earth with us, and their survival is essential to the well-being of the entire Earth community. For example, forests are one of its integral parts. Although they cannot speak in human language, they cry out in their own way every day, reminding us that they are in danger. In addition, countless animals are now endangered and exploited, and extinction rates are only increasing. In the last five minutes, while you were reading this passage, one animal species may already have gone extinct. The rate is almost 10,000 times higher than the historical average, and human activity is almost entirely to blame.

We have a duty to protect the most vulnerable members of our earthly community. By extending care and solidarity beyond familiar boundaries, we ensure a more just and sustainable future for generations to come.

What We Will Read

Unit 9. Animals
Unit 10. Our Earth
Unit 11. Sacrifice and Service
Unit 12. The Young and the Old
Unit 13. Men and Women

Further Reading 1: Excerpts from "Remarks at the Security Council Briefing on Children and Armed Conflict"
Further Reading 2: Excerpts from "A Voice for the Voiceless: Animal Rights and Human Responsibility" from the Universal Declaration of Animal Rights
Further Reading 3: Excerpts from "A Sacred Vow to Remember: Memorial Day Address"

Unit 9

Animals

"Cats are a mysterious kind of folk."

—Sir Walter Scott

Preview 1. Main Ideas

1. Human attitudes toward animals are changing.
2. Animals play an essential role in Earth's ecosystems.
3. Humans and animals are indispensable companions.

Preview 2. Keywords

Define the words below in your own words. Then, search online for example sentences that show how each word is used. Share your definitions and sentences with your partner.

1. domestication of animals

   ____

2. game (animal):

   ____

3. ecosystem:

   ____

4. companion:

   ____

5. embrace:

   ____

Preview 3. Talking About

Look at the following questions and discuss your ideas with a partner.

1. How have humans historically viewed and treated animals?
2. Do you think people's attitudes toward animals have changed over time? If so, how? Can you provide an example?
3. Do you think caring for animals can help people grow and become better?
4. If you have a pet, how would you describe your relationship with it? What does this relationship mean to you?

Preview 4. Further Discussion

1. How does animal extinction affect global ecosystems and biodiversity?
2. What actions can people take to help protect balanced ecosystems?

Throughout history, humans have coexisted with plants and animals, sharing space and resources in the struggle for survival. Yet, despite living side by side, people have generally regarded animals as inferior. This view is reflected even in language, where animals are often referred to impersonally as *it*. The domestication of animals, which began about 10,000 years ago, transformed the lives of many species to serve human needs in agriculture, transportation, and food production. While this process benefited humans, it deprived animals of freedom and reduced the numbers of their wild counterparts.

In Greek mythology, the goddess Artemis was associated not only with abundance but also with hunting because people believed the two were inseparable. Ancient societies viewed animals primarily as sources of leather, meat, labor, and even entertainment. This perception persists today, as sport fishing and hunting of deer or other animals remain popular in many regions. Such practices have been so widespread and enduring, and as a result, the animals most frequently hunted came to be known as "game."

In modern times, however, attitudes toward animals have begun to shift. Many people now regard animals as companions and friends rather than resources. Unlike before, pets are often referred to as *he* or *she*, not *it*. Eckhart Tolle, the German-born bestselling author, once said, "When the dog looks at you, the dog is not thinking what kind of a person you are. The dog is not judging you."[33] For this reason, many people willingly share their lives with animals as partners. The pet industry reflects this change as pet ownership in South Korea reaches record levels. For the first time in human history, humans and animals are living together in such deep physical and emotional closeness. Let us explore this transformation further.

9A: Sir Walter Scott

Pre-Reading 1. General Questions

1. Search for information about Sir Walter Scott online.
2. What is Romanticism?
3. Explore the historical relationship between Scotland and England.
4. Examine the portrait of Sir Scott with his hound(s) on the next page. What kind of relationship do you think existed between them?

Pre-Reading 2. Vocabulary

Guess the meaning of each underlined word and choose its definition from the list below.

1. He was made the baronet of Abbotsford in Roxburgh County, Scotland in <u>recognition</u> of his literary achievements. ________
2. He unfortunately <u>contracted</u> polio at the age of two. ________
3. His grandfather <u>regaled</u> him with many stories and legends of Scotland. ________
4. Loyal <u>hounds</u> formed strong bonds with their owners. ________
5. His <u>legacy</u> continues to inspire new generations of writers. ________

A. (n) something passed down from the past, such as achievements, ideas, or traditions.
B. (n) dogs that are trained and used for hunting animals
C. (n) the act of showing official appreciation for (something)
D. (v) to entertain someone with talks such as stories, jokes, etc.
E. (v) to become sick or fall ill with a disease

Sir Walter Scott by Sir William Allan

Sir Walter Scott was an important figure in the history of English literature. He was born in 1771 in the Old Town of Edinburgh, which is still home to many historical buildings and monuments reflecting Scotland's rich history. Scott spent his entire life in Scotland and died in 1832, which marked the end of the Romantic era in English literature. His poetical works and historical novels are still regarded as an important part of Romanticism.

Scott was a highly respected literary figure during his time. He received much recognition for his literary achievements and was made the baronet of Abbotsford in Roxburgh County, Scotland, on April 22, 1820. This title honored his contributions to the literary world, leaving a lasting legacy.

Scott's life and fame are inseparable from the spirit of Scotland. Although born into a respected Scottish family, he unfortunately contracted polio at the age of two and was sent to his grandfather's farm on the Scottish Borders in the hope of healing his leg. There, his grandfather regaled him with many stories and legends of Scotland, which had a lasting impact on his imagination and later his literary world. His illness, however, left him with a permanent disability. At the age of 12, he began formal studies in Edinburgh and later entered the University of Edinburgh to study the classics, which was considered the most intellectually demanding discipline at the time. Despite being considered too young by his classmates, Scott managed to complete the course.

After completing his education, Scott studied law and became a lawyer in Edinburgh. His work led him to visit the Scottish Highlands several times. During these journeys, he was inspired to renew his creativity and began writing poetry. His poetry is based on Scottish folk songs, tales, and legends. Unlike the speculative and philosophical poetry of his contemporaries such as Wordsworth and Coleridge, Scott appealed to readers with his more familiar themes.

Scott's poetry swiftly garnered the spotlight, and he became the most beloved British poet until Lord Byron rose to sudden prominence in literary circles. He then broadened the scope of his artistic activity to novels. The early 1800s were a time when novels began to gain popularity, thanks to advancements in printing technology and new intellectual needs among people. Many early novels tried to impose moral lessons on readers, but Scott tried to fire up their imagination by pioneering a new genre at the time—historical fiction.

His first and most famous novel was *Waverley* (1814). Its story follows a non-fictional event, the Battle of Culloden—a bloody battle fought in 1745 between English soldiers and the Jacobites, a Scottish rebel group that opposed English rule over Scotland. In this battle, almost 2,000 Jacobites were killed or wounded, and even those who managed to hide were executed after being relentlessly pursued. This brutal incident left a lasting scar on the hearts of the Scottish people. Scott brought this tragic collective memory to life by adding imaginary characters. He understood how imagination, when combined with well-known historical events, could deeply move and comfort people.

Scott was also known for his love of animals, especially dogs. He was often depicted in portraits with his favorite hunting dog, Bran. Hounds were indispensable for hunting, a favorite sport among the upper class. Loyal and trustworthy hounds formed strong bonds and interacted closely with their owners while hunting. Bran was not only a faithful hunting companion but also a great friend. He accompanied Scott almost everywhere, not just on the hunting grounds. In the poem we read, it is easy to imagine Bran sitting by Scott's side. His love of Scotland, his affection for animals, and his enduring contributions to literature have firmly secured his place in history.

The Abbotsford Family by Sir David Wilkie, 1817, depicting Scott and his family

Sir Scott's Poem:

Hunting Song

Waken, lords and ladies gay,
On the mountain dawns the day;
All the jolly chase is here
With hawk and horse and hunting-spear,
Hounds are in their couples yelling,
Hawks are whistling, horns are knelling,
Merrily, merrily mingle they
Waken, lords and ladies gay.

Waken, lords and ladies gay,
The mist has left the mountain gray;
Springlets in the dawn are steaming,
Diamonds on the brake are gleaming;
And foresters have busy been
To track the buck in thicket green;
Now we come to chant our lay,
Waken, lords and ladies gay.

Waken, lords and ladies gay,
To the greenwood haste away;
We can show you where he lies,
Fleet of foot and tall of size;
We can show the marks he made
When 'gainst the oak his antlers fray'd;
You shall see him brought to bay
Waken, lords and ladies gay.

Louder, louder chant the lay,
Waken, lords and ladies gay!
Tell them youth and mirth and glee
Run a course as well as we;
Time, stern huntsman! who can balk,
Staunch as hound and fleet as hawk:
Think of this, and rise with day,
Gentle lords and ladies gay!

- steaming: doing its work with energy
- diamond: dewdrop in this context
- brake: a cluttered, tangled bush or a forest
- buck: a male deer
- lay: a narrative poem meant to be sung
- he: refers to the buck
- fray'd; old-fashioned spelling of frayed

Duck Shooting by Horace Vernet, 1824

Post-Reading 1. Review

1. What did Sir Scott study at the University of Edinburgh?
2. What changes in the 1800s helped novels become more popular?
3. How was his way of writing novels different from other writers of his time, and which historical event is central to *Waverley*?

Post-Reading 2. Paraphrasing

Rewrite Sir Scott's idea as seen in the lines below in simpler, everyday English.

Waken, lords and ladies gay,
On the mountain dawns the day;
All the jolly chase is here
With hawk and horse and hunting-spear,
Hounds are in their couples yelling,
Hawks are whistling, horns are knelling,
Merrily, merrily mingle they
Waken, lords and ladies gay.

Post-Reading 3. Discussion

1. Scott was a gifted storyteller. Do you think this ability is innate, or can it be developed through practice and experience?
2. *Waverley* was immediately celebrated by readers. What parts of the novel do you think appealed to them the most?
3. In this poem, which part is described most vividly?

Post-Reading 4. Critical Thinking

1. Scott loved dogs. Many people love animals but also depend on them for work or food. How can we keep this relationship in balance?
2. More people today have pets, but sometimes we treat them as property. How can we see animals as real members of our community?
3. Animal farming often causes suffering. How can we make it more humane and still affordable?

9B: Christopher Smart

Pre-Reading 1. General Questions

1. Search for information on Christopher Smart online.
2. If you were to have a pet, which would you choose — a dog or a cat? Explain your preference.
3. Explore the positive impact that pets have on human psychology.

Pre-Reading 2. Vocabulary

Guess the meaning of each underlined word and choose its definition from the list below.

1. Smart's father, Peter, was a <u>steward</u> of a private estate in England. ________
2. Grace Vane, a duchess, <u>sponsored</u> Smart's education. ________
3. Modernism was <u>established</u> and his poetry was considered outdated. ________
4. He stayed in a <u>mental institution</u> for a while. ________
5. He seems <u>eccentric</u> enough to exceed the ordinary standards of the time. ________

A. (v) to pay for or support someone's education, activity, or project
B. (a) showing behavior or ideas that are unusual or different from what is normal
C. (n) a person who manages another person's property, land, or estate.
D. (n) a hospital or facility where people with mental illnesses are treated and cared for.
E. (v) to start or set up something important, such as a system, movement, or institution.

Christopher Smart

Christopher Smart was a poet who lived from 1722 to 1771, about 300 years ago. Because of the time gap, we may assume that his way of thinking was very different from ours today. However, when we read his poetry, we may feel that he was modern in many ways. Smart's father, Peter, was a steward of a private estate in England, so he couldn't afford to give Smart a good education. As a result, Smart grew up on a farm until the age of 11, spending much of his time close to nature and developing a vivid imagination. He then attended Maidstone Grammar School, but after his father died, he had to pause his education. The family was left in heavy debt. Smart's mother sold their possessions and moved the family closer to relatives in Durham.

While staying at the mansion of Henry Vane, the Earl of Darlington, Smart wrote poems for Henrietta, the Duchess of Cleveland, who was the sister of Grace Vane, the Earl's wife. Smart's intelligence soon caught the attention of the Duke and Duchess, who later sponsored his education at Pembroke College, Cambridge University.

Smart was not well-known as a poet during his lifetime, but rather as a publisher. His writings were introduced under the female pseudonym "Mrs. Mary Midnight." It was unusual for male writers to use female pen names, which reflects his uniqueness. His poetic works were collected in only two books. One of them did not receive public or critical attention until the 19th century, and the other was not even published until 1939. When they were finally published, only a few critics showed interests in them because modernism was already being established, and his poetry was seen as outdated.

Despite this, Smart's poetry remains relevant today with three main themes that are often studied: hymns, madness, and cats. In the strict religious society after the Puritan revolution, faith was rigid and served as the guiding principle of life. Smart was also deeply religious and wanted to use his poetic talents for his faith. Thanks to his determination, his hymns such as "I Sing of God—the World He Made" can still be found today, even on the Internet.[34]

The second theme, madness, is often linked to Smart because of rumors that he was mentally ill. However, this remains uncertain as there is little evidence to support this claim. He stayed in a mental institution for a while, but it is not clear whether he suffered from a psychological disorder. It was an era when even people without mental illness could be imprisoned in such places, and those who broke social norms were often considered to be psychotic. Rumors about Smart's mental illness seem to have begun with a publisher's remark suggesting that

Smart had some personal issues. However, several historical documents that support the claim of his mental illness do not match the known facts. Christopher Hunter, Smart's nephew and first biographer, was also uncertain about the nature of his alleged madness and his confinement. It is therefore highly likely that Smart was not mentally ill.

Even so, he appeared eccentric by the standards of his time, as demonstrated by his famous poem about his cat, Jeoffry. This depiction appears in a 74-line passage within *Jubilate Agno*, a religious poem of more than 1,200 lines, where Smart intentionally breaks the regular rhythm. The unusual choice of subject and bold departure from convention also reveal his eccentric nature. Still, it is clear that he had a genuine affection for his feline companion. Through his eyes, the cat's grace and dignity, admired by cat lovers today, are vividly portrayed.

Christopher Smart was a distinctive poet who was not well received in his time, but whose work remains significant today. His themes of faith, mental health, and love for animals continue to be studied and appreciated by readers and scholars alike.

Title page of *Hymns for the Amusement of Children* (3rd ed., 1775) by Christopher Smart

Smart's Poem:

For I Will Consider My Cat Jeoffry*

For he is the cleanest in the use of his forepaws of any quadruped.
For the dexterity of his defense is an instance of the love of God to him exceedingly.
For he is the quickest to his mark of any creature.
For he is tenacious of his point.
For he is a mixture of gravity and waggery.
For he knows that God is his Saviour.
For there is nothing sweeter than his peace when at rest.
For there is nothing brisker than his life when in motion.
For he is of the Lord's poor, and so indeed is he called by benevolence perpetually–
    Poor Jeoffry! poor Jeoffry! the rat has bit thy throat.
For I bless the name of the Lord Jesus that Jeoffry is better.
For the divine spirit comes about his body to sustain it in complete cat.
For his tongue is exceeding pure so that it has in purity what it wants in music.
For he is docile and can learn certain things.
For he can sit up with gravity, which is patience upon approbation.
For he can fetch and carry, which is patience in employment.
For he can jump over a stick, which is patience upon proof positive.
For he can spraggle upon waggle at the word of command.

……

- gravity: seriousness
- waggery: playful or mischievous humor; joking behavior
- spraggle: to move loosely, awkwardly, or spread out in an irregular way.

* "For I Will Consider My Cat Jeoffry" corresponds to lines 732-748 from Fragment B in *Jubilate Agno,* a religious poem written between 1759 and 1763 by Smart.

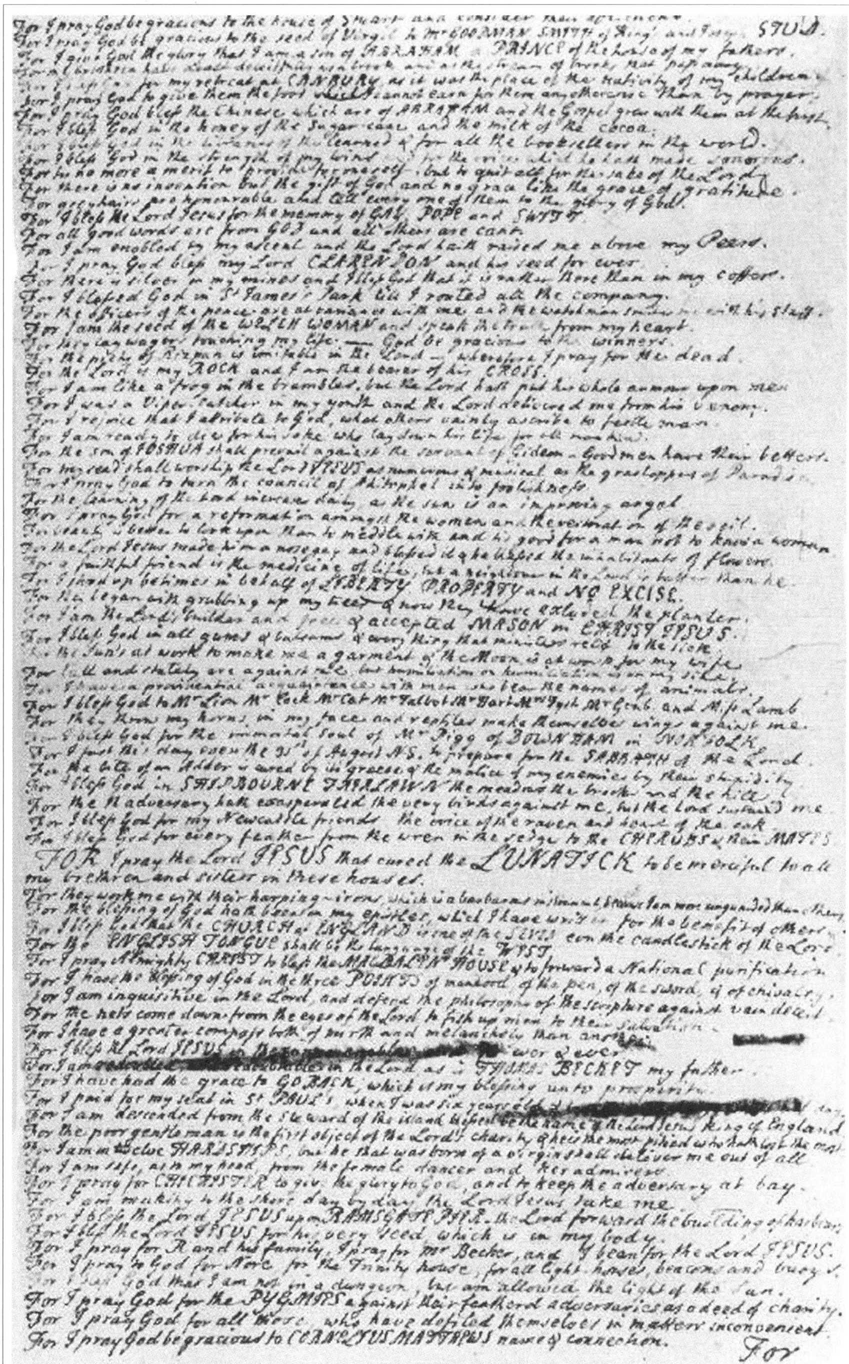

Manuscript page from Christopher Smart's *Jubilate Agno*

Post-Reading 1. Review

1. Explain why Christopher Smart dropped out of school and how he was able to continue his education.
2. What was Smart's occupation?
3. Find instances that show Christopher Smart's unique or exceptional qualities in his writings or personal life.

Post-Reading 2. Paraphrasing

Rewrite Smart's idea as seen in the lines below in simpler, everyday English.

For he is a mixture of gravity and waggery.
For he knows that God is his Saviour.
For there is nothing sweeter than his peace when at rest.
For there is nothing brisker than his life when in motion.

Post-Reading 3. Discussion

1. Explore how cats are perceived differently in Western and Eastern cultures.
2. Which characteristics of cats are highlighted in his poetry? Do these aspects match your own views on cats?
3. Share your experiences of having or raising animals, including both the most rewarding and challenging moments.
4. Discuss why Smart was portrayed as a madman. Do you think this label was justified, given what you know about his mental health?

Post-Reading 4. Critical Thinking

1. In the past, people with different ideas were often mistreated. How can we make sure that, today, diverse ideas are accepted and respected?
2. Why do you think some people abandon their pets? Brainstorm creative ways—both individual- and community-based—to solve this problem.
3. How might animal cruelty reflect deeper social or cultural problems? Share examples or stories to support your view.

Unit 10
Our Earth

"The best thing one can do when it's raining is to let it rain."

—Henry Wadsworth Longfellow

Pre-Reading 1. Main Ideas

1. Nature is the perfect place for us to rest and regain our own primordial energy.
2. The fates of humanity and the Earth are inseparable.
3. The Earth is, and will always be, our first and last community.

Pre-Reading 2. Keywords

Define the words below in your own words. Then, search online for example sentences that show how each word is used. Share your definitions and sentences with your partner.

1. solitude: ______________________________

2. an organic system: ______________________________

3. inhabitants: ______________________________

4. The Amazon: ______________________________

5. Mother Nature: ______________________________

Pre-Reading 3. Talking About

Look at the following questions and discuss your ideas with a partner.

1. Talk about an impressive experience you recently had in nature (such as exploring a forest, hiking, or camping).
2. Give examples of current environmental problems that the Earth is facing.

Pre-Reading 4. Further Discussion

1. Study about Greta Thunberg's campaign and discuss its influence on societal attitudes toward climate change.
2. Do you see the Earth as part of our human community? Share your reasons for your viewpoint.
3. What actions do you think are necessary to ensure the well-being and sustainability of the planet?

Albert Einstein once said, "Look deep, deep into nature, and then you will understand everything better."[35] What did he mean by this? By spending time in nature, we can find a sense of peace and solitude. Despite the sounds of the wind through the trees, birds singing, and water flowing, we do not consider these noises to be disruptive or distracting. Rather, we experience a moment of liberation from the hustle and bustle of city life. Thus, nature has long been seen as the perfect place for humans to regain their energy.

Ecology, or ecocriticism, moves beyond the traditional view of nature as merely a resting place for humans, and instead sees the Earth as an organic system in which human life is deeply interconnected with all living things. This perspective is closely reflected in the Gaia theory, which originated in the 1970s and was named after the Greek goddess Gaia. The theory portrays the Earth as the mother of all living things, including humanity itself. According to the idea, all living things, including humans, are sustained and supported by Gaia.

As inhabitants of planet Earth, we share a special bond with our planet. However, we often take it for granted and harm it to serve our greed. For example, the Amazon is often called the "lungs of the Earth" because it produces a significant amount of the world's oxygen. Nonetheless, driven by the pursuit of profit, people continue to destroy it at an alarming rate. The melting of glaciers at the poles is also a sign of human-caused damage. Mother Nature continually sends us warning signs that we should heed, but we constantly ignore them.

Fortunately, there are ongoing efforts to raise awareness and minimize the negative impact of humans on the Earth. Most notably, a young Swedish environmentalist, Greta Thunberg, is known for her campaign with the slogan, "Our House Is on Fire," raising awareness about climate change and the urgent need for action to protect the environment. Such ongoing discussions regarding the fate of the planet are all around us. Let's talk about how to treat the Earth with respect, since it is our first and last community.

10A: Henry Wadsworth Longfellow

Pre-Reading 1. General Questions

1. Search for information on Henry Wadsworth Longfellow online.
2. Have you ever felt comforted or refreshed by spending time in nature? Talk about this with your partner.
3. Talk about the lessons we learn from nature. Are there any famous sayings or proverbs related to nature?

Pre-Reading 2. Vocabulary

Guess the meaning of each underlined word and choose its definition from the list below.

1. He was born in a so-called <u>cradle of gold</u>. ________
2. <u>Constrained</u> by the harsh environment, early Americans found it difficult to create a unique culture. ________
3. It is often regarded as the first <u>authentic</u> piece of American literature. ________
4. His deep sorrow was not easily <u>abated</u>. ________
5. His poetry was <u>replete</u> with feelings of solitude. ________

A. (a) real or genuine
B. (idiom) being born into wealth and privilege
C. (v) to limit or control something, especially by rules, conditions, or circumstances
D. (v) to become weakened or less intense
E. (a) filled or well-supplied with something

Longfellow, one of America's most celebrated poets, was born in Portland, Maine, in 1807. His family descended from settlers who arrived on the *Mayflower* in the early 1600s. His mother was the daughter of General Peleg Wadsworth, who served in the Continental Army during the American Revolutionary War. Longfellow's middle name, Wadsworth, shows the pride he took in his family's role in the history of the United States. Thanks to his prestigious family background, Longfellow was raised in a supportive environment and received a good education. He entered a dame school, which was similar to a kindergarten today, at the age of three, and later attended Bowdoin College at 15. His grandfather was one of the founders of the college, and his father served as one of its trustees. Needless to say, he was born into a cradle of gold.

Henry Wadsworth Longfellow

Upon graduating from Bowdoin, Longfellow was offered a teaching position at Bowdoin College. He accepted the position only on the condition that he could first travel to Europe to study languages. His travels lasted much longer than expected, and the three years he spent there were full of new cultural experiences and surprises. After learning much about the sophisticated cultures of Europe, he returned to Bowdoin College but declined the teaching position because he felt that the salary was too low for his qualifications and status. He later accepted another offer with a higher salary and began his career as a professor.

Following its independence from Britain, Americans could not yet establish their own culture. Constrained by the harsh environment and the struggles of daily life, they were still heavily influenced by European models. However, as time passed, their own cultural identity began to shine through in their works. In 1850, Nathaniel Hawthorne published *The Scarlet Letter*, vividly portraying the Puritan atmosphere that dominated 17th-century New England. Today, this work is considered the first authentic piece of American literature. Longfellow was also one of the pioneers of this era. He combined the knowledge and experience he had gained in Europe with his unique American sensibility, hoping that the younger generation would help open up a rich and diverse future for America.

About five years later, he was offered a teaching position at Harvard University, which allowed him to travel to Europe

Longfellow's first wife Mary Storer Potter

and experience its refined culture before taking up his position. However, this second journey to Europe proved a misfortune. His pregnant wife, Mary Storer Potter, died of exhaustion during the trip at the young age of 22. Longfellow returned alone.

After he began teaching at Harvard, his grief did not easily abate. During this period, his writings began to reflect emotional turmoil marked by unbearable loneliness and pain. However, his poetry did not become as dark as Poe's. Instead, he transformed his sorrow into works that gave American poetry a new and distinctive character. His poems were written in clear, easy-to-read English, and he expressed a sensibility well suited to Puritan and patriotic American tastes.

Longfellow is especially loved for the way he writes about the simple emotions of the heart with purity, sweetness, and tenderness. Moreover, he wrote more poems about nature than any other American poet, and many of the best-known short descriptions of nature—phrases or single lines—originate in his work.[36] Nature comforted him in his deep loneliness and sorrow, and he shared that comfort with his contemporaries.

In his time, he became America's most beloved poet, and his gentle nature endeared him to the public. Though a sense of solitude remains in his poetry, his social relationships did not suffer. A European visitor who once spoke with him remarked, "This is the pleasantest man I ever met. He is a first-class gentleman. But where is Longfellow? Where's the American poet?"[37] It is often believed that artists and poets have eccentric personalities or peculiar tastes, yet Longfellow was different. Perhaps his pleasant character mirrored the gentle spirit that also permeates his poetry.

Longfellow's Poem:

A Day of Sunshine

O gift of God! O perfect day:
Whereon shall no man work, but play;
Whereon it is enough for me,
Not to be doing, but to be!
Through every fibre of my brain,
Through every nerve, through every vein,
I feel the electric thrill, the touch
Of life, that seems almost too much.
I hear the wind among the trees
Playing celestial symphonies;
I see the branches downward bent,
Like keys of some great instrument.
And over me unrolls on high
The splendid scenery of the sky,
Where through a sapphire sea the sun
Sails like a golden galleon,
Towards yonder cloud-land in the West,
Towards yonder Islands of the Blest,
Whose steep sierra far uplifts
Its craggy summits white with drifts.

- keys: the keys on a keyboard instrument (e.g., a piano or an organ)
- galleon: large Spanish sailing ships in use from the 16th to the 17th centuries
- blest: blessed
- drifts: snow blown by the wind

Longfellow and his family on European tour, 1869

Post-Reading 1. Review

1. Explain why Longfellow wanted to study European culture.
2. Talk about his family background.
3. What were the main themes of his poems?

Post-Reading 2. Paraphrasing

Rewrite Longfellow's idea as seen in the lines below in simpler, everyday English.

Through every fibre of my brain,
Through every nerve, through every vein,
I feel the electric thrill, the touch
Of life, that seems almost too much.
I hear the wind among the trees
Playing celestial symphonies;
I see the branches downward bent,
Like keys of some great instrument.

Post-Reading 3. Discussion

1. Longfellow is often described as a gentle and kind poet, unlike the eccentric personality of Edgar Allan Poe. Discuss the main factors that may have contributed to these characteristics in Longfellow.
2. Examine his poetry and identify passages that show how nature brings comfort.

Post-Reading 4. Critical Thinking

1. Longfellow sought to develop a distinctive American culture by embracing refined European culture. What is the difference between imitation and creation?
2. When does cultural exchange become enrichment, and when does it risk cultural loss? Discuss the balance between external influences and local creativity.
3. Which do you think has a greater influence on a person's success, innate personality or environment?

10B. Gerard Manley Hopkins

Pre-Reading 1. General Questions

1. Search for information about Gerard Manley Hopkins online.
2. Find a song or poem that warns of the destruction of nature.
3. Talk about the key work or goals of an environmental organization or activist you are familiar with.

Pre-Reading 2. Vocabulary

Guess the meaning of each underlined word and choose its definition from the list below.

1. His father Manley and mother Kate came from successful <u>entrepreneurial</u> families.

   ____

2. He was a <u>bane</u> to the principal, yet received the full support of his classmates.

   ____

3. The beauty of nature is continually destroyed in the name of <u>urban expansion</u> and industrial development. ________

4. He was appointed a professor in recognition of his <u>aptitude</u> as a scholar. ________

5. His father never understood the <u>conversion</u> of his son. ________

A. (n) someone or something that causes continuous problems
B. (a) involved in running their own businesses and pioneering new opportunities in the market
C. (n) the act of changing beliefs, habits, or ways of thinking
D. (n) the growth or increase of urban areas and industries
E. (n) a person's innate ability or skill in a field

Gerard Manley Hopkins

Hopkins, a renowned poet and Catholic Jesuit priest, was born in 1844 and died in 1889. Although he is widely recognized today as one of the most celebrated English poets of the late nineteenth century, he received little recognition during his lifetime. This is largely because his mature poems were not published until after his death. Hopkins was the eldest child of Manley and Kate Hopkins; his parents came from successful entrepreneurial backgrounds. As the eldest child and the first grandchild on both sides of the family, he grew up surrounded by the care and affection of his relatives. His childhood was full of joyful activities, such as tree climbing, and he also received a well-rounded education in music and art.

At the age of 10, Hopkins entered a boarding school called Highgate School. This school was well known for its effective teaching and was popular with middle-class parents who hoped to send their children to prestigious universities. To enforce these high standards, physical punishment, such as caning, was common. Hopkins strongly opposed such discipline and at times openly defied the headmaster, challenging his authority with reasoned arguments. Hopkins later recalled that, after an argument with the headmaster, he was even struck hard "with his riding whip."[38] He became the bane of the headmaster's existence, yet he also won popularity among his peers and enjoyed the full support of his classmates. After being admitted to Balliol College, Oxford, he maintained a large circle of friends while displaying a remarkable range of academic talents. He was called *the star of Balliol*. A friend once described him as "one of the cleverest and most original men at Oxford in his time."[39] In short, he was a very promising young man.

His life took a very different path after his conversion. In the 19th century, individualism was thriving, and people were increasingly focused on developing their sense of self. Hopkins felt that the Anglican Church (the Church of England) did not meet his own spiritual needs, though he had attended it with his parents since childhood. At that time, the Anglican Church was dominant in England, and joining another church often made it difficult to enter the mainstream of society. This remained true even for someone with an Oxford education. When Hopkins decided to leave the Anglican Church—even at the cost of a promising career, his father strongly opposed the decision. However, ultimately, Hopkins converted to Catholicism and became a Jesuit priest.

In the period immediately before and just after his ordination as a priest, Hopkins wrote poems that praised the pure and beautiful aspects of nature, seeing in them reflections of God's glory. Some years later, while serving as a parish priest in large industrial cities, his poems expressed a much deeper concern about the impending environmental crisis, which he saw as the result of reckless development. One of his poems, which we will examine, describes how the beauty of nature is continually destroyed in the name of urban expansion and industrial development. He also witnessed the urban poor losing their health and natural vitality to heavy labor and poverty. His grief over these injustices deepened, and his own health began to decline.

Subsequently, the Society of Jesus appointed him as a professor at University College Dublin in recognition of his scholarly aptitude. In Ireland, however, his health worsened, and he was unhappy about being far from England—a homeland he loved as deeply as he loved the beauty of nature. Moreover, teaching did not suit him as well as others had expected. "He was a man of great intellectual gifts, who had much difficulty in putting them to systematic use in an institutional context."[40] Hopkins' health continued to decline, and he eventually passed away in Ireland, with his parents having come to be by his side. His last words are reported to have been, "I am so happy. I am so happy."[41] His father, who had never understood his son's conversion, finally realized how deeply his son was loved and respected.

Nearly 30 years after Hopkins' death, his friend, Robert Bridges, edited and published his handwritten manuscripts. Around a decade later, the world began to celebrate his poetry. In 1975, *The Month*—a Jesuit magazine—issued a formal apology for refusing to publish his masterpiece, "The Wreck of the Deutschland," on the grounds that it was too experimental. By 1975, exactly a hundred years had passed since Hopkins had first written the poem. Hopkins had hoped that one day his poetry would be recognized by the grace of God. His dream was fulfilled.

Hopkins's final resting place in Dublin

Hopkins' Poem:

Binsey Poplars: Felled 1879

O if we but knew what we do
When we delve or hew
Hack and rack the growing green!
Since country is so tender
To touch, her being so slender,
That, like this sleek and seeing ball
But a prick will make eye at all,

Where we, even where we mean
To mend her we end her,
When we hew or delve:
After-comers cannot guess the beauty been.
Ten or twelve, only ten or twelve
Strokes of havoc unselve
The sweet especial scene,
Rural scene, a rural scene,
Sweet especial rural scene.

- delve: dig
- country: countryside where natural scenery remains, or nature
- slender: weak
- this sleek and seeing ball: human's eyeballs
- make: to cause to be broken
- unselve: lose or undo one's sense of self
- sweet: beautiful

St Beuno's and the Welsh landscape
—Hopkins's most beloved place of inspiration

Post-Reading 1. Review

1. Who was Gerard Manley Hopkins?
2. Talk about Hopkins' school days.
3. What is the most critical turning point in Hopkins' life? Why?

Post-Reading 2. Paraphrasing

Rewrite Hopkins' idea as seen in the lines below in simpler, everyday English.

> Where we, even where we mean
>   To mend her we end her,
>   When we hew or delve:
> After-comers cannot guess the beauty been.

Post-Reading 3. Discussion

1. What do you think influenced his decision to convert to Catholicism?
2. Talk about the environmental destruction that Hopkins witnessed while serving as a priest in industrial cities.
3. Discuss how Hopkins' poems reflect his view of nature as God's creation.

Post-Reading 4. Critical Thinking

1. Can you think of examples of artists whose work was not recognized during their lifetime? What might be the reasons?
2. Considering Hopkins' struggles with teaching, discuss the importance of choosing a career that matches one's aptitude. How can one identify and pursue a suitable career path?
3. Hopkins' poem expresses the pain of seeing a tree cut down. Do you think artists often use nature to express broader emotional or societal concerns? Why or why not?
4. What do concern for nature and concern for the poor have in common? Or are the two completely separate issues?

Unit 11
Sacrifice and Service

> **"Firefighters save more than homes. They save hearts, memories, and dreams."**
>
> —The Hellenic Initiative

Pre-Reading 1. Main Ideas

1. In the past, communities were often understood as single entities, characterized by a simple and repetitive daily routine.
2. Today, a community is defined by more than just its location.
3. The greatness of a community is shaped by its members' commitment and compassion.

Pre-Reading 2. Keywords

Define the words below in your own words. Then, search online for example sentences that show how each word is used. Share your definitions and sentences with your partner.

1. a geographical boundary:

   ____

2. absolute authority:

   ____

3. mutual support:

   ____

4. marginalized:

   ____

5. compassionate actions:

   ____

Pre-Reading 3. Talking About

Look at the following questions and discuss your ideas with a partner.

1. Discuss how you contribute to the communities you are involved in, and explain what they mean to you.
2. Look for examples of the communities we are familiar with. How are they maintained?

Pre-Reading 4. Further Discussion

1. Share your experiences with communities focused on building relationships. What values or aspects do you find most significant in these communities?
2. Online communities—such as those on Facebook, Kakao, X (formerly Twitter), and Instagram—are now widely used. What benefits do they offer, and what challenges do they pose for human connection?

Historically, communities in traditional societies were relatively easy to define. People seldom ventured beyond the borders of their towns, and most lived their entire lives without traveling more than twenty miles from their birthplace. Life was marked by monotony and the challenges of daily survival. Within these simple and repetitive routines, confined by narrow geographical boundaries, local community life functioned as a tightly bounded unit. It exercised strict control, binding its members to the absolute authority of a distant sovereign—a king or feudal monarch. They acknowledged his power but rarely, if ever, saw him in person.

On the other hand, in modern society, location alone is not enough to define a community. We now see a shift toward communities based on personal relationships and common interests. We often don't know or even care about our next-door neighbors. Instead, we look for and join online communities—sometimes offline ones, too—of people who share our hobbies or concerns. We often feel closer to them than to those next door. We now live in an era in which we choose and even define our own communities. What a remarkable change this is! We can share the same culture with people in other countries and create communities with them, as seen in the global popularity of groups such as the BTS ARMY or Blackpink's Blinks.

This newfound freedom comes at a price: we tend to remain ignorant of, or worse, ignore the pain and sorrow of people we do not see. During the COVID-19 pandemic and beyond, many marginalized people suffered from being isolated from their societies and were left struggling through this crisis. Even in those challenging times, stories of empathy and compassion emerged, as many quietly dedicated themselves to helping their communities endure and overcome the hardships. Coretta Scott King, once said that the greatness of a community is best measured by the compassionate actions of its members.[42] The true strength of a community is revealed through its kindness and empathy. When people are willing to make sacrifices for the sake of others, their dedication deserves our respect and gratitude. This spirit of empathy and mutual support shows the true value of a caring community.

11A: Alfred Edward Housman

Pre-Reading 1. General Questions

1. Search for information about Alfred Edward Housman online.
2. Are there examples of literary works that have been used to convey political messages or propaganda?
3. How can literary works have a significant impact on society and politics?

Pre-Reading 2. Vocabulary

Guess the meaning of each underlined word and choose its definition from the list below.

1. He received first-class honors in <u>Moderations</u>, a set of comprehensive examinations.

   ____

2. He could not immediately <u>pursue</u> a career as a scholar. ________

3. Housman had an <u>unparalleled</u> reputation as a classical scholar. ________

4. As a result, he became an <u>atheist</u>. ________

5. There have been many horrific wars resulting in <u>mass casualties</u> throughout history.

   ____

A. (a) unmatched or without equal in quality or reputation
B. (n) someone who does not believe in the existence of God or any gods
C. (n) preliminary examinations in certain fields of study that assess a wide range of knowledge
D. (n) a very large number of people killed or injured at the same time, usually because of war, disaster, or violence.
E. (v) to follow or engage in a particular path or career over a period of time

Alfred Edward Housman

Alfred Edward Housman, the eldest of seven children in a middle-class family, was born in a small town in Worcestershire, Britain in 1859. His mother died of cancer when he was just 12 years old. After his father's remarriage, Housman attended King Edward's School and later Bromsgrove School. It was there that his poetic talent first appeared, but he still prioritized his studies. With his outstanding academic skills and achievements, he gained admission to Oxford University on an open scholarship. Once enrolled, he earned first-class honours in Moderations, a set of comprehensive examinations taken early in some Oxford degree courses. It seemed as if Housman was destined for a bright academic career.

However, to many people's surprise, he failed to obtain honors on his final exam for graduation. This was a severe disappointment not only to Housman but also to his family, who had placed high hopes on him. As a result, he could not immediately pursue an academic career. Instead, he began work as a civil servant in London, a position he held for about 10 years. Whenever he could find spare time from his work in a government office in London, Housman spent it in the library, determined to triumph one day over the classical scholars who had rejected him.[43] Finally, in 1892, he was appointed Professor of Latin at University College London. Later, in 1911, he was appointed to a professorship at Trinity College, Cambridge.

During his lifetime, Housman was better known as a classical scholar, with an unparalleled reputation, than as a poet, even refusing to permit his first collection, *A Shropshire Lad*, to appear in the "Smaller Classics" series.[44] He considered it inappropriate to put his poetry on the same level as the classics. In addition, he bluntly rejected a publisher's request to write an autobiography, underscoring his preference to be regarded as a scholar rather than as a poet.

However, despite how he wished to be known, he was undoubtedly a poet. While he was alive, two collections of his poetry were published, and a third was released posthumously by his younger brother, making a total of 175 poems. Housman's poetic inspiration largely came from the tragic deaths in his family. The first shock came from the death of his mother who passed away on the very day of his 12th birthday. This loss resulted in the deepest wounds, leaving him feeling that his earnest prayers to God had been unanswered. As a result, he became an atheist, and his poems avoided the religious language common among his contemporaries. This may have made his poetry appear more modern to the next generation of readers. The second great loss was the death of his youngest brother Herbert, who served in the

Second Boer War in 1901 in South Africa. That loss further deepened the central themes of his poetry, such as sadness, death, soldiers, and patriotism. His works often paid tribute to bravery and self-sacrifice on the battlefield, expressing admiration and compassion for those who died honorably at a young age. Over time, he came to be recognized as one of the most prominent war poets in the West.

Since Housman's death in 1936, several generations have passed, and the world has witnessed even more horrific wars with mass casualties. Many people firmly oppose war, yet they also believe that those who sacrificed their lives on the battlefield for their communities should be remembered and honored. Let us consider how communities can remember such sacrifices without glorifying war.

An illustration of the Battle of Modder River during the Second Boer War, 1899

Housman's Poem:

Farewell to a Name and Number

Farewell to a name and a number
    Recalled again
To darkness and silence and slumber
    In blood and pain.

So ceases and turns to the thing
    He was born to be
A soldier cheap to the King
    And dear to me;

So smothers in blood the burning
    And flaming flight
Of valour and truth returning
    To dust and night.

number: military serial number

South African War Memorial in Toronto, commemorating Canadian soldiers who served in the Second Boer War (1899–1902). Photo by Taxiarchos228, licensed under the Free Art License.

Post-Reading 1. Review

1. Who was Alfred Edward Housman?
2. How did he prepare for a career as a classical scholar while working as a civil servant?
3. What experiences influenced the main themes of his poems?

Post-Reading 2. Paraphrasing

Rewrite Houseman's idea as seen in the lines below in simpler, everyday English.

> So ceases and turns to the thing
>   He was born to be
> A soldier cheap to the King
>   And dear to me;

Post-Reading 3. Discussion

1. What mood does the poem convey?
2. If you were Housman, would you emphasize your identity as a poet as well as that of a scholar? Why?
3. Do you think personal struggles are necessary for creating powerful art, as seen in Housman's life and poetry? Why or why not?

Post-Reading 4. Critical Thinking

1. Discuss how literary works can be used in contexts of war and politics. Provide examples.
2. Do you think poets and writers have a responsibility to take a moral or political stance in their work, or should art remain neutral? Why?

11B. Jane Taylor

Pre-Reading 1. General Questions

1. Search for information about Jane Taylor online.
2. Are there any female writers you know? Do they have any distinctive characteristics?
3. Do you know the song "Twinkle, Twinkle, Little Star"? If you don't, let's learn it together.

Pre-Reading 2. Vocabulary

Guess the meaning of each underlined word and choose its definition from the list below.

1. She regained the color and vitality of full health. ________
2. Jane Taylor may not be a household name. ________
3. The volumes were published posthumously by her brother. ________
4. Jane Taylor strongly criticized economic monopoly in her essays. ________
5. She dreamed of a world in which all people can live without deprivation. ________

A. (adv) after a person's death
B. (n) a state in which people lack what they need
C. (n) energy and strength; the quality of being full of life and active
D. (a) familiar to most families or people
E. (n) a situation where one group completely controls trade or resources

Jane Taylor may not be a household name. Without her brother's efforts to compile and publish her handwritten manuscripts posthumously in five volumes in 1824, her legacy might have been forgotten. According to the records left by her brother, Jane was born on September 23, 1783, while her parents were living in London. From birth through her first two years, her health was so weak and fragile that many doubted she would survive that difficult period. Fortunately, before she turned three, Mr. Taylor moved his family to the countryside. After that, Jane seemed to gain new energy and soon regained the color and vitality of full health.[45]

The Taylor Family by Isaac Taylor, featuring Jane and Ann Taylor

In 1806, Jane and her sister Ann published a collection of poetry that enjoyed modest success. Encouraged by this, they released another volume four years later, but this was their last collaboration. When Ann married and left home in 1813, Jane's literary pursuits slowed down. However, she continued on her own, writing essays, poems, and numerous letters expressing her views on social issues. They demonstrate a depth and breadth of knowledge that surpassed her sister Ann's, who had devoted her whole life to literature. Still, Jane's writings were not widely recognized since the literary world of her time was dominated by male Romantic poets.

Jane Taylor is best known for her poem "Twinkle, Twinkle, Little Star." It first appeared in a collection of poems in 1806, but it was not popular during her lifetime. That changed when it was included in Lewis Carroll's *Alice's Adventures in Wonderland* published in 1865. In Chapter 7, "A Mad Tea-Party," the Hatter performs a playful version of the rhyme: "Twinkle, twinkle, little bat, how I wonder what you're at."[46] He then asks Alice if she knows the song, and she replies that she has heard something similar. After the rise of Darwinism, British society took a deep interest in human progress and began to pay special attention to children, who were seen as the generation that would shape the future. This broader cultural shift fueled a boom in children's books in Britain and beyond. Among them, Lewis Carroll's *Alice's Adventures in Wonderland* was the most popular. People became interested in the song mentioned by the Hatter and Alice. "Twinkle, Twinkle, Little Star" became famous along with it.

While Jane Taylor is often linked to children's literature, her work goes far beyond nursery rhymes and lullabies. She also explored a wide range of important themes such as freedom, slavery, justice, humanity, war, moral judgment, voluntarism, and even the problem of economic monopoly. These ideas reflected her vision for a world in which all people could live free from deprivation. She urged people to consider those who are marginalized in society, reminding them not to take their own comfort for granted.* Even today, her words continue to resonate with readers, encouraging us to care for the less privileged and to work toward a fairer future.

Cover of *The Original Poems and Others* by Ann and Jane Taylor and Adelaide O'Keeffe

* This line echoes Jane Taylor's poem "The Beggar Boy," whose original wording includes: "while you in plenty all comforts enjoy, Oh think upon."

Taylor's Poem:

Poverty

I saw an old cottage of clay,
And only of mud was the floor;
'T was all falling into decay,
And the snow drifted in at the door.

Yet there a poor family dwelt,
In a cottage so dismal and rude;
And though gnawing hunger they felt,
They 'd not a morsel of food.

The children were crying for bread,
And to their poor mother they run;
"O give us some breakfast," they said,
Alas! their poor mother had none.

She view'd them with looks of despair,
She said (and I'm sure it was true),
"'Tis not for myself that I care,
But, my poor little children, for you,"

O, then, let the wealthy and gay
But see such a hovel as this,
That in a poor cottage of clay
They may learn what true misery is.

And the little that I may have to bestow
I never will squander away,
While many poor people there are,
As poor and as wretched as they.[47]

An engraving of impoverished residents in Wentworth Street, Whitechapel, from *London: A Pilgrimage* (1872) by Gustave Doré.

- gnawing: continuously painful
- 'Tis: It is
- morsel: a small amount of food
- hovel: a small, unpleasant, and often dirty house or room
- bestow: give something as a sign of respect
- squander away: to waste money or time in a foolish way

Post-Reading 1. Review

1. What insights or previously unknown facts did you discover about Jane Taylor?
2. Provide a concise summary of Jane Taylor's career.
3. What themes or issues was Jane Taylor most concerned with as a writer?

Post-Reading 2. Paraphrasing

Rewrite Taylor's idea as seen in the lines below in simpler, everyday English.

O, then, let the wealthy and gay
But see such a hovel as this,
That in a poor cottage of clay
They may learn what true misery is.

Post-Reading 3. Discussion

1. Children's literature became popular after the rise of Darwinism. How do you think Darwin's ideas may have influenced this genre?
2. What virtues do Taylor's poems emphasize? Why were those virtues significant in her time?

Post-Reading 4. Critical Thinking

1. If Jane Taylor lived today, how would her work be received differently? What would make her popular now?
2. Imagine you are wealthy in Taylor's time. How would you design an effective way to support the poor beyond charity?
3. In today's world, where public welfare systems exist, what role can individual charitable action play in reducing poverty?

Unit 12

The Young and the Old

"The freethinking of one age is the common sense of the next."

—Matthew Arnold

Pre-Reading 1. Main Ideas

1. People see childhood as the happiest time in life.
2. There are many cases of children suffering from exploitation.
3. The elderly are highly likely to be excluded from accessing new information.

Pre-Reading 2. Keywords

Define the words below in your own words. Then, search online for example sentences that show how each word is used. Share your definitions and sentences with your partner.

1. vulnerable: ______________________________

2. worldly knowledge: ______________________________

3. exploitation and abuse: ______________________________

4. true character: ______________________________

5. fast-changing world: ______________________________

Pre-Reading 3. Talking About

Look at the following questions and discuss your ideas with a partner.

1. What do you think is the most serious problem that children face today?
2. Give examples of difficulties experienced by the elderly in modern society.

Pre-Reading 4. Further Discussion

1. What do you think children need most as they grow up?
2. What do you believe are the most harmful influences on children?
3. What significant obstacles do you think older people face in today's society?
4. How can society better include older people and encourage them to take part in community life?

In literature, children are often depicted as innocent, with their only role being to play, which is why childhood is often seen as a happy time in life. However, in reality, children are among the weakest and most vulnerable members of society. They usually have no money, very few rights, and almost no way to make their voices heard in the world around them.[48] Because of their lack of worldly knowledge, they are easy targets for exploitation and abuse by adults. Bong Joon-ho's film *Snowpiercer* (2013) shows a striking image of this: a small boy trapped under a train, forced to remove engine waste until he dies. This reminds us that the exploitation of children has been a repeated problem throughout history, especially since the Industrial Revolution. Nelson Mandela, former president of South Africa, said that nothing reveals a society's true character more clearly than the way it treats its children.[49]

On the other hand, the elderly have long been the most respected members of a community. In the past, survival knowledge remained largely unchanged. As a result, accumulated wisdom and experience were valued and passed down, helping society maintain a strong system of knowledge transfer. The elderly served as leaders and teachers and often held powerful positions in their communities. However, in today's fast-changing world, older people are often left behind as they try to keep up with new knowledge and technology. Each day brings new changes, and the world of tomorrow will again be different from today. Because of this constant change, many elderly people feel disconnected and struggle to adjust to the world around them. As people live longer and society gets older, this problem will only become more serious.

Children and the elderly! Children remind us of a stage of life we have already passed, while the elderly point to the stage we will reach someday. Let us think about these two groups who may seem far from us and yet are, in fact, very close.

12A: Christina Georgina Rossetti

Pre-Reading 1. General Questions

1. Explore the life and works of Christina Georgina Rossetti online.
2. Investigate the Pre-Raphaelite Brotherhood. What were their main artistic principles?
3. Find information about the Oxford Movement.

Pre-Reading 2. Vocabulary

Guess the meaning of each underlined word and choose its definition from the list below.

1. The Pre-Raphaelite Brotherhood was the most famous artistic movement of the Victorian era. ________

2. When she turned 13, her father contracted tuberculosis. ________

3. She kept to the movement's emphasis on self-sacrifice and discipline. ________

4. Her poetic talent was already well known to contemporary artists. ________

5. She actively took part in addressing the issues of those deprived.________

A. (v) to become infected with a disease
B. (a) existing or occurring at the same time period as another event or person
C. (a) lacking basic needs like food, housing, education, or social opportunities
D. (n) a collective effort by a group of people to achieve artistic or social objectives
E. (n) the practice of following rules or controlling one's behavior, often to achieve improvement or maintain order.

Christina Rossetti, portrayed by her brother Dante Gabriel Rossetti

Christina Georgina Rossetti was born in London in 1830 into an extraordinarily artistic family. Her father, Gabriel Rossetti, was a poet and scholar who fled Italy to England for political reasons. Her mother, Frances, also came from an artistic family: her brother, John William Polidori, was a physician and writer, and a friend to several of the most prominent poets of the late Romantic period. Among Christina's siblings, Dante Gabriel Rossetti stood out as a poet, painter, and leader of the Pre-Raphaelite Brotherhood, one of the most influential artistic movements of the Victorian era, while her other brother William and her sister Maria were also writers.

Christina grew up surrounded by art and literature. Her mother educated her at home instead of sending her to school. She enjoyed reading books from her father's library, which was filled with volumes he had brought from Italy. This experience enriched her artistic inspiration and broadened her imagination.

Tragedy struck the Rossetti family when Christina turned 13. Her father contracted tuberculosis, and complications from the illness caused him to lose his sight. As a result, he had to resign from his professorship at King's College London. This marked a significant break with Christina's once-vibrant, happy childhood. To support the family, her mother ran a nursery school. Her older sister Maria worked as a resident tutor, and her brother William took a position in the excise tax office. Meanwhile, her brother Dante was attending an art school, which often left Christina alone at home. Around the age of fourteen, she experienced severe emotional distress that led to depression and other related health problems.

She overcame this difficult period by embracing the principles of the Oxford Movement. This movement, which began at Oxford University, aimed to restore spirituality within the Anglican Church. It spread across Britain during the 1830s and 1840s and had a lasting influence on both her beliefs and lifestyle. In keeping with the movement's emphasis on self-sacrifice and discipline, she pursued a more profound spiritual life. As part of this commitment, she chose to remain unmarried.

She began writing poetry at the age of 12 and published her first collection at 18. Unlike many female authors of the 19th century, she published under her own name rather than using a pseudonym. As the younger sister of the renowned artist Dante Rossetti, she was already well known among many contemporary artists who admired her brother. At 31, she published her most famous and successful work, *Goblin Market and Other Poems*. This collection received rave reviews from critics and firmly secured her place among the most significant poets of the time. Today, she is recognized as an important religious poet whose works are still studied by scholars.

Toward the end of her life, Christina suffered from Graves' disease, a form of hyperthyroidism, breast cancer, and several other chronic illnesses before finally passing away in 1894. Despite her health struggles, she put her religious beliefs—human beings are the recipients of salvation and part of God's plan—into action. She strongly opposed slavery in the southern United States, the cruelty of using animals for experiments, and the exploitation of minors as prostitutes.[50] She volunteered for over 10 years at the St. Mary Magdalene charity home in Highgate, a shelter for prostitutes. She also placed particular value on childhood, the purest period of life, and therefore believed that children should be protected from abusive environments. In the poem that we will read, her sympathy for children is expressed through her belief in human dignity and universal compassion. Let us share her concern for the most vulnerable and marginalized, and reflect on how we can build a more caring society.

Frontispiece of *Goblin Market and Other Poems* by Christina Rossetti, illustrated by Dante Gabriel Rossetti

Rossetti's Poem:

Is it Well with the Child?*

Safe where I cannot die yet,
    Safe where I hope to lie too,
Safe from the fume and the fret;
        You, and you,
    Whom I never forget.
Safe from the frost and the snow,
    Safe from the storm and the sun,
Safe where the seeds wait to grow
        One by one,
    And to come back in blow.

The Girlhood of Mary Virgin, painted by Dante Gabriel Rossetti, with Christina Rossetti as the model

* Quoted from "Run at once to meet her and say to her, 'Is all well with you? Is all well with your husband? Is all well with the child?'" And she answered, "All is well" in 2 Kings 4:26, the Bible (New International Version)

Post-Reading 1. Review

1. Discuss Christina Georgina Rossetti and her family background. What were the main fields of work they were involved in?
2. What stage of life did Rossetti consider the most innocent or pure?
3. What social issues did she care about, and what volunteer work did she do for many years?

Post-Reading 2. Paraphrasing

Rewrite Rossetti's idea as seen in the lines below in simpler, everyday English.

Safe from the frost and the snow,
Safe from the storm and the sun,
Safe where the seeds wait to grow
One by one,
And to come back in blow.

Post-Reading 3. Discussion

1. Unlike other female writers of the time, Rossetti published her collection of poetry under her own name. Why do you think she made this choice?
2. In what ways might Rossetti's family situation have shaped her emotional struggles and her creative work?
3. Rossetti chose to remain unmarried to follow her religious beliefs and personal values. Do you think it can sometimes be better to stay single to focus on your goals, or to marry and still pursue them? Why?

Post-Reading 4. Critical Thinking

1. Rossetti's poetry often dealt with strong social concerns and compassion for others. How can literature or art today inspire people to think differently about society?
2. Rossetti continued to write poetry even in the last years of her life. What helps people stay creative and passionate when facing illness or hardship?

12B: Matthew Arnold

Pre-Reading 1. General Questions

1. Search online for information on Matthew Arnold.
2. Can you think of a historical or modern figure whose life was strongly shaped by their parents? How did that influence affect their choices or achievements?
3. Who are some social reformers you know, and how successful do you think they were in bringing about change?

Pre-Reading 2. Vocabulary

Guess the meaning of each underlined word and choose its definition from the list below.

1. He was the eldest son of Thomas Arnold, who was a renowned educator. ________
2. Rugby football is derived from the name of the school. ________
3. His rebellious courage came to a halt when his father died. ________
4. People are portrayed as being atomized and isolated from the mainstream of society. ________
5. He made an appeal for us to enjoy our full humanity without division or discrimination of any kind. ________

A. (v) to be separated from others and feel alone in society
B. (v) originated from or based on something
C. (n) a stop or pause in progress or movement
D. (n) a strong request for help or agreement on something important
E. (a) famous and respected for a particular skill, achievement, or quality

Matthew Arnold

Matthew Arnold, who lived from 1822 to 1888, was a poet, educator, and critic. He was the eldest son of Thomas Arnold, who was a renowned educator and the principal of Rugby School in England. Rugby School was founded in 1567 as a grammar school and later developed into a boarding school for boys aged 13 to 18. The term 'rugby football' is derived from the name of the school, as the sport is thought to have originated there. In the 1820s, a new convention gradually emerged among students, permitting them to catch and run with the ball.

Soon after, Thomas Arnold was appointed headmaster of Rugby School. He is often described as a natural radical reformer who constantly sought ways to improve whatever he observed.[51] His appointment marked a turning point in the school's history. He reformed the traditional school into a more modern educational institution. As a result, Rugby gained a solid reputation as Britain's premier secondary educational institution. Today, it stands as one of the UK's top private schools, comparable to other esteemed institutions such as Eton College.

Thomas's educational beliefs and his role as a social reformer had, for better or worse, a profound effect on his son. Matthew was awarded a scholarship when he entered Balliol College, Oxford, in 1841. However, his lifestyle was quite different from that of a typical hardworking student. According to his contemporaries, he seemed to rebel against his strict and well-known father. Living like a dandy, he dressed elegantly, often in bright colors, looked relaxed and cheerful, and refused to take things seriously. His irreverent jokes frequently annoyed his more serious undergraduate friends and acquaintances. His flamboyant behavior came to a halt when his father died of a heart attack. After graduating from Oxford, he taught at Rugby for a while as if trying to follow in his father's footsteps. Then, he was elected a fellow of Oriel College, Oxford.

From this time on, Matthew began to establish himself as a talented writer and critic. He published a collection of poems and numerous essays and articles as a literary and social critic. His social critiques resembled his father's in the way he identified social issues and proposed solutions. In fact, Matthew came to surpass his father in renown, becoming a herald of a new era. After publishing *Culture and Anarchy*, a calm and deliberate exploration of contemporary social and political problems, he came to be seen as something of a prophet in his time. As a poet, he also served as a powerful inspiration to many younger writers. In his poetry, human beings are portrayed as atomized and cut off from the mainstream, lacking the sense of belonging that comes from being part of a community. It may have been the first time this depiction of isolated humanity appeared in English poetry. That is why some people call him the father of modern poetry.

Like his father, he was very much a reformer. He not only diagnosed problems in society but also proposed practical solutions. He made a passionate appeal for people to embrace their shared humanity, free from division or discrimination of any kind. In the poem featured in this unit, even the elderly—often the most overlooked members of society—are given full attention. Having watched his own father grow old and later experiencing aging himself, he reflected deeply on the lives of the elderly and the neglect they often face. He passed away in 1888. What would he say if he saw people living in today's society? What would he think about the way we treat the elderly?

Painting of a Cricket Match at Rugby School, by Henry Jamyn Brooks

Arnold's Poem:

Growing Old

What is it to grow old?
Is it to lose the glory of the form,
The luster of the eye?
Is it for beauty to forego her wreath?
—Yes, but not this alone.

Is it to feel our strength—
Not our bloom only, but our strength—decay?
Is it to feel each limb
Grow stiffer, every function less exact,
Each nerve more loosely strung?

Yes, this, and more; but not
Ah, 'tis not what in youth we dreamed 'twould be!
'Tis not to have our life
Mellowed and softened as with sunset glow,
A golden day's decline.

'Tis not to see the world
As from a height, with rapt prophetic eyes,
And heart profoundly stirred;
And weep, and feel the fullness of the past,
The years that are no more.

……

Thomas Arnold, father of Matthew Arnold, by Thomas Phillips

- forego: forgo, give up
- bloom: healthy facial complexion.
- 'tis: It is
- 'twould: it would
- mellow: to become softer, especially with age

Post-Reading 1. Review

1. What did you learn about Matthew Arnold that you didn't know before?
2. Who was Matthew Arnold's father, and what was he known for?
3. What were Matthew Arnold's school days like?

Post-Reading 2. Paraphrasing

Rewrite Arnold's idea as seen in the lines below in simpler, everyday English.

> Yes, this, and more; but not
> Ah, 'tis not what in youth we dreamed 'twould be!
> 'Tis not to have our life
> Mellowed and softened as with sunset glow,
> A golden day's decline.

Post-Reading 3. Discussion

1. In what ways did Thomas' life influence Matthew, both positively and negatively?
2. How does Arnold's poem portray old age? Do you agree with his ideas?
3. According to Arnold's poem, what do the elderly need in order to live happier and less lonely lives?

Post-Reading 4. Critical Thinking

1. How does parental influence on children differ between traditional and modern societies?
2. What do you think about the current policies for the elderly in Korea? How effective are they, and what areas need improvement?
3. What do you think is the greatest challenge caused by the rapid aging of our society. What solutions can you propose to address this issue?

Unit 13

Men and Women

"I am no bird; and no net ensnares me: I am a free human being with an independent will."

—Charlotte Brontë, in *Jane Eyre*

Pre-Reading 1. Main Ideas

1. People tend to prefer classifying rather than integrating.
2. Society today is so complex that we need integration more than classification.
3. We should live as global citizens who can overcome barriers that divide us.

Pre-Reading 2. Keywords

Define the words below in your own words. Then, search online for example sentences that show how each word is used. Share your definitions and sentences with your partner.

1. categorize:

___

2. criteria:

___

3. classify:

___

4. integrate:

___

5. individual identity:

___

6. converge:

___

Pre-Reading 3. Talking About

Look at the following questions and discuss your ideas with a partner.

1. People tend to prefer classifying rather than integrating. Do you agree or disagree? Why?
2. Do you think society still expects men and women to have different roles? Give reasons for your opinion.

Pre-Reading 4. Further Discussion

1. Have you ever felt pressure to act in certain ways because of your gender?
2. Have you ever experienced discrimination because you were seen as different from others?
3. What benefits can integration across different fields bring to society?

After the Academy Awards ceremony, Oscar-winning actress Youn Yuh-Jung emphasized the importance of equality, saying that people should not be judged or separated based on skin color, gender, or sexual orientation.* She expressed her belief that all human beings share the same warm heart and should be treated as equals. Her words received worldwide acclaim and recognition.

People have a natural tendency to divide and categorize aspects of life rather than integrate them. Over time, knowledge has been separated into many different fields. Similarly, people are divided based on various criteria, with gender being one of the most prominent. Traditionally, adults and children have been separated only by age, whereas men and women have been separated by almost everything.[52] Until recently, this difference affected almost every part of life. For example, we can see this in English personal pronouns, which have long distinguished men and women without question. The gender roles prescribed to men and women in the past have been as different as the clothes they have worn. Men were typically given roles outside the home, while women were limited to roles inside it. Men and women received the education needed for them to fulfill their socially accepted roles. The more educated they became, the more strongly they were expected to act masculine or feminine. The concept still influences society today, as men are expected to be 'manly' while women are praised for being 'ladylike.'

However, we have largely abandoned these outdated views and come to the realization that sex, gender, and sexuality are three separate aspects that can vary independently in any individual. As democratic citizens, we know that our individual identities are more important than any other values. Society has become so complex that it seems the time has come to start looking at ways to integrate rather than divide and classify. In many academic fields integration is required, and each field is being asked to converge with others. In such a world, how ironic it would be if we still lived trapped in gender stereotypes that divide people. In this unit, we will talk more about this.

* In a backstage interview uploaded by Entertainment Tonight on YouTube in March 2021, titled "Oscars: Yuh-Jung Youn REACTS to Making History During Backstage Interview", Youn said: "We people are categorized like a black, white, yellow, brown, something like that. That's not a nice way to just divide like that. You know, I think if we put all colors together, make it more prettier. Even a rainbow has seven colors. So color doesn't matter. Gender doesn't matter. All then what, what else, men and women or I don't like to divide… divide like, you know, like this man, woman or black, and white, yellow, brown, or some other word, the gender, you know, gay or straight or something like that. I don't want that kind of things. Just we are equal human beings. We have the same warm heart." (Accessed 20 Aug. 2025)

13A: Coventry Patmore

Pre-Reading 1. General Questions

1. Search for information on Coventry Patmore online.
2. What roles and characteristics are traditionally assigned to men and women?
3. Is it possible to change the older generation's views on gender roles and social matters? What strategies could be successful?

Pre-Reading 2. Vocabulary

Guess the meaning of each underlined word and choose its definition from the list below.

1. His poetry contains outdated concepts. ________
2. Considering the literacy rate and the publishing market conditions at the time, it could legitimately be called a great bestseller. ________
3. The woman shows her devotion to the man by being virtuous. ________
4. Patmore had converted from Anglican to Roman Catholic to marry her. ________
5. Some say 'The Angel in the Houses' is made through the wife's self-sacrificing spirit. ________

A. (a) showing a willingness to give up your own interests or happiness so that other people can be helped or benefit
B. (v) to change one's religious faith or beliefs to another
C. (adv) in a manner that is fair, reasonable, and follows accepted standards
D. (a) no longer current or considered old-fashioned; behind the times
E. (a) having high moral standards; behaving in a morally good and honest way

Coventry Patmore by John Singer Sargent

Patmore, a British poet born in 1823 and died in 1896, is now largely forgotten, but he was once quite famous. Some critics who still remember him no longer appreciate him and his works because his poetry contains outdated concepts. Patmore lived in the 19th century, and his ideas reflected the values of that era. He enjoyed a positive reputation not only in the 19th century but also in the early 20th century when traditional thinking was still dominant.

His most famous and representative poetic work is *The Angel in the House,* a trilogy of poems that took about eight years to complete. It became famous not only in the UK but also in the US and sold about 200,000 copies in the forty years following its publication. Considering the literacy rate and the publishing market conditions at the time, it was a legitimate bestseller.

With four volumes published in three parts from 1854 to 1862,* this collection of poems tells of a man and woman's first time falling in love, getting engaged, and finally ending up in a happy marriage. The man believes in the power of love and fully dedicates himself to it. The woman shows her devotion to the man by being virtuous. Their marriage allows them to become fully realized individuals. Readers were touched by the story of the happy and loving couple portrayed in these volumes. They found it to be the perfect example of marriage grounded on Christian ideals of love and beliefs.

Knowing that Patmore's poem was based on his own marriage, readers became interested in his wife as she was thought to be the ideal woman he described in the poem. Before marrying, Patmore was only 23 years old and a thin, hungry-looking young man who had published only a little-known collection of poems. It was Emily who was determined to marry him. According to a memoir about Patmore, his wife, Emily Augusta, had a natural talent for languages and studied Greek and Latin well enough to help her sons prepare for school and for the Navy.[53] At that time, it was unusual for a woman to take an active role in important life events, such as her marriage, or to be educated enough to teach her children.

* *The Angel in the House* was published in four parts: *The Betrothal* (1854), *The Espousals* (1856), and *The Victories of Love* in two volumes (1860 and 1862).

She was someone who transcended the standards set for women.

After marriage, however, she embodied the ideal of her time and devoted her brilliance and courage to supporting her husband and children. "To her children she was a most devoted mother, training them to be, like herself, 'simple, truthful, honourable.'"[54] She was said to have lived as though she had been blessed with a happy marriage and family. This image was reinforced by the popularity of Patmore's poetry, which led her to be regarded as the ideal woman of her time.

When Emily died in 1862 at the young age of 38, Patmore lost both his wife and his muse. After her death, his poetry became less creative and original, often echoing his earlier work. Two years later, Patmore married Marianne Caroline Byles, whom he had met by chance in Rome. Patmore had converted from Anglican to Roman Catholic to marry her. Although Marianne differed from Emily in character, she also generously devoted her wealth and wholehearted support to helping Patmore live more comfortably. He eventually retired from the British Museum, where he had worked since his youth. He focused only on spreading his ideas through his poems, which promoted love, happiness, and religion. Throughout that time, Marianne was always mindful of his former wife, Emily, and tried to live up to the standards that Emily had set. Eventually, she was also regarded as the ideal wife and mother by supporting her husband and caring for her stepchildren.

Portrait of Emily, the first wife of Coventry Patmore, by John Everett Millais

Patmore has often been criticized for emphasizing gender stereotypes and fixed identities. For example, his idea of "The Angel in the House" has been seen as a representation of a woman's self-sacrificing nature, while others view it as a forced illusion. What is your opinion on this matter?

Patmore's Poem:

The Angel in the House[*]

Yet is it now my chosen task
  To sing her worth as Maid and Wife;
Nor happier post than this I ask,
  To live her laureate all my life.
On wings of love up lifted free,
  And by her gentleness made great,
I'll teach how noble man should be
  To match with such a lovely mate;
And then in her may move the more
  The woman's wish to be desired,
(By praise increased,) till both shall soar,
  With blissful emulations fired.
And, as geranium, pink, or rose
  Is thrice itself through power of art,
So may my happy skill disclose
  New fairness even in her fair heart;

- laureate: a poet honored with awards for outstanding achievement
- pink: a type of flower, especially common in Britain
- thrice: an old-fashioned word meaning "three times"; sometimes used poetically to mean 'greatly' or 'with blessing'

The Lodge, Lymington, home of Coventry Patmore, from *Coventry Patmore* (1905) by Edmund Gosse

* The quote is taken from Canto II, "Mary and Mildred," in Book I of *The Angel in the House.*

Post-Reading 1. Review

1. Discuss the reasons for the popularity of his poems among the public during his lifetime.
2. Why do his poems no longer appeal to critics and ordinary readers today?
3. What were the primary sources of inspiration for his poetry?

Post-Reading 2. Paraphrasing

Rewrite Patmore's idea as seen in the lines below in simpler, everyday English.

> Yet is it now my chosen task
>   To sing her worth as Maid and Wife;
> Nor happier post than this I ask,
>   To live her laureate all my life.
> On wings of love up lifted free,
>   And by her gentleness made great,
> I'll teach how noble man should be
>   To match with such a lovely mate;

Post-Reading 3. Discussion

1. Patmore's ideas or notions were appropriate for the social norms of his time. Do you think it's difficult for individuals to break free from the dominant social norms of their time?
2. Patmore wrote about love and marriage. Do you think people today view love and marriage in the same way as people did in Patmore's time? What similarities or differences do you notice?

Post-Reading 4. Critical Thinking

1. How have the social norms for men and women changed over time? Give some examples.
2. Do you think flexible thinking is necessary for integration and cooperation? What role does it play?
3. Some people have had pioneering ideas that were ahead of their time. Can you give examples of such people and explain the impact they had on society?

13B. Sir Henry Newbolt

Pre-Reading 1. General Questions

1. Search online for information about Sir Henry Newbolt.
2. Find a story or song that promotes patriotism.
3. Find a movie or TV show that mainly features male characters.
4. What are the most common stereotypes for men's and women's roles in pop culture?

Pre-Reading 2. Vocabulary

Guess the meaning of each underlined word and choose its definition from the list below.

1. He passed the bar and began a career as a barrister. ________

2. He was knighted in recognition of his commitment. ________

3. He was a man of great enthusiasm, optimism, and intense sociability. ________

4. They needed to strengthen the physical health and mental toughness of boys who would become soldiers. ________

5. The war did not end quickly despite a great number of casualties. ________

A. (v) to make something stronger or more effective; to improve in power, ability, or firmness
B. (a) showing a high level of energy, enthusiasm, or effort; very strong or serious in quality
C. (n) the act of officially acknowledging someone's achievements or services, often leading to honors such as knighthood
D. (n) a lawyer in some countries who is qualified to provide specialist legal advice and represent individuals in higher courts
E. (n) people who were injured or killed in an accident, war, or other event

Sir Henry John Newbolt was born in 1862, the son of an Anglican priest Henry Francis Newbolt. When he was only four, his father passed away. His mother, unable to bear the grief, moved to the town where her parents lived. Newbolt spent the next nine years there and received his education at a grammar school. When he was 14, his family moved to Bristol, where he enrolled in Clifton College. After graduating from Corpus Christi College, Oxford in 1885, he passed the bar and began a career as a barrister.

Sir Henry John Newbolt

He published his first collection *Admirals All* (1897), 10 years later. Although it contained only 12 poems, it brought him great fame. He followed this up with *The Island Race* (1899), which was also a financial success. With these two consecutive successes, Newbolt was able to leave his legal career and become a full-time writer.

Newbolt's career as a writer flourished. He became a Fellow of the Royal Society of Literature, a group of well-known and respected contemporary literary figures. He was also a founding member of its Academic Committee. After achieving great success, he began devoting his energy to community service, which suited his prestigious position. Newbolt launched a campaign to raise the standard of English among ordinary British people. In recognition of his commitment, he was knighted in 1915.

His distinctively bright personality also influenced his social achievements. He was described as a man of great enthusiasm, zeal, and optimism, with an intense sociability that shaped his social life. Beyond literature, he was an excellent marksman and showed passionate interests in fishing, birdwatching, and heraldry from a young age. In his intellectual pursuits, he was known as a careful and thorough researcher, widely read in many fields but especially in poetry—both traditional and contemporary. Although he engaged in various literary activities over the years, poetry always remained his deepest passion and the core of his life.[55]

The themes of his poetry can be summarized as patriotism, communal courage, and heroic sacrifice. These ideas deeply moved the British people, who were carried along by a wave of patriotic enthusiasm at the time. His most famous poem "Play up! Play up! And play the game!" made him a household name all over the UK, as well as in the US and Canada. At first glance, it seems to describe boys playing sports at school. However, the ideology of imperialism at the time is hidden within it. Britain waged two Boer Wars in South Africa to expand its empire but did not achieve the victories it expected. The British were shocked by their defeat and attributed it to the weak minds and frail bodies of the soldiers of the Empire. For its glory, they came to the conclusion that they needed to strengthen the physical health and mental toughness of their men, especially the boys who would one day become soldiers. This led British public education to focus on "the organization and dissemination of sport as a tool of Spartan practice and imperialism."[56] With such a trend, Newbolt's "Play up! Play up! And play the game!" and the ideals of patriotism came to be understood as almost synonymous. These sentiments spread to every part of the world where nationalism was prevalent. Newbolt became well-known and one of the most influential figures of his time.

Newbolt's poetry began to lose popularity midway through World War I (1914-1918) when Britain entered the war in Europe with the idealistic aim of defending world peace. The war dragged on despite the heavy casualties. People grew sick of the war and skeptical about its purpose. As the war lost support among the public, Newbolt's poetry, full of ideas of patriotism and heroism, failed to inspire people any longer. Yet, in some corners of the world, the stereotype remains that boys should be brave, strong, and ready to fight for their community.

Clifton College Close, Bristol

Newbolt's Poem:

Play up! Play up! And play the game!

There's a breathless hush in the Close to-night
Ten to make and the match to win
A bumping pitch and a blinding light,
An hour to play, and the last man in.
And it's not for the sake of a ribboned coat,
Or the selfish hope of a season's fame,
But his Captain's hand on his shoulder smote
"Play up! Play up! And play the game!"

The sand of the desert is sodden red-
Red with the wreck of the square that broke;
The Gatling's jammed and the colonel dead,
And the regiment blind with dust and smoke.
The river of death has brimmed its banks,
And England's far and Honour a name,
But the voice of a schoolboy rallies the ranks:
"Play up! Play up! And play the game!"

This is the word that year by year,
While in her place the School is set,
Every one of her sons must hear,
And none that hears it dare forget.
This they all with joyful mind
And bear through life like a torch in flame,
falling fling to the host behind-
"Play up! Play up! And play the game!"

A moment from a 1928 American football game, described by Coach Alexander as "the smartest play of the game"

- a ribboned coat: signifying a private school uniform in Britain.
- Gatling: a machine gun model used in the late 1800s
- her: Britain's
- host: army

Post-Reading 1. Review

1. What new information about Henry Newbolt did you learn from this article compared to what you found online?
2. How would you describe Newbolt's personality?
3. What made Newbolt's poetry widely admired in his time?

Post-Reading 2. Paraphrasing

Rewrite Newbolt's idea as seen in the lines below in simpler, everyday English.

> The river of death has brimmed its banks,
> And England's far and Honour a name,
> But the voice of a schoolboy rallies the ranks-
> "Play up! Play up! And play the game!"

Post-Reading 3. Discussion

1. The text suggests that Newbolt's personality played a major role in his social success. Do you think a person's personality can influence their social success? How might this happen?
2. What stereotypes about boys or men are emphasized in Newbolt's work? Do you consider these stereotypes to be still relevant today?

Post-Reading 4. Critical Thinking

1. Newbolt's poem suggests that society needs people with healthy bodies and sound minds. Is this idea outdated today? Or is it still a necessary concept?
2. Newbolt's poem shows that national circumstances can shape the direction of education. Can you give some examples and discuss how they might affect children's lives?

Further Reading 1

Excerpts from "Remarks at the Security Council Briefing on Children and Armed Conflict" *

António Guterres, United Nations Secretary-General

[...] As Graca Machel said in her landmark 1996 report: "Millions of children are caught up in conflicts in which they are not merely bystanders, but targets." Children ... are among the most vulnerable, unable to protect themselves from its impact. [...] 2018 saw more than 12,000 children killed or maimed in conflict – the highest recorded figures since 1996. [...]

Attacks on hospitals and schools deny children education, healthcare and lifesaving emergency assistance and force families from their homes. Children may be subjected to horrific abuses in war zones, including sexual violence and abduction. They may be trained to use deadly weapons, or exploited as cooks and messengers. These violations cause lasting damage to the children themselves, and to their communities and societies. [...]

Campaigns including 'Children, Not Soldiers' and the new 'Act to Protect' have helped to bring about a global consensus that children should never be used in conflict. However, despite these efforts, the figures for grave violations against children in conflict continue to rise. [...] By integrating specific measures to protect children into peace processes, we can achieve concrete results for children, and for peace. [...]

Discussion Questions

1. How does war affect children differently from adults, according to the speech?
2. Why is protecting children an important part of achieving sustainable peace?
3. What responsibilities do the international community and governments have to prevent children from being exploited in conflicts?

---

* António Guterres delivered this speech on February 12, 2020, at the United Nations Headquarters in New York during a Security Council briefing on Children and Armed Conflict. He emphasized the urgent need to protect children in war, describing them as the most vulnerable victims—facing death, injury, abduction, and exploitation. Attacks on schools and hospitals strip children of education, healthcare, and safety, leaving long-term scars on communities and societies. Guterres highlighted that safeguarding children is not only a moral duty but also a crucial step toward building sustainable peace. By integrating child protection into peace processes and international cooperation, the global community can break the cycle of violence and give children a chance to live with dignity and hope.

Further Reading 2

Excerpts from "A Voice for the Voiceless: Animal Rights and Human Responsibility," from the Universal Declaration of Animal Rights*

In 1978, a group of international advocates gathered in Paris to proclaim a powerful idea: animals, like humans, have rights. They called on the world to recognize that animals are not property, but fellow beings who deserve respect, protection, and compassion.

Some of the key messages include:

- All animals are born equal and have the right to exist.
- No animal should be subjected to cruelty or exploitation.
- Animals raised for food or work must be treated humanely.
- Wild animals deserve freedom in their natural environment.
- Companion animals have the right to live out their natural lifespans and not be abandoned.
- Using animals for entertainment or scientific experiments, or in any way that causes unnecessary suffering is unethical.
- Respect for animals reflects the depth of our respect for one another.

This declaration challenged the belief that humans are above all other species. Instead, it called for coexistence, care, and education—starting from childhood—to build a more compassionate world.

Discussion Questions

1. Do you think animals should be given legal rights? Why or why not?
2. What does it mean to say that "respect for animals is linked to respect for humans"?
3. What responsibilities do people have toward pets, wild animals, or animals raised for food?

---

* The Universal Declaration of Animal Rights was first proclaimed in 1978 at UNESCO headquarters, revised in 1989, and publicly released in 1990. It emphasizes that all animals are entitled to life, liberty, and protection from human cruelty. The declaration condemns exploitation, inhumane treatment, and unnecessary suffering, while urging humanity to respect animals in everyday life, industry, and scientific research. Its message calls for global awareness and responsible action to ensure peaceful coexistence between humans and other species. This excerpt is adapted from the public release of the declaration for educational use.

Chapter 4

Self-Awareness in the Community

Warm-Up!

Talk about the following questions with your partners.

1. How would your friends or family describe you?
2. What are some communities or groups you are part of?
3. How do you usually contribute to your community?

Humanity has achieved remarkable progress, yet many challenges remain. Despite hopes for a better future, there are concerns that these challenges may persist or even grow worse. One such challenge is inequality. It has become so deeply rooted that, in some communities, the oppression and exploitation of minorities are almost taken for granted. Many thinkers and activists have fought against inequality, but the problem remains unresolved. Furthermore, today's technological age is expected to create deeper divides between those who have access to information and technology and those who do not.

Another major concern is that, with advances in technology, violence has become more destructive than ever before. War represents its most extreme form, threatening the peace and safety of entire communities, and humanity has long sought to avoid it. Yet with the rise of artificial intelligence, technological advances are already being used in warfare, and the damage will likely grow even greater in the future.

These threats may seem remote, but people are already experiencing the negative effects of technological advances in their daily lives. Studies suggest that teenagers who spend long hours on electronic devices are at a significantly higher risk of suicide.[57] They also struggle to understand themselves, as research shows that self-concept is acquired through patterns of interaction with others.[58]

In a hyper-connected society, people can paradoxically feel more isolated online, and communities become increasingly fragmented. As genuine interaction becomes harder, developing a healthy sense of self also becomes more difficult. Without strong connections, neither personal happiness nor collective well-being can be guaranteed. Technology may transform our world; however, to truly thrive, we must ask how we can build better relationships between ourselves and our communities.

What We Will Read

Unit 14. Life and Inequality
Unit 15. War and Peace
Unit 16. Self and Identity
Unit 17. Self and Community

Further Reading 1: Excerpts from "A Just and Lasting Peace"
Further Reading 2: Excerpts from "The Smile That Builds Community"

Unit 14

Life and Inequality

"If you want to see the true measure of a man, watch how he treats his inferiors, not his equals."

—Joanne K. Rowling

Preview 1. Main Ideas

1. All human beings are born free and equal.
2. There are still many people in desperate conditions on our planet.
3. Some often violate and undermine the dignity of others.

Preview 2. Keywords

Define the words below in your own words. Then, search online for example sentences that show how each word is used. Share your definitions and sentences with your partner.

1. dignity:

2. entitled:

3. distinction:

4. sovereignty:

5. marginalized:

Preview 3. Talking About

Look at the following questions and discuss your ideas with a partner.

1. Talk about a historical event that showed widespread inequality in a certain period or community.
2. Look up the UN Charter online and summarize its main idea.

Preview 4. Further Discussion

1. Do you think inequality still exists in today's world?
2. What do you think are the essential conditions for living a life with dignity?
3. How would you define modern slavery?

In 1948, the United Nations adopted the Universal Declaration of Human Rights, which states the following:

> Article 1. All human beings are born free and equal in dignity and rights. They are endowed with reason and conscience and should act towards one another in a spirit of brotherhood.
>
> Article 2. Everyone is entitled to all the rights and freedoms set forth in this Declaration, without distinction of any kind, such as race, colour, sex, language, religion, political or other opinion, national or social origin, property, birth or other status.
>
> Furthermore, no distinction shall be made on the basis of the political, jurisdictional or international status of the country or territory to which a person belongs, whether it be independent, trust, non-self-governing or under any other limitation of sovereignty.
>
> Article 3. Everyone has the right to life, liberty, and security of the person.

In total, the Declaration contains 30 articles. The first three articles firmly declare that every human being is born with inherent dignity. They also set out specific conditions under which such dignity can be guaranteed. Today, in most parts of the world, few people would disagree with these ideas.

However, in some parts of the world—still far too many—there are people who are marginalized and denied the basic conditions necessary to live with dignity. The Trafficking Victims Protection Act (TVPA) of 2000, issued by the US government, explains that terms such as "trafficking in persons," "human trafficking," and "modern slavery" are umbrella terms that include both sex trafficking and forced labor.[59] This terminology implies that there are still many people on our planet who are in such desperate conditions.

Inequality, however, is not limited to such extreme cases; it also appears in our daily lives. For example, when COVID-19 was at its peak, the poor and marginalized were in greater danger. In addition, the safety of many Asian Americans was threatened because of the color of their skin. The problems faced by marginalized groups were further highlighted when an African-American male was shot and killed by police. He was found to have dozens of gunshot wounds, even though he was unarmed.[60] While many agree that every human being has inherent worth, some still violate the dignity of others because of a false belief in their superiority or power. We need to discuss what more we can do to address these issues as global citizens.

14A: William Blake

Pre-Reading 1. General Questions

1. Search for information about William Blake online.
2. What was the working environment like during the Industrial Revolution?
3. Have you ever considered what life was like for enslaved people during the Industrial Revolution?

Pre-Reading 2. Vocabulary

Guess the meaning of each underlined word and choose its definition from the list below.

1. A great number of people lost their farmland and <u>flocked</u> to the city. ________

2. They earned very low wages and had to work hard under <u>harsh</u> conditions. ________

3. <u>Throughout</u> Britain, London had the largest population of African slaves. ________

4. Blake's illustrations were unique and unconventional, <u>challenging</u> the expectations of the common people. ________

5. He is one of the earliest British poets to express the ideal of equality with genuine <u>compassion</u> for others. ________

A. (a) very severe, unpleasant, or difficult to endure
B. (prep.) in every part of (something or a place)
C. (v) to gather in a large group
D. (n) a deep awareness of and sympathy for another's suffering, coupled with a desire to alleviate it
E. (v) to question, dispute, or call into doubt; to test the strength, skill, or truth of something

William Blake

Blake was born in London in 1757 around the beginning of the Industrial Revolution. Newly invented steam engines were being introduced to the textile industry and contributed to the establishment of mass production systems. Exporting wool and importing grain were of great benefit to the British economy, and much of England's farmland was turned into pasture to meet the demand for wool. Many people lost their farmland and flocked to the cities in large numbers. In these urban areas, they faced harsh living conditions, earned very low wages, and had to endure dangerous working environments.

The industrial capitalists' greed for cheaper labor and greater profits knew no bounds, and neither conscience nor humanity guided their decision-making. If a worker's health declined or something went wrong on the job, they were treated like broken machine parts and simply replaced. Sadly, few cared about these tragic realities. London was filled with people who had no choice but to work for a living despite inhumane treatment.

The lives of enslaved people at that time were even more miserable. Though we often associate slavery with the United States, the practice has a long history. In fact, the large-scale trade of African slaves had existed and expanded in Britain long before it reached the Americas. The British Empire banned the slave trade in 1807 under the Slave Trade Act. However, slavery itself was not abolished across the empire until 1833.[61] This was just slightly earlier than in the United States. Yet, slave trading continued in secret throughout Britain, and London had the largest number of African slaves. Blake grew up as an artist and spent most of his life in London, witnessing the dreadful acts humans committed against others.

Blake was not only a talented poet but also a gifted painter and printmaker. He used his prints as illustrations when publishing his collections of poetry. It was common to include illustrations to help readers better understand the text. However, Blake's illustrations were unique and unconventional, challenging the expectations of ordinary people. In many cases, they did not match the themes of the poems, which made them difficult for readers to understand. He often depicted scenes from Hell, even in bright and hopeful poems. Blake used these images because he saw the world he lived in as a kind of hell, or sometimes even worse.

Through them, he showed that reality was full of wickedness, oppression, and suffering so severe that people could lose their very humanity.

Blake's unusual way of seeing and depicting the world led many to regard him as a mystic. He revealed that he had several mysterious experiences, including frequent spontaneous visions that he later turned into poetry, which many people found hard to understand. According to some records, he once said, "I am under the direction of messengers from heaven, daily and nightly,"[62] and "I have written this poem … from immediate dictation, twelve or sometimes twenty or thirty lines at a time, without premeditation, and even against my will."[63] If taken literally, these words suggest that his poetry was not entirely his own creation but rather a form of divine revelation. In fact, some scholars still debate the origin and nature of these visions. Unfortunately, Blake's work did not gain popularity until after his death in 1827, and no one ever attempted to interview him or record his views on the matter while he was alive.

Today, people recognize the brilliance of his imagination. "Blake still influences contemporary creativity and ideas. He is seen by many as one of the great synthesizers of cultural experience, attracting a myriad of followers with interests ranging from literature, painting, book design, politics, mysticism, philosophy, mythology through to music and filmmaking … it seems safe to say that the illustrators for *The Lord of the Rings*, *Conan the Barbarian* and similar books have also been heavily influenced by William Blake."[64] Also, his painting *The Great Red Dragon and the Woman Clothed in Sun* and the poem "Auguries of Innocence" both play prominent roles in Thomas Harris's novel *Red Dragon* (1981), and the 2002 cinematic thriller by the same name.[65]

Equally important is that he was among the earliest British poets to express the ideal of equality with genuine compassion for others. Blake's poems expose the cruelty that humans have inflicted on one another throughout history. At the same time, they reveal his deep resentment toward such a world and his profound sympathy for those stripped of their dignity.

Etching by William Blake, *Flagellation of a Female Samboe Slave* (1796), from Stedman's *Narrative*

Blake's Poem:

The Little Black Boy

My mother bore me in the southern wild,
And I am black, but O! my soul is white;
White as an angel is the English child:
But I am black as if bereav'd of light.

My mother taught me underneath a tree
And sitting down before the heat of day,
She took me on her lap and kissed me,
And pointing to the east began to say.

Look on the rising sun: there God does live
And gives his light, and gives his heat away.
And flowers and trees and beasts and men receive
Comfort in morning joy in the noonday.

And we are put on earth a little space,
That we may learn to bear the beams of love,
And these black bodies and this sun-burnt face
Is but a cloud, and like a shady grove.

For when our souls have learn'd the heat to bear
The cloud will vanish we shall hear his voice.
Saying: come out from the grove my love & care,
And round my golden tent like lambs rejoice.

Thus did my mother say and kissed me,
And thus I say to little English boy.
When I from black and he from white cloud free,
And round the tent of God like lambs we joy:

I'll shade him from the heat till he can bear,
To lean in joy upon our fathers knee.
And then I'll stand and stroke his silver hair,
And be like him and he will then love me.

- bereav'd: bereaved
- learn'd: learned

William Blake, *Our Time is Fix'd, and All Our Are Number'd* (c.1805), watercolor illustration for Robert Blair's poem "The Grave"

Post-Reading 1. Review

1. Describe in detail the impact that the Industrial Revolution had on British society during Blake's lifetime.
2. In what ways did Blake's illustrations for his poetry collections differ from the typical ones of his era?
3. What message did Blake aim to convey through his illustrations?

Post-Reading 2. Paraphrasing

Rewrite Blake's idea as seen in the lines below in simpler, everyday English.

My mother bore me in the southern wild,
And I am black, but O! my soul is white;
White as an angel is the English child:
But I am black as if bereav'd of light.

My mother taught me underneath a tree
And sitting down before the heat of day,
She took me on her lap and kissed me,
And pointing to the east began to say.

Post-Reading 3. Discussion

1. In the fourth stanza, Blake uses the phrases "black bodies" and a "sun-burnt face." What meaning do you think he intended to convey through these images?
2. It is said that the imagery in several aforementioned books and films was heavily influenced by Blake. Have you seen any of these works? Do they effectively capture the essence of Hell?

Post-Reading 4. Critical Thinking

1. "Blake was ranked number 38 on the BBC's 100 Greatest Britons in a poll. Shakespeare was the only British poet who ranked higher than him. No other British artist was ranked higher."[66] Discuss what made Blake such an important figure in British history.
2. Where do you think Blake's extraordinary imagination and insight originated?
3. In what ways do you think Blake's views have influenced human life and the modern understanding of equality?

14B: Rudyard Kipling

Pre-Reading 1. General Questions

1. Search for information about Rudyard Kipling online.
2. Find out what *The Jungle Book* is about.
3. Let's briefly define the term imperialism.

Pre-Reading 2. Vocabulary

Guess the meaning of each underlined word and choose its definition from the list below.

1. They believed that India was not a <u>suitable</u> environment for his education. ________
2. his parents left Kipling in Britain to <u>pursue</u> his education. ________
3. His fame and celebrated works have undergone a significant <u>devaluation.</u> ________
4. Kipling's public reputation is often associated with <u>jingoistic</u> and imperialistic traditions. ________
5. His works lent strength to the <u>propaganda</u> of imperialism and racism. ________

A. (a) characterized by extreme patriotism, especially in the form of aggressive or warlike foreign policy
B. (a) appropriate or fitting for a particular purpose, person, or situation
C. (n) A reduction in the value, importance, or reputation of something
D. (n) information, especially of a biased or misleading nature, used to promote a political cause or point of view
E. (v) to follow or try to achieve something over a period of time, such as a goal, dream, or career

Rudyard Kipling

Rudyard Kipling was born in 1865 in Bombay, now Mumbai. Though his parents married in London, they soon moved to India. Their first child, born there, was named Rudyard after Rudyard Lake in Staffordshire, where the couple had first met.[67] It is an artificial lake that remains a popular site today. Kipling's given name, Rudyard, reflects his parents' affection and their nostalgia for their homeland. He spent his childhood both in Britain and India. At the age of six, he moved from India to England with his parents. The following year, when his father had to return to India, his parents left Kipling in Britain to pursue his education, considering that India was not a suitable environment for it at the time. The routine of living apart from his parents was repeated several times until he reached adulthood.

Kipling's childhood in India left a deep impression on him, shaping his literary basis and allowing him as an adult to adapt easily to foreign cultures. He traveled extensively in many countries in Asia and Africa, which stimulated his boundless imagination. Kipling wrote poetry and novels while working as a journalist. His most famous works include the poem "The White Man's Burden" (1899) and the novel *The Jungle Book* (1894). When *The Jungle Book* was first published, it achieved great popularity and soon became a must-read for children in the US and the UK.

It continues to appear in various forms, still inspiring the imaginations of children around the world. It was adapted once again into a film by Walt Disney Pictures, featuring stunning special effects. It grossed about $1 billion worldwide the same year and won critical acclaim and awards at several major film festivals.

As everyone knows, *The Jungle Book* is the story of a boy or 'man-cub,' Mowgli, who is raised in the jungle by wolves, builds friendships and overcomes the dangers of the Indian jungle. Parents hope that their children learn from Mowgli's courage and innocence and are not intimidated by terrifying opponents such as Shere Khan. Kipling's *The Jungle Book* remains a timeless masterpiece of children's literature.

Gaining wide recognition through many of his works, he rose to prominence as one of Britain's most renowned writers in the late 19th and early 20th centuries. In 1907, he became the youngest and even the first

English-speaking author to receive the Nobel Prize for Literature. Briefly describing his life, the author of his biography says, "Of the later incidents of his life there is no need to speak."[68] In other words, he had smooth sailing for most of his life.

Even today, his poetry as well as his novels is loved by many. His poetry appeals to the universal sensibility of human beings while providing an easy-to-understand sense of familiarity and comfort. Nevertheless, in recent years his fame and successful works have faced harsh re-evaluations from critics. According to those new perspectives, "The public reputation of Kipling and the outspoken jingoistic imperialistic tradition came to be thought of as synonymous."[69] Jingoists were those who showed fierce and aggressive support for the expansion of the Empire. Kipling was undoubtedly a jingoist in that he believed that the Empire should take on the role of enlightening all so-called 'savage' peoples in the world and, for this mission, should enlarge its practical and military power.

Critics have identified the jingoism hidden in several of Kipling's works. For example, "White Man's burden," his most beloved poem, has also been re-evaluated. They argue that "White Man's burden" is either hypocrisy or racism[70] because it fueled propaganda by calling on the white race, above all others, to take responsibility for caring for the whole world. Some critics argue that *The Jungle Book* was intended "to prove that white people are the superior race,"[71] and that Mowgli's eventual rise as the little king of the jungle can be interpreted as symbolizing what "the British do to the Indian."[72] These perspectives have resulted in a devaluation of Kipling's literary reputation, leaving many admirers of *The Jungle Book* and his poetry with mixed feelings and uncertainty.

Time passes, and thoughts change. Kipling caused little controversy in his time and in his country. However, when we read his poems from the perspective of minorities or the marginalized today, Kipling's work can be understood in a different way. Let's explore this perspective together as we read his poem.

Kipling as guardian of empire and subject peoples, depicted by William Strang, 1901

Kipling's Poem:

The White Man's Burden

Take up the White Man's burden--
  Send forth the best ye breed--
Go bind your sons to exile
  To serve your captives' need;
To wait in heavy harness
  On fluttered folk and wild--
Your new-caught, sullen peoples,
  Half devil and half child.

Take up the White Man's burden--
  In patience to abide,
To veil the threat of terror
  And check the show of pride;
By open speech and simple,
  An hundred times made plain,
To seek another's profit,
  And work another's gain.

Take up the White Man's burden--
  The savage wars of peace--
Fill full the mouth of Famine
  And bid the sickness cease;
And when your goal is nearest
  The end for others sought,
Watch Sloth and heathen Folly
  Bring all your hope to nought.

Take up the White Man's burden--
  No tawdry rule of kings,
But toil of serf and sweeper--
  The tale of common things.
The ports ye shall not enter,
  The roads ye shall not tread,
Go make them with your living,
  And mark them with your dead!

……

- ye: you (in an old-fashioned style)
- sloth: laziness
- heathen: a person who does not believe in Christian God (old-fashioned, often offensive)
- tawdry: cheap and of low quality; showy but poor in style or value

1910 illustration from Rudyard Kipling's *The Jungle Book*, with the caption: "He would get his torch and wave it, and yell with the best."

Post-Reading 1. Review

1. What did you learn about Kipling from the article?
2. How did Kipling's childhood influence his work?
3. What explains the lasting popularity of *The Jungle Book*?

Post-Reading 2. Paraphrasing

Rewrite Kipling's idea as seen in the lines below in simpler, everyday English.

Take up the White Man's burden--
  Send forth the best ye breed--
Go bind your sons to exile
  To serve your captives' need;
To wait in heavy harness
  On fluttered folk and wild--
Your new-caught, sullen peoples,
  Half devil and half child.

Post-Reading 3. Discussion

1. According to Kipling's poem, what is "The White Man's Burden?"
2. To what extent can Kipling be regarded as supporting white supremacy? Provide reasons for your view.

Post-Reading 4. Critical Thinking

1. Reflecting on Kipling's significance in the literary context of his era, what impact do you think his works had on society and literature?
2. Identify expressions of racial prejudice in Kipling's poems. How do these contribute to reinforcing existing inequalities?
3. Public perception of Kipling's contributions shifted dramatically from the early to the late 20th century. Compare this shift with similar cases in your country.
4. Over time, many thoughts and works are re-evaluated. Do you think this is necessary? If so, what criteria should such re-evaluation be carried out?

Unit 15

War and Peace

"In peace, sons bury their fathers. In war, fathers bury their sons."

—Herodotus

Preview 1. Main Ideas

1. All human beings belong to a community and share its destiny.
2. The development of modern civilization has heightened fears of war.
3. We are all part of a global community.

Preview 2. Vocabulary

Define the words below in your own words. Then, search online for example sentences to see how each word is used. Share your definitions and sentences with your partner.

1. earnest endeavors:

   ____

2. bombardment:

   ____

3. skepticism:

   ____

4. a supranational federation:

   ____

5. devastation:

   ____

Preview 3. Talking About

Look at the following questions and discuss your ideas with a partner.

1. Are there examples of negative uses of our accumulated scientific knowledge?
2. What negative, and possibly positive, effects does war have on humanity?

Preview 4. Further Discussion

1. Discuss what can be done to prevent wars from breaking out.
2. What responsibilities or contributions can individuals make toward peace?
3. Share your personal views on the future ahead of us.

All human beings are interconnected and share a common destiny with their communities. Our views on various issues such as geography, climate, politics, and economy are shared collectively. Acknowledging our common destiny, we make every effort to cultivate harmony with other nations. Despite our best efforts, conflicts often arise between countries or even within a single country.

War has some of the most profound and most tragic impacts on human life. The development of modern civilization has brought with it an increase in the horrors of warfare. World War I, the first modern global conflict after the Industrial Revolution, became a feast for mass-production systems. With the rise of automation, there was no chance of running out of supplies as factories produced weapons on a constantly spinning conveyor belt. Bombardment could go on without end and occur at any time day or night. Newly acquired knowledge of biology and chemistry enabled the development of horrific poison gases used as weapons of war. For the first time in history, mankind experienced battlefields where they fought an invisible enemy at such an immense scale.

Amid endless deaths, skepticism about the war itself and the fear about the course of civilization grew in the minds of people. This awakening led to the creation of a supranational federation called the League of Nations, which was founded in 1920 as a response to war. Unfortunately, humanity repeated its mistakes, plunging into World War II just two decades later.

The period from the end of World War II to the early 21st century was once called the "Long Peace," a time largely free from global conflict. However, that peace has long ended, as we now face numerous regional wars and escalating global tensions. With the rise of media and the internet, we are able to witness devastation firsthand. We see civilians and children sacrificed in bombings, used as human shields on the battlefield. In such moments, we wonder whether humanity can ever truly achieve lasting peace. How will we accomplish this task?

15A: Wilfred Owen

Pre-Reading 1. General Questions

1. Search online for information about Wilfred Owen.
2. Discuss the relationship between the pursuit of scientific knowledge and wars such as World War I and World War II.
3. Examine the wars currently taking place around the world and discuss their root causes.

Pre-Reading 2. Vocabulary

Guess the meaning of each underlined word and choose its definition from the list below.

1. He audited classes at a nearby university. ________

2. He was transported to a hospital in the rear. ________

3. He suffered the common symptoms of shell shock, such as repeated nightmares, numbness, and short-term paralysis. ________

4. Eventually, he began turning those traumatic experiences into poetry. ________

5. In Britain, it was touted as a glorious war. ________

   A. (n) the state of being unable to feel sensations
   B. (n) an area located far behind the front line, the back part of something
   C. (v) to attend a class informally (not to receive credit)
   D. (v) to promote or praise actively; to highlight one's strengths (usually to persuade others)
   E. (a) causing emotionally disturbing or distressing problems

Owen's life was tragically short. Born to a middle-class family in 1893, he died at the age of 25 in 1918. He attended a technical school. Although he passed the entrance exam for University of London in 1911, he was unable to enroll because his grades were not high enough for a scholarship. His family also could not afford the cost of a university education. He then worked as a lay assistant for a priest for about two years and audited classes at a nearby university. Despite having no university degree, he was considered sufficiently educated to support himself as a tutor.

Wilfred Owen
(Photo by Allex Langié, licensed under CC BY-SA 3.0 via Wikimedia Commons)

Owen was drafted in May 1916, while working as a tutor in France. Thanks to his academic background, he was selected and trained as an officer, and later sent to the front lines as a lieutenant. He embraced his role as the leader of his crew with a strong sense of responsibility. Born without a silver spoon in his mouth, he saw his military service as a chance to rise above the lower middle class, with its constant struggle against poverty and the threat of debt.[73] The experience made him more alert and brave; "This morning I was hit! We were bombing and a fragment from somewhere hit my thumb knuckle. I coaxed out one drop of blood. Alas! No more!! There is a fine heroic feeling about being in France, and I am in perfect spirits."[74] He wrote as if he were still fully in control of his mind, but in fact, he was beginning to suffer from mental illness.

The war turned out to be very different from what he had imagined. In Britain, it had been touted as a glorious war, but what he saw on the battlefield had nothing to do with glory or honor. Amid the constant bombardment, Owen could only watch helplessly as his men were killed, blinded, or left choking on blood in clouds of poison gas. Even on days without shelling, he worried about when the bombs would start falling again. The fear of death and the guilt over letting his men die weighed heavily on his mind. As an officer, he could not speak openly about his suffering and fear. He described the terrible scene he experienced in these words: "For twelve days I did not wash my face, nor take off my boots, nor sleep a deep sleep. For twelve days we lay in holes, where at any moment a shell might put us out. I think the worst incident was one wet night when we lay up against a railway embankment. A big shell lit on the top of the bank, just 2 yards from my head. Before I awoke, I was blown in the air right away from the bank!"[75]

It is said that grief and fear are universal parts of human experience, but in the trenches, soldiers had no time to grieve before facing another loss and no relief from the constant fear for their survival.[76] The term *trench warfare* symbolizes World War I. A *trench* refers to a ditch, about two meters deep and over a mile long, dug to defend against enemy attacks. The front line is a long stretch where these trenches seemed to go on forever. Life in the trenches was a daily struggle for survival for the soldiers, with mud, bugs, viruses, and, above all, bombing and poisonous gas attacks. That is why World War I is remembered for trench warfare.

Eventually, Owen collapsed from what was then called 'shell shock.' Today, we know it as post-traumatic stress disorder (PTSD), but at the time, there was no term to capture the psychological collapse of young soldiers. People just assumed it was the effect of being shelled, hence the name.

British soldiers of the 11th Battalion, Cheshire Regiment in a captured German trench during the Battle of the Somme, July 1916.

He was transported to a hospital in the rear—the area behind the front lines. When he first arrived there, he suffered the common symptoms of shell shock, such as repeated nightmares, numbness, and short-term paralysis. He also felt deep guilt because many people at the time misunderstood shell shock, seeing its victims as weak or even cowardly. He received psychological and hypnotherapy treatments to deal with his trauma, but the memories of war still haunted him. Eventually, he began turning those traumatic experiences into poetry. He wrote in a preface to his poetic collection that "My subject is War, and the pity of War. The poetry is in the pity. Yet these elegies are to this generation in no sense consolatory. They may be to the next. All a poet can do today is warn. That is why true Poets must be truthful."[77] As he said, his poetry stands as one of the most powerful warnings against the horrors of war. Around the end of August 1918, he returned to the battlefield, saying that "I do so because I have my duty to perform towards War."[78]

Just two months later, in early November, he was killed in battle. He was posthumously awarded the Military Cross.

Owen's Poem:

Exposure

……

Watching, we hear the mad gusts tugging on the wire,
Like twitching agonies of men among its brambles.
Northward, incessantly, the flickering gunnery rumbles,
Far off, like a dull rumour of some other war.
　　What are we doing here?

The poignant misery of dawn begins to grow…
We only know war lasts, rain soaks, and clouds sag stormy.
Dawn massing in the east her melancholy army
Attacks once more in ranks on shivering ranks of grey,
　　But nothing happens.

British soldiers wearing
early gas helmets during World War I

Sudden successive flights of bullets streak the silence.
Less deadly than the air that shudders black with snow,
With sidelong flowing flakes that flock, pause, and renew,
We watch them wandering up and down the wind's nonchalance,
　　But nothing happens.

Pale flakes with fingering stealth come feeling for our faces—
We cringe in holes, back on forgotten dreams, and stare, snow-dazed,
Deep into grassier ditches. So we drowse, sun-dozed,
Littered with blossoms trickling where the blackbird fusses.
　—Is it that we are dying?

……

- exposure: being subjected to harmful conditions, such as poison gas
- watching: keeping guard, staying on watch
- wire: barbed wire used as a barrier in war
- ranks: lines of soldiers or a person or thing stretching in length.
- nonchalance: calm indifference, showing little concern
- holes, ditches: symbolizing the trenches on the battlefield in World War I

Post-Reading 1. Review

1. Explain why he was unable to continue his higher education.
2. What kind of person do you think he was?
3. How would you describe the challenges he faced in the hospital, considering both his physical and psychological struggles?

Post-Reading 2. Paraphrasing

Rewrite Owen's idea as seen in the lines below in simpler, everyday English.

> The poignant misery of dawn begins to grow…
> We only know war lasts, rain soaks, and clouds sag stormy.
> Dawn massing in the east her melancholy army
> Attacks once more in ranks on shivering ranks of grey,
> But nothing happens.

Post-Reading 3. Discussion

1. Owen wrote poetry while in the hospital. Do you think writing poetry helped him overcome his war trauma? Why or why not?
2. What aspects of war does his poem portray? Which parts moved you the most, and why?
3. Owen repeatedly says "But nothing happens" in his poem "Exposure." What was he waiting for, and what did he hope would not happen amid the horrors of war?

Post-Reading 4. Critical Thinking

1. What is the true value of honor or wealth gained after death? Do you think they hold any real meaning for those who have passed away?
2. Can war ever be justified as a necessary means to maintain peace?

15B: John Donne

Pre-Reading 1. General Questions

1. Search for information about John Donne online.
2. Learn about the Reformation in England and its historical background.
3. Review the storyline of *For Whom the Bell Tolls* written by Hemingway.

Pre-Reading 2. Vocabulary

Guess the meaning of each underlined word and choose its definition from the list below.

1. At that time, Roman Catholics were subject to political persecution. ________
2. He was unable to find a social position suitable for his talents and intelligence. ________
3. Donne's behavior was no different from dishonoring a noblewoman. ________
4. As a Roman Catholic, he refused to swear the oath of allegiance to the King. ________
5. The novel reflected his experiences as a war correspondent during the Spanish Civil War, opposing a fascist dictator. ________

A. (a) ideal or appropriate for particular circumstances or conditions
B. (n) a journalist who reports from areas of conflict or warfare, providing firsthand accounts of events
C. (n) the act of systematically discriminating against or mistreating individuals based on their political beliefs or religious practices
D. (n) a formal promise of loyalty to a sovereign or government
E. (v) to bring shame or disgrace upon someone, especially by violating their dignity or honor

John Donne

Born in 1572, John Donne lived a dramatic life. At that time, Roman Catholics in Britain faced political persecution. This was because, in 1534, Henry VIII declared himself the Supreme Head of the Church of England and separated it from the authority of the Pope. Donne's parents were Roman Catholic, which limited his chances of rising to a higher social status. At the age of 11, Donne entered Oxford University, where he studied for three years, and later continued his studies at the University of Cambridge for another three years. However, he was unable to graduate from either university because, as a Roman Catholic, he refused to swear the oath of allegiance to the king, which was required of all students at the time. He then entered Lincoln's Inn, one of the Inns of Court, to become a barrister. However, he eventually gave up his promising legal career, disappointed in the Church of England and the English legal system after his younger brother Henry was executed for his religious activities.

Unable to find a social position that matched his talents and intelligence, he joined the Earl of Essex on the Spanish expedition. This led to his appointment as secretary to Sir Thomas Egerton, Lord Keeper of the Great Seal. Egerton was one of the most powerful nobles, trusted by the king and respected at court. Donne's life at last seemed to be sailing smoothly under Sir Egerton's patronage.

However, life rarely goes as planned. He fell in love with Anne More, a niece of Sir Egerton's wife. The social status of Donne's family was much lower than Anne's, which made their marriage impossible. Nevertheless, they married in secret. Given the social norms of the time, Donne's behavior was seen as no different from dishonoring a noblewoman. He was eventually sentenced to prison but, thanks to those who valued his talents, he was soon released. For years, he endured many hardships and suffered both financial and emotional distress, which eventually left him seriously ill and deeply depressed. He expressed the melancholy and emptiness of this period in a book called *Biathanatos*, which means 'violent death' in Greek.

After experiencing all these troubles and hardships, he profoundly changed his attitude toward life and even religion. He wrote a letter supporting King James I's authority over the Church of England. This earned him the king's favor. From this point on, he gradually gained better opportunities and social standing. In 1615, he was ordained a priest in the Church of England. Afterwards, his writings, poems, and sermons changed completely, gaining him great respect as a clergyman. His poverty soon came to an end.

There is a clear distinction between the character of his writings before and after his appointment to the clergy. Before becoming a priest, his poetry was characterized by intellectual playfulness and ingenious use of metaphor. For example, in "The Flea," one of his best-known poems, the flea serves as a metaphor for love, symbolizing the consummation of the lovers' union after it has sucked their blood. Killing it is likened to destroying the very fruit of their love. This logic is absurd and even ridiculous, yet oddly persuasive. In another poem, "A Valediction: Forbidding Mourning," a pair of stiff twin compasses symbolizes a man and a woman—the man wandering far away while the woman remains in the center.

After becoming a priest, his poetry took on a deeply spiritual and reflective tone. Even today, his religious poetry is loved for its depth and devotion. The novelist Ernest Hemingway was one of those who helped revive modern interest in Donne. Hemingway published a novel *For Whom the Bell Tolls* (1940), drawing on his experiences as a war correspondent in the Spanish Civil War. The protagonist, Robert Jordan, travels to Spain—just as Hemingway once did—and joins an anti-Franco resistance group. Through Jordan's journey, the story depicts countless deaths and realistically conveys the horrors and meaninglessness of the civil war. It became a major bestseller and was made into a film, starring Ingrid Bergman.

The movie as well as the novel was loved around the world. A question arose about the origin and meaning of the title. Hemingway answered that it came from a short religious prose piece "No Man Is an Island" by John Donne. In the prose, Donne emphasizes that every human life is as precious as our own and that all lives are interconnected. The phrase, "for whom the bell tolls" seems one of the most appropriate titles to grieve the civil war, a feast of death and hatred. Now, shall we read it?

John Donne depicted in his burial shroud, engraved by Martin Droeshout. Donne posed for this portrait while still alive and continued to wear the shroud until his death five weeks later.

Donne's Poem:

No Man Is an Island

No man is an island entire of itself; every man
is a piece of the continent, a part of the main;
if a clod be washed away by the sea, Europe
is the less, as well as if a promontory were, as
well as any manner of thy friends or of thine
own were; any man's death diminishes me,
because I am involved in mankind.
And therefore never send to know for whom
the bell tolls; it tolls for thee.

- clod; a lump of soil or earth
- promontory: a high point of land that juts out into the sea
- thine: yours in an old form
- the bell: a church bell rung to announce a death

A scene from *For Whom the Bell Tolls* (1943), based on Ernest Hemingway's novel

Post-Reading 1. Review

1. What did you learn about John Donne from the reading?
2. What kept Donne from getting his degree?
3. Why did Donne get married in secret?

Post-Reading 2. Paraphrasing

Rewrite Donne's idea as seen in the lines below in simpler, everyday English.

> … any man's death diminishes me,
> because I am involved in mankind.
> And therefore never send to know for whom
> the bell tolls; it tolls for thee.

Post-Reading 3. Discussion

1. What do you think was the most difficult moment in Donne's life?
2. Why did Donne say that the death of another person was also his own?
3. Why do you think Hemingway, an American, chose to take part in the Spanish Civil War, a conflict in another country?

Post-Reading 4. Critical Thinking

1. How does the title "No Man Is an Island" show human nature during war? Think about it in terms of both violence and compassion.
2. Evaluate whether a nation's involvement in foreign wars can ever be justified.
3. How can literature both represent the reality of war and encourage peace?

Unit 16

Self and Identity

"Never forget what you are, for surely the world will not. Make it your strength. Then it can never be your weakness. Armour yourself in it, and it will never be used to hurt you."

—George R. R. Martin

Preview 1. Main Ideas

1. Many thinkers and artists have sought inner freedom beyond the boundaries of reality.
2. For the first time, individualism was considered taboo, as it was believed to weaken the unity of the community.
3. People began to see themselves as whole, unique individuals, possessing an identity that could not be shared with anyone else.

Preview 2. Vocabulary

Define the words below in your own words. Then, search online for example sentences to see how each word is used. Share your definitions and sentences with your partner.

1. an unstable society: ____________________

2. blossom: ____________________

3. individuality: ____________________

4. unity: ____________________

5. whole: ____________________

Preview 3. Talking About

Look at the following questions and discuss your ideas with a partner.

1. How are individualism and collectivism different?
2. Can you think of a time when your opinion or choice was respected by others?
3. Have you ever taken a personality test like the MBTI? How could the results help you?

Preview 4. Further Discussion

1. Is individualism good for the growth of a community?
2. Do you think self-awareness helps personal growth?
3. How does knowing yourself help you understand others better?
4. Why are individuality and personality becoming more important in today's society?

Emily Brontë says that she is happiest when she feels most distant from reality,[79] expressing her longing for inner freedom beyond its limits. John Clare describes his self-image in a marginalized and unstable society, saying that he consumes his own sorrows.[80] Henry David Thoreau writes that he has heard "cheerful morning news" within his inmost soul,[81] capturing those beautiful moments that pass through his inner self. Brontë, Clare, and Thoreau were all writers of the 19th century.

The idea of viewing the world from the perspective of the 'individual' dates back to ancient Greece. However, the modern concept of individualism first appeared in the 18th century and blossomed during the 19th century. In its early days, individualism was considered taboo, as many believed it weakened the unity of communities. Beginning in the 1840s, many thinkers and philosophers began to view individualism more positively. Concepts such as "individual" and "individuality" gained wider acceptance among the public. *On Liberty* written by John Stuart Mill and *Self-Help* by Samuel Smiles, both published in 1859, were central to this trend, marking a shift toward individuality as a key social principle. Smiles wrote that each individual is responsible for their own destiny, arguing that "The spirit of self-help is the root of all genuine growth in the individual."[82] People increasingly came to see themselves as unique beings, each with distinct qualities and personalities unlike anyone else's.

Since the 19th century, this perspective on individuality has continued to evolve. Today, we believe that understanding ourselves as whole individuals helps us understand the world better and build healthier relationships with others. Each of us is the starting point of the world we live in. Now, let's look within ourselves, the true beginning of the world.

16A: Walt Whitman

Pre-Reading 1. General Questions

1. Search for information about Walt Whitman online.
2. Name some American poets and novelists you know and describe what they wrote.
3. What important events in 19th-century American history do you know about?

Pre-Reading 2. Vocabulary

Guess the meaning of each underlined word and choose its definition from the list below.

1. Whitman was the kind of man who built his career through persistence and sincerity. ________
2. He worked only as much as was necessary in pursuit of a simple life. ________
3. Later, it became the wellspring of his poetry. ________
4. Whitman's poetry centers on a celebration of democracy, freedom, and individuality. ________
5. He speaks as an ordinary American, in a voice that is plain and humble. ________

A. (a) simple and ordinary in appearance; not decorated or elaborate
B. (n) a source or origin from which something continually flows or develops
C. (v) to have something as the main subject, focus, or interest
D. (n) the act of striving toward or seeking out a specific goal or objective
E. (n) continuous and determined effort over time.

Walt Whitman

Walt Whitman was born in 1819 on Long Island, New York. His father, Walter, was a home builder. Whitman received little formal schooling as he began working in a printing house at the age of twelve. He was largely self-taught and particularly interested in reading the classical works of Homer, Dante, Shakespeare, and others. He learned about human nature and the world through these books. After the printing house burned down when he was 17, he started working as a teacher at an elementary school and kept teaching full-time until he became a journalist in 1841.

Whitman built his career by focusing on one thing with persistence and sincerity. This attitude was evident even when he built his own house: He gathered the necessary materials for the construction and completed it step by step on his own. Although this episode shows his diligence, he never worked more than was necessary in pursuit of a simple life. In his spare time, he traveled, met people from various professions, and talked about life. At the time, people did not understand his way of thinking or his lifestyle. Some even considered him lazy, but he used those times of rest to refine and enrich his spirit. This simple way of life nurtured his inner self and granted him freedom that later became the wellspring of his poetry.

After becoming a journalist, he wrote for several magazines and gradually developed his own poetic style. In 1855, his collection of poems, *Leaves of Grass,* was published. Although it contains only a dozen poems, it is considered his masterpiece and remains a lasting legacy of American literature to this day.

By the mid-19th century, American literature was still seen as less developed, and few writers were thought to capture their culture as fully as British authors did. With the publication of *The Scarlet Letter* in 1850, American literature entered a new phase, beginning to reflect its unique culture and identity. Around this time, Ralph Waldo Emerson, a poet and philosopher, laid the intellectual foundation for this new spirit. It was within this newly formed literary landscape that Whitman's poetry stood out. After reading *Leaves of Grass,* Emerson immediately recognized it as a classic. He wrote a letter of praise to Whitman, "I am not blind to the worth of the wonderful gift of *Leaves of Grass.* I find it the most extraordinary piece of wit

& wisdom that America has yet contributed. I am very happy in reading it, as great power makes us happy."[83] Whitman's poetry soon spread throughout Europe and Britain. He became the leading poet of American literature, celebrating not only its natural beauty but also its ideas and spirit.

Whitman's poetry centers on the celebration of democracy, freedom, and individuality. Before him, no poet had praised the value of the individual so openly and positively. His poem "Song of Myself" begins with the line "I celebrate myself, and sing myself." Yet he does not portray himself as a noble or heroic figure. Instead, he speaks as an ordinary American—plain and humble, finding beauty and strength in such simplicity. His praise in this poem extends beyond himself to every common person. The belief that everyone deserves respect as an individual reflects the basic spirit of humanism and democracy, which has become a core value and remains a source of pride for Americans.

Even after suffering a paralytic stroke later in life, Whitman's spirit remained strong and free. He continued to write poetry until he died in 1892. "O Captain! My Captain!," Whitman's poem written in tribute to Abraham Lincoln's death, was famously quoted in the film *Dead Poets Society* (1989). By celebrating free thought and individuality, the film highlights how Whitman's spirit resonates with the ideals of freedom and human rights. He is now called the father of modern American poetry.

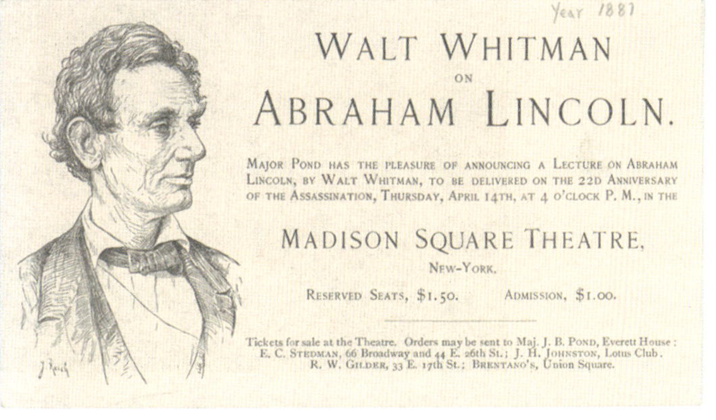

Walt Whitman's 1887 lecture poster commemorating Abraham Lincoln

Whitman's Poem:

Song of Myself

I celebrate myself, and sing myself,
And what I assume you shall assume,
For every atom belonging to me as good belongs to you.

I loafe and invite my soul,
I lean and loafe at my ease observing a spear of summer grass.

My tongue, every atom of my blood, form'd from this soil, this air,
Born here of parents born here from parents the same, and their parents the same,
I, now thirty-seven years old in perfect health begin,
Hoping to cease not till death.

Creeds and schools in abeyance,
Retiring back a while sufficed at what they are, but never forgotten,
I harbor for good or bad, I permit to speak at every hazard,
Nature without check with original energy.

The County Election (1852) by George Caleb Bingham—a visual emblem of democratic participation and individual dignity in Whitmanian America

Post-Reading 1. Review

1. What was Whitman's lifestyle like?
2. Although *Leaves of Grass* contains only a dozen poems, why does it remain a lasting legacy of American literature to this day?
3. Which movie quotes Whitman's poem which was written in honor of Lincoln's death?

Post-Reading 2. Paraphrasing

Rewrite Whitman's idea as seen in the lines below in simpler, everyday English.

> I celebrate myself, and sing myself,
> And what I assume you shall assume,
> For every atom belonging to me as good belongs to you.

Post-Reading 3. Discussion

1. Do you think Whitman's choice to work only as much as needed to live a simple life is still relevant today? Why or why not?
2. Is it better to work just enough to enjoy a fulfilling personal life, or to work hard to reach your full career potential? Which choice do you think leads to a happier life?

Post-Reading 4. Critical Thinking

1. Why is the concept of the 'self' important in human relationships and in society?
2. What are the key factors for building healthy self-esteem?
3. In what ways can contributing to your community help you discover who you are?

16B: William Ernest Henley

Pre-Reading 1. General Questions

1. Search online for information about William Ernest Henley.
2. Find out the storyline of the movie *Invictus* (2010).

Pre-Reading 2. Vocabulary

Guess the meaning of each underlined word and choose its definition from the list below.

1. He contracted tuberculosis, which continued to plague him until his death.

   ____

2. The school principal recognized Henley's talent and sympathized with his suffering.

   ____

3. He suggested possibilities in life and strength of character that Henley had never imagined.

   ____

4. Doctors told him that one of his legs would have to be amputated immediately.

   ____

5. He resisted South Africa's system of white supremacy and racial segregation.

   ____

A. (n) a person's natural abilities or qualities
B. (v) to feel the same way about another person's feelings or opinions
C. (n) a system that keeps people of different races separate and treats them unequally
D. (v) to surgically remove a limb or part of the body
E. (v) to cause persistent pain or distress

William Ernest Henley

Henley was born in Gloucester, Britain, in 1849. He enjoyed a peaceful childhood. His father was a bookseller in that city; not, it seems, a very successful businessman, but gifted with ability and a singular charm of manner.[84] At the age of 12, he entered the Crypt Grammar School, where he contracted tuberculosis that continued to plague him until his death in 1903. The disease, which by modern standards poses no significant threat, was incurable then. Even when it seemed to have been cured, it kept coming back, causing him unbearable pain.

This caused him to limp and suffer from depression. He almost lost hope for his future. However, Thomas Edward Brown, the school principal, recognized Henley's talent and sympathized with his suffering. Brown had already been a renowned theologian and writer and, with keen insight, recognized what would truly help Henley. Brown gave him great comfort and courage—enough for Henley to keep going. Later, Henley recalled that Brown had opened new horizons for him, helping him discover his true self and suggesting possibilities in life and strength of character he had never imagined.* The two became friends beyond social positions, and their friendship lasted for their lifetime. When Brown died, Henley wrote an epitaph in memory of Brown.

At the age of eighteen, Henley passed the Oxford Local Examination as a senior student.[86] It seemed as though a new stage had begun, but unfortunately, he suffered a serious relapse. Doctors told him that his leg would have to be amputated immediately if he was to survive. However, Henley refused to lose his only leg since the other had already been lost. He went to Edinburgh to see a doctor who was renowned for working on a new treatment. Despite his poor health, he endured the very painful journey, and after 20 months in a hospital in Edinburgh, he finally managed to save his leg.

Even during that painful period, he did not waste his time. He studied Spanish, German, and Italian on his own and began writing poetry. One of his fellow patients admired the poems he had written during this time and sent the manuscripts to a magazine. Fortunately, they caught the attention of the editor.

---

* The original memoir reads, "He opened to me ways of thought and speech that … helped me discover me the beginnings, the true materials, of myself….What he did for me, practically, was to suggest such possibilities in life and character as I had never dreamed. He was singularly kind to me at a moment when I needed kindness even more than I needed encouragement."[85]

This led Henley to become the editor of a weekly magazine called *London* at the age of 28. The following year, he married a young woman named Anna. Her family did not welcome their marriage. Henley walked with a limp, had five younger siblings, and was very poor. Becoming the editor of a weekly magazine did not immediately improve his financial situation. Moreover, his father died while Henley was in the hospital, leaving nothing because the treatment had been so expensive. Henley's situation at the time was described as follows: "There was, for instance, one occasion when he and his brother Anthony were absolutely penniless. Henley, exhausted from hunger, lay on his bed; towards evening, Anthony, in desperation, went out."[87]

The north front of the Royal Infirmary of Edinburgh, where William Ernest Henley was hospitalized for 20 months in the 1870s.

Under these circumstances, Henley continued to publish poetry. No matter what difficulties he encountered, they never discouraged him from writing. He pressed on and grew stronger through every hardship.

Henley's life, full of courage and determination, was brought to life in the film *Invictus*, which is based on the story of Nelson Mandela. In the film, Mandela refers to Henley's poem "Invictus," saying, "When things got very bad, I found inspiration in the poem." Mandela spent for about 27 years in prison for "advocating nonviolent resistance to apartheid—South Africa's institutionalized system of white supremacy and racial segregation … Confined to a small cell without a bed or plumbing, he was forced to do hard labor in a quarry. He could write and receive a letter once every six months, and once a year he was allowed to meet with a visitor for 30 minutes."[88] The film shows that during this horrible time, Henley's poem "Invictus" inspired Mandela to keep going. Like Henley and Mandela, people may also face moments of deep despair. Even then, it is up to each individual to rebuild their own life. This is the central message of Henley's life and poetry. Now, let us read the poem.

Henley's Poem:

Invictus

Out of the night that covers me,
  Black as the pit from pole to pole,
I thank whatever gods may be
  For my unconquerable soul.

In the fell clutch of circumstance
  I have not winced nor cried aloud.
Under the bludgeonings of chance
  My head is bloody, but unbowed.

Beyond this place of wrath and tears
  Looms but the Horror of the shade,
And yet the menace of the years
  Finds and shall find me unafraid.

It matters not how strait the gate,
  How charged with punishments the scroll,
I am the master of my fate,
  I am the captain of my soul.

- fell: (a) vicious or violent
- wince: to make a slight shrinking movement because of pain or distress
- bludgeonings: a heavy beating or attack, as if with a thick stick
- chance: luck, fate
- menace: Things or situations that bother, annoy, or cause pain to a person
- scroll: A heavenly book with names and deeds written on it.

William Ernest Henley, who bore a life of adversity with resilience, portrayed in his final years

Post-Reading 1. Review

1. What caused the greatest suffering in Henley's life?
2. What role did Thomas Edward Brown play in Henley's life?
3. What effect did Henley's poem quoted in the movie *Invictus* have on the main character?

Post-Reading 2. Paraphrasing

Rewrite Henley's idea as seen in the lines below in simpler, everyday English.

> It matters not how strait the gate,
> How charged with punishments the scroll,
> I am the master of my fate,
> I am the captain of my soul.

Post-Reading 3. Discussion

1. What do you think was the most important factor that helped Henley overcome the hardships of his life?
2. Do you think Henley's song, Invictus, reflects the main character's life journey well? If so, in what way?

Post-Reading 4. Critical Thinking

1. Henley's poem suggests that courage and resilience are the keys to overcoming life's challenges. Do you agree with this idea, or do you think something more is needed?
2. What specific factors or changes do you think could improve your life, and why?
3. Do you think the strength of character that can overcome life's hardships is innate or developed?
4. How can self-awareness help a person navigate through life's challenges?

Unit 17

Self and Community

"In every community, there is work to be done. In every nation, there are wounds to heal. In every heart, there is the power to do it."

—Marianne Williamson

Preview 1. Main Ideas

1. As individuals, we are unique, authentic, and invaluable.
2. Every person deserves respect as an individual, but at the same time, we need to cooperate with others in the community.
3. Our destinies are closely linked to the fate of the community.

Preview 2. Vocabulary

Define the words below in your own words. Then, search online for example sentences to see how each word is used. Share your definitions and sentences with your partner.

1. self-awareness:

   ____

2. a strong sense of values:

   ____

3. authentic:

   ____

4. the well-being of the community:

   ____

5. collaborate:

   ____

Preview 3. Talking About

Look at the following questions and discuss your ideas with a partner.

1. Have you ever thought about what the word "we" really means? When does this idea become important?
2. How can you and your community thrive together in a rapidly changing world?

Preview 4. Further Discussion

1. Describe in detail what values are important to you and how you apply them in your daily life.
2. As a member of your community, explain the values that matter most to you and share how you put them into practice.

Each of us is unique, authentic, and invaluable. Every person is a whole being, not something that can be broken into parts. The more this truth is understood, the deeper one can reach into the heart of their being and the more clearly one can see the nature of the world around them.

It goes without saying that human beings do not exist alone. Each person must be fully respected as an individual, but at the same time, they need to cooperate with other members of the community. Paradoxically, this is why self-awareness is so important: only by understanding ourselves can we truly balance our individuality with the needs of the community. However, when pursuing shared goals and meeting society's demands, personal happiness, individuality, and a strong sense of values are often overlooked or even distorted. On the other hand, focusing only on individual interests and happiness can destroy the well-being of the community. Self-awareness and harmony with others may seem like opposing goals, but they must be pursued together.

Herman Melville, best known for writing *Moby-Dick* (1851), once said, "We cannot live only for ourselves. A thousand fibers connect us with our fellow men."[89] These words remind us that we are all connected. Each of us is part of a larger "we," and our lives are intertwined with those around us.

As much as we care for ourselves, we need to remember our destinies are closely tied to the fate of the community. As members of a community, we should keep two things in mind. First, never treat the two separately. The more beautiful, fruitful, and peaceful the community is, the more prosperous our future will be. Second, respect other members of the community and be willing to work with them. It may be helpful to remember that a true community is made by harmony and balance among its members, not by the sacrifice of just one side. Our past, present, and future as connected with those of the others, and as the community grows, so do we.

17A: Douglas Malloch

Pre-Reading 1. General Questions

1. Search online for information about Douglas Malloch.
2. Read his well-known "Good Timber" and share your impressions.
3. What does it mean to live in harmony with others within a community?

Pre-Reading 2. Vocabulary

Guess the meaning of each underlined word and choose its definition from the list below.

1. Muskegon is considered one of Michigan's best vacation spots for its wide, <u>untouched</u> beaches. ________
2. His love for his homeland is <u>reflected</u> in the poem. ________
3. The city was the center of the <u>timber industry</u>. ________
4. Malloch's poetry does not follow new cultural <u>paradigms</u> like modernism. ________
5. It also lacks the kind of rich <u>metaphors</u> that many poets liked to employ. ________

A. (n) a model, a distinctive pattern, or an example of something
B. (n) a way to describe something by saying it is something else
C. (n) the business of growing, cutting, and selling trees for wood products
D. (v) to show or express (properties of things, people's attitudes or emotions)
E. (a) in its natural (original) conditions, unspoiled

Douglas Malloch was born in 1877 in Muskegon, Michigan, which was a port city. Today, it is considered one of Michigan's best vacation spots for its wide, untouched beaches. During Malloch's childhood, however, the town was once the center of the timber industry. Its geographical position between the forests and the sea gave it an advantage in transporting timber. Malloch grew up in logging camps. For him, the forest was his playground and a friend throughout his childhood.

He never left Michigan, even in adulthood. His love for his homeland is reflected in the poem "Michigan my Michigan," which later became the unofficial anthem of the state. This heartfelt devotion is beautifully expressed in the lines, "Thy lakes so clear, thy forests grand, thy fertile fields and golden sand—Michigan, my Michigan!" His career also began and ended in Michigan. For 13 years, he worked for *The Muskegon Chronicle*, a local newspaper covering the Muskegon area. He also wrote weekly articles for *The American Lumberman* in Chicago, a business magazine focusing on the lumber industry. Continuing his journalism career, he became an influential figure in the American media, serving as President of the Chicago Press Club, the largest media group in the United States, and as Master of the Writers Guild of Chicago.

Meanwhile, he occasionally contributed his writings to another magazine, *The Journal of Education.* Among these works is the famous poem "Good Timber,"[90] which earned him the nickname 'Lumberman.'

> Good timber does not grow with ease:
> The stronger wind, the stronger trees;
> The further sky, the greater length;
> The more the storm, the more the strength.
> By sun and cold, by rain and snow,
> In trees and men good timbers grow.

Twin Lakes State Park, Michigan. Public domain image by Yinan Chen

He sings about the life of a tree growing in the forest, yet he is actually describing human life. To become good timber, a tree in the forest must withstand the wind and rain and receive enough sunlight. The more sunlight it gets and the stronger the wind blows, the stronger the wood grows. Just as trees in the forest grow stronger through trials, so too do humans. The harsher the storms they endure, the deeper their roots and the stronger they grow. His idea—that we become better people by facing challenges without fear—is simple yet profoundly enlightening. *The Journal of Education* published a series of poems by Malloch. The editor seems to have found his poetry suitable for an educational magazine. Soon, his poetry became well-known across the country, and he gained nationwide recognition.

As his nickname 'Lumberman' implies, he was like a tree that does not move once it takes root. He worked for the magazine *The American Lumberman* for decades until he died of a heart attack in 1938, at the age of 61. Malloch's poetry does not follow cultural paradigms like modernism. His poems avoid contemporary issues, like social or political debates, and make no use of academic terminology. It also lacks the kind of rich metaphors that many poets liked to employ. Becaused of this, his poetry did not receive a lot of attention from scholars at the time. Nevertheless, his poems were loved by many at that time and are still loved today. His simple poetic touch makes it much easier for us to understand and reflect on its meaning as we look inward. At its heart lies the principle that each of us is part of a community, and we become more complete and beautiful beings when we are in harmony.

Northwestern Lumberman cover, forerunner of *The American Lumberman*

Malloch's Poem:

Be the Best of Whatever You Are

If you can't be a pine on the top of the hill,
Be a scrub in the valley—but be
The best little scrub by the side of the rill;
Be a bush if you can't be a tree.

If you can't be a bush be a bit of the grass,
And some highway happier make;
If you can't be a muskie then just be a bass—
But the liveliest bass in the lake!

We can't all be captains, we've got to be crew,
There's something for all of us here,
There's big work to do, and there's lesser to do,
And the task you must do is the near.

If you can't be a highway then just be a trail,
If you can't be the sun be a star;
It isn't by size that you win or you fail—
Be the best of whatever you are!

- scrub: a small, branchy tree
- rill: a small and narrow stream
- muskie: a type of fish called the muskellunge

Workers cutting trees in Ontario, using a crosscut saw, ca. 1870–1930. Public domain image

Post-Reading 1. Review

1. What was Malloch's occupation?
2. What was the the central theme of his poetry?
3. Why were his poems so loved?

Post-Reading 2. Paraphrasing

Rewrite Malloch's idea as seen in the lines below in simpler, everyday English.

> If you can't be a highway then just be a trail,
> If you can't be the sun be a star;
> It isn't by size that you win or you fail—
> Be the best of whatever you are!

Post-Reading 3. Discussion

1. Summarize Malloch's life and explain what he valued most.
2. Malloch believed that challenges help people grow stronger, just as storms make trees take deeper roots. Do you agree that hardship is necessary for personal growth? Why or why not?
3. What does a bush symbolize in his poem "Be The Best of Whatever You Are"?

Post-Reading 4. Critical Thinking

1. What lessons do you think we can learn from nature?
2. Malloch's poems often emphasize harmony and cooperation, like trees growing together in a forest. How can teamwork help you experience this kind of harmony in your group projects or classes?
3. Malloch encourages us to do our best in whatever we do, even when we face difficulties. What kinds of things make it hard for you to do your best, and how do you try to overcome them?

17B: T. S. Eliot

Pre-Reading 1. General Questions

1. Search online for information about T. S. Eliot.
2. Find out what modernism is.
3. Why was T. S. Eliot awarded the Novel Prize?

Pre-Reading 2. Vocabulary

Guess the meaning of each underlined word and choose its definition from the list below.

1. Eliot is a part of the heritage of both America and Britain. ________

2. He became a naturalized British citizen at the age of 39. ________

3. He was a fairly prominent elite even among writers. ________

4. He is regarded as a representative of modernism in literature. ________

5. His works are recognized for their profound insights into human existence.

A. (n) an object or culture passed down from previous generations
B. (v) to acquire the nationality of another country and become a citizen of that country
C. (a) standing out or important; easily noticeable
D. (n) a person who speaks or acts for others, or a typical example of a group or quality
E. (n) the ability to clearly understand the true nature of something or someone

T. S. Eliot

Thomas Stearns Eliot is his full name. Many people know him by his surname, Eliot, and by the famous line "April is the cruelest month." In Western literature, he is considered one of the most prominent poets in America and Britain, along with Wordsworth and Yeats. He was born in the United States in 1888 and died in London in 1965. Thus, Eliot can be seen as part of the heritage of both America and Britain. Strictly speaking, however, he is seen more as a British figure because he lived in the U.K. longer and became a naturalized British citizen at the age of 39. He even converted to the Church of England.

Eliot's literary talent was influenced by his mother, who had published a few poetic works. His father ran a brick company, providing him with full financial support so that he could devote himself to his studies. With such a background, he became a fairly prominent figure even among writers. He entered Harvard University at the age of 18 and obtained a master's degree there at 22. After studying for a year at the Sorbonne in France, he returned to Harvard and started his doctoral course. He chose philosophy as his major. In the process, he broadened his intellectual interests to include English literature, French literature, Western modern philosophy, Indian philosophy, and more. He is recognized not only for his poetry but also for his philosophical depth, as his works express profound insights into human existence.

While working on his thesis, Eliot married a beautiful ballerina, Vivienne Haigh-Wood. He fell in love with Vivienne, but their personalities were very different. She was very sensitive and emotionally unstable. Eliot was rather reserved and detached, unable to provide her with the emotional support she needed. Over time, the conflicts between them deepened, and they could not find a way to bridge their differences. After 14 years, they formally separated, a step often taken by couples who, for religious reasons, could not divorce. With some distance from her, Eliot's world of poetry deepened, reflecting a newfound sense of emotional tranquility. Yet Vivienne's life ended tragically in a psychiatric hospital.

Nowadays, he is regarded as a representative of modernism in literature. At the beginning of the 20th century, many people in the Western world grew skeptical about modern civilization. The rise of science and technology was breaking down traditional ways of life, leading to a new approach to understanding people and civilization. The area of literature and art, too, was breaking away from traditional techniques and conventions, and modern civilization became a target of criticism. This artistic movement of critically examining the negative features of modern society is called modernism. Each period has its own *zeitgeist*,* which is difficult to define in simple terms. In the same way, modernism also has various meanings, and different modernist writers interpret it in their own ways. Eliot was different from many other writers of his time. Instead of breaking away from the past to create something new, he respected tradition and tried to find solutions to modern problems in it. His poem "The Waste Land" is representative of this tendency. In the poem, he explored the problems of modern civilization and even suggested some answers based on the long traditions of Europe and the East.

He respected traditions from both the West and the East. However, when he focused on the West, he believed that Britain had a much longer history than the United States and that its traditions were better preserved. His becoming a British citizen and joining the Anglican Church were clear evidence of how much he valued them.

"The Waste Land"(1922) is his most famous poem, but *Four Quartets* (1943) is considered his greatest work, which is a series of four major poems written and published over six years. There is a gap of nearly two decades between these two masterpieces. However, they are similar because both try to offer guidance to a modern civilization that is losing its human values. First, in "The Waste Land," Eliot offers a message to people who had lost their way after World War I: Give, sympathize, and control.** This idea, drawn from an ancient Indian scripture, conveys three key principles—generosity, compassion, and self-control. Second, in *Four Quartets*, Eliot encourages us to keep seeking and to stay hopeful about the future, reminding us that we are the makers of history.

Vivienne Haigh-Wood, wife of T. S. Eliot

Eliot was awarded the Nobel Prize for Literature in 1948 in recognition of all his poetry, critical essays, and philosophical visions. His legacy remains an enduring treasure for humanity.

* *Zeitgeist* means "the spirit of the time." It refers to the general cultural, intellectual, and moral climate of a particular era.

** The phrase "Datta. Dayadhvam. Damyata." comes from the *Brihadaranyaka Upanishad*, one of the oldest and most important Hindu scriptures, which contains ancient teachings about how humans should live in harmony with others and with themselves.

Eliot's Poem:

Little Gidding*

What we call the beginning is often the end
And to make an end is to make a beginning.
The end is where we start from. And every phrase
And sentence that is right (where every word is at home,
Taking its place to support the others,
The word neither diffident nor ostentatious,
An easy commerce of the old and the new,
The common word exact without vulgarity,
The formal word precise but not pedantic,
The complete consort dancing together)
Every phrase and every sentence is an end and a beginning,
Every poem an epitaph. And any action
Is a step to the block, to the fire, down the sea's throat
Or to an illegible stone: and that is where we start.
We die with the dying:
See, they depart, and we go with them.
We are born with the dead:
See, they return, and bring us with them.
The moment of the rose and the moment of the yew-tree
Are of equal duration. A people without history
Is not redeemed from time, for history is a pattern
Of timeless moments.

……

And the end of all our exploring
Will be to arrive where we started
And know the place for the first time.
Through the unknown, unremembered gate
When the last of earth left to discover
Is that which was the beginning;
At the source of the longest river

---

* *Little Gidding* is the fourth and final of *Four Quartets* by T. S. Eliot.

The voice of the hidden waterfall

And the children in the apple-tree
Not known, because not looked for
But heard, half-heard, in the stillness
Between two waves of the sea.
Quick now, here, now, always--
A condition of complete simplicity
(Costing not less than everything)
And all shall be well and
All manner of thing shall be well
When the tongues of flames are in-folded
Into the crowned knot of fire
And the fire and the rose are one.

- ostentatious: showy or extravagant, meant to attract attention
- vulgarity: rude or offensive behavior or language
- pedantic: obsessed with rules
- two waves: a pair of waves that rise and fall in turn
- knot: a hard or tangled spot in wood, rope, or something similar

St John's Church at Little Gidding, seen in April.
Photo by John Sutton, licensed under CC BY-SA 2.0 via Wikimedia Commons

Post-Reading 1. Review

1. Talk about Eliot's family background and the environment in which he grew up.
2. Which unique qualities or approaches set Eliot apart from other modernist writers?
3. What is the shared theme in Eliot's "The Waste Land" and *Four Quartets*?

Post-Reading 2. Paraphrasing

Rewrite Eliot's idea as seen in the lines below in simpler, everyday English.

> Every phrase and every sentence is an end and a beginning,
> Every poem an epitaph. And any action
> Is a step to the block, to the fire, down the sea's throat
> Or to an illegible stone: and that is where we start.

Post-Reading 3. Discussion

1. Eliot believed we can learn important lessons from tradition and history.
   What are some traditional values that you think are still meaningful today?
2. Eliot worried that modern people were losing their human values.
   In today's world of technology and social media, do you think that's true? Why or why not?
3. How can we find harmony and balance in our modern lives, as Eliot suggested in his works? Think about your daily life—study, relationships, or personal goals—and share what helps you stay centered.

Post-Reading 4. Critical Thinking

1. Eliot looked to Eastern traditions for answers to Western problems.
   What do you think are the benefits and risks of learning from other cultures?
2. Eliot became a British citizen to find new meaning and growth in life.
   Would you choose to join a new community to grow personally, or would you try to improve the one you belong to now? Explain your choice.
3. In today's fast-changing world, what traditional values do you think are still worth keeping, and why?
4. Eliot believed that humans play a key role in shaping history.
   Do you agree? How can this idea affect how you live your life or make decisions?

Further Reading 1

*Excerpts from "A Just and Lasting Peace"**

Barack Obama

[...] For all the cruelty and hardship of our world, we are not mere prisoners of fate. Our actions matter, and can bend history in the direction of justice. [...]

But perhaps the most profound issue surrounding my receipt of this prize is the fact that I am the Commander-in-Chief of the military of a nation in the midst of two wars. [...] I come here with an acute sense of the costs of armed conflict – filled with difficult questions about the relationship between war and peace. [...]

The concept of a "just war" emerged, suggesting that war is justified only when certain conditions are met: if it is waged as a last resort or in self-defense; if the force used is proportional; and if, whenever possible, civilians are spared from violence. [...]

So yes, the instruments of war do have a role to play in preserving the peace. And yet this truth must coexist with another – that no matter how justified, war promises human tragedy.

Part of our challenge is reconciling these two truths – that war is sometimes necessary, and war at some level is an expression of human folly. [...] Let us focus on a more practical, more attainable peace, based not on a sudden revolution in human nature but on a gradual evolution in human institutions. [...]

Discussion Questions

1. Obama describes the idea of a "just war." What conditions does he believe are necessary for war to be morally justified?
2. President Obama received the Nobel Peace Prize while the U.S. was involved in two wars. Do you think this is paradoxical or justified? Why?
3. He states that "war promises human tragedy." How does this recognition shape his vision of peace?

* Barack H. Obama delivered his Nobel Lecture on December 10, 2009, in Oslo as the 44th U.S. President and wartime Commander-in-Chief. Speaking during the Iraq and Afghanistan wars, he reflected on the moral complexities of war—that war may sometimes be necessary to protect nations and uphold justice, yet it always brings human tragedy. He emphasized the idea of "just war," the responsibility that comes with using force, and ultimately called for a "just and lasting peace" built on the gradual evolution of human institutions. His message urged the world to face the realities of conflict while striving for humanity's highest aspiration—peace.

Further Reading 2

*Excerpts from "The Smile That Builds Community"**

Mother Teresa

[...] I believe that love begins at home, and if we can create a home for the poor – I think that more and more love will spread. And we will be able through this understanding love to bring peace, be the good news to the poor. The poor in our own family first, in our country and in the world. [...]

Today there is so much suffering – and I feel that the passion of Christ is being relived all over again – are we there to share that passion, to share that suffering of people. Around the world, not only in the poor countries, but I found the poverty of the West so much more difficult to remove. When I pick up a person from the street, hungry, I give him a plate of rice, a piece of bread, I have satisfied. I have removed that hunger. [...]

And so let us always meet each other with a smile, for the smile is the beginning of love, and once we begin to love each other naturally we want to do something. So you pray for our Sisters and for me and for our Brothers, and for our Co-Workers that are around the world. That we may remain faithful to the gift of God, to love Him and serve Him in the poor together with you. [...]

Discussion Questions

1. Mother Teresa says, "a smile is the beginning of love." Why do you think a simple smile can build community?
2. She compares material poverty with the "poverty of being unwanted." Which do you think is harder to overcome, and why?
3. What small acts of love can you practice in your home or community that could create peace?

* Mother Teresa delivered this Nobel Peace Prize Lecture in Oslo, Norway, in 1979. She emphasized that true peace begins with small acts of love—especially within families and local communities—and that the "poverty of being unwanted and unloved" is deeper than material poverty. Her message highlighted that a smile and simple acts of care can spread love and build peace. This excerpt is adapted from Mother Teresa's Nobel Peace Prize Lecture delivered on December 11, 1979, at Oslo City Hall, Norway.

End Notes

Chapter 1: Creative Thinking and Imagination

1 김현철. (2016, Feburary 22). "이준익 감독은 왜 윤동주여야만 했나." *SBS News.* https://news.sbs.co.kr/news/endPage.do?news_id=N1003427611(Accessed June 25, 2025)

2 잠보니, 쥬세뻬(Zamboni, G). (1996). *토마스 아퀴나스의 인식론* (이재룡 역, p. 12). 가톨릭대학교출판부.

3 Shaw, G. B. (2003) *Pygmalion.* London: Penguin. p. 104.

4 Shaw, G. B. (n.d.). Imagination is the beginning of creation. *QuotePark.* https://quotepark.com/quotes/872895-george-bernard-shaw-imagination-is-the-beginning-of-creation-you-imag/(Accessed July 25, 2025)

5 Quote Investigator. (2017, September 8). *New dreams require new habits.* https://quoteinvestigator.com/2017/09/08/new-dream/(Accessed July 25, 2025)

6 Boyle, L. E. (1977). Saints, scholars and others, 500–800 A.D. In J. Ronsley (Ed.), *Myth and reality in Irish literature*(p. 17). Wilfrid Laurier University Press.

7 Yeats, W. B. (2010). *The collected works of W. B. Yeats: Autobiographies (*W. H. O'Donnell & D. Archibald, Eds.; Vol. 3, p. 89). Scribner.

8 Carroll, L. (1998). *Alice's adventures in Wonderland and Through the Looking-Glass and what Alice found there*(p. 52). Penguin Books.

9 Carroll, L. (1998). p. 14.

10 Klein, E. (Director). (2018, June 13). *케이팝의 모든 것*(Season 1, Episode 4) [TV series episode]. In Vox Media (Producer), *Explained: 세계를 해설하다.* Netflix.

11 Brontë Parsonage Museum. (n.d.). *About the Brontë.* https://www.bronte.org.uk/about-the-brontes (Accessed July 25, 2025)

12 이응복 (Director), & 김은숙 (Writer). (2018, July 14). 제3화[TV series episode]. In Studio Dragon (Producer), 미스터 션샤인. tvN.

13 Guérard, Albert. (1934) Herder's Spiritual Heritage: Nationalism, Romanticism, Democracy. *The Annals of the American Academy of Political and Social Science*, 174. pp. 1–8.

Chapter 2: Empathy and love

14 Locke, J. (n.d.). *An essay concerning human understanding.* William Tegg & Co.

15 Fromm, E. (2006). *The art of loving*(p. 19). Harper Perennial.

16 바론, H., & 바론, K. (2009). "서문." In *아들과 연인* (정상준, Trans., Vol. 1, pp. 5-10, p. 7). 민음사.

17 "First Letter Robert Browning Wrote to Elizabeth Barrett Browning." *British Literature Wiki*, https://britishliterature.fandom.com/wiki/ElizabethandRobertBrowning(Accessed August 20, 2025)

18 Fromm, E. (2006). The art of loving(p. 92). Harper Perennial.

19\. 정규웅. (2007). "해설: 환상과 미의 세계." In *애너벨 리*(pp. 102–111, p. 102). 민음사.

20 Carhart, M. S. (1924). *The life and work of Joanna Baillie*(p. 5). Yale University Press.

21 Shakespeare's Birthplace Trust. (n.d.). *Shakespeare's words.* https://www.shakespeare.org.uk/explore-shakespeare/shakespedia/shakespeares-words/(Accessed November 18, 2024)

22 ProFlowers. (n.d.). *Friendship quotes.* https://www.proflowers.com/blog/friendship-quotes(Accessed December 12, 2023)

23 황동규. (2012). "해설: 인간 바이런과 시인 바이런." In *순례: 조지 고든 바이런*(pp. 137-142, p. 137). 민음사.

24 Moore, T. (1830). *Letters and journals of Lord Byron*(Chap. 14). https://quotefancy.com/quotes/1893023-george-gordon-byron-i-awoke-one-morning-and-found-myself-famous(Accessed April 1, 2022)

25 Awondo, P., Geschiere, P., & Reid, G. (2012). *Homophobic Africa?: Toward a more nuanced view.* African Studies Review, 55(3), 145–168. p. 147.

26 Kirby, M. (2021). The sodomy offence: England's least lovely criminal law export? In C. Lennox & M. Waites (Eds.), *Human rights, sexual orientation and gender identity in the Commonwealth*(p. 74). University of London Press; Institute of Commonwealth Studies. https://www.jstor.org/stable/j.ctv512st2.6(Accessed May 29, 2022)

27 Boyd, D. (2013). The problem with freedom: Homosexuality and human rights in Uganda. *Anthropological Quarterly*, 86(3), 697–724. https://doi.org/10.1353/anq.2013.0047

28 Adut, A. (2005). A theory of scandal: Victorians, homosexuality, and the fall of Wilde. *American Journal of Sociology*, 111(1), 213–248. p. 227. https://doi.org/10.1086/428817

29 Adut, A. (2005). p. 214.

30 와일드, 와일드(Oscar Wilde). (2022). *심연으로부터* (박명숙, Trans., pp.23-24). 문학동네.

31 Rutherford, E. (2014). Impossible love and Victorian values : J. A. Symonds and the intellectual history of homosexuality. *Journal of the History of Ideas*, 75(4), 605–627. p. 624.

32 Robbins, T. (n.d.). Tom Robbins Quotes. *BrainyQuote*. https://www.brainyquote.com/quotes/tom_robbins_387517. (Accessed September, 30 2024)

33 Tolle, E. (n.d.). *When the dog looks at you, the dog is not thinking what kind of a person you are. The dog is not judging you.* https://elevatesociety.com/when-the-dog-looks-at/(Accessed August 18, 2025)

Chapter 3: Living in Harmony

34 Hymnary.org. (n.d.). *Christopher Smart.* https://hymnary.org/person/Smart_Christopher(Accessed November 18, 2024)

35 Bright Drops. (n.d.). *Nature quotes.* https://brightdrops.com/nature-quotes(Accessed November 18, 2024)

36 Charton, M. (1915). Descriptions of nature in Longfellow's poems. *Proceedings*, 10. p. 117. https://historycambridge.org/wp-content/uploads/2017/08/Proceedings-Volume-10-1915-2.pdf(Accessed November 18, 2024)

37 Trollope, A. (1881, April). Henry Wadsworth Longfellow. *The North American Review*, 132(293), 383–406. p. 384.

38 Hopkins, G. M. (1956). *Further letters of Gerard Manley Hopkins*(C. C. Abbott, Ed.). Oxford University Press. p. 2.

39 Arkins, B. (1997). Heraclitean fire: Greek themes in Hopkins. *International Journal of the Classical Tradition*, 4(3), 458-472. p.429.

40 Arkins, B. (1997). p. 461.

41 Mariani, P. (2008). *Gerard Manley Hopkins: A life*(p. 425). Viking.

42 King's widow urges acts of compassion. (2000, January 17). *Los Angeles Times.* https://www.latimes.com/archives/la-xpm-2000-jan-17-mn-54832-story.html(Accessed November 18, 2024)

43. Rockwell, K. A. (1957). A. E. Housman, poet-scholar. *The Classical Journal*, 52(4), 145–148. p. 146.

44 Rockwell, K. A. (1957). p. 45.

45 Taylor, I. (1832). *The writings of Jane Taylor: Memoirs and poetical remains*(Vol. 1, p. 13). Perkins & Marvin.

46 Carroll, L. (1998). *Alice's adventures in Wonderland and Through the Looking-Glass.* Penguin Books. p. 63.

47 Taylor, J. (1834). "Poverty." *Original poems for infant minds.* T. Ash. p. 11.

48 Nelson, C. (2012). *Precocious children & childish adults: An inversion in Victorian literature.* Johns Hopkins University Press. p. 152.
Nelson, Claudia. Precocious Children & Childish Adults: An Inversion in Victorian Literature. The Johns Hopkins UP, 2012.

49 BrainyQuote. (n.d.). *Nelson Mandela quotes.* https://www.brainyquote.com/quotes/nelson_mandela_178795 (Accessed November 18, 2024)

50 윤명옥. (2013). p. 256.

51 Nicholls, D. (1967). The totalitarianism of Thomas Arnold. *The Review of Politics*, 29(4), 518–525. p. 519.

52 Kincaid, J. R. (1994). *Child-loving: The erotic child and Victorian culture.* Routledge. p. 13.

53 Champneys, B. (1900). *Memoirs and correspondence of Coventry Patmore*(Vol. 1, p. 127). George Bell and Sons.

54 Champneys, B. (1900). p. 131.

55 Jackson, V. F. (1990). *Patriotism is not enough: A reappraisal of the poetry of Henry Newbolt*(Doctoral dissertation). Bowling Green State University. pp. 10–11.

56 박형지, & 설혜심. (2016). *제국주의와 남성성: 19세기 영국의 젠더 형성*. 아카넷. p. 12.

Part 4: Self-Awareness in the Community

57 The Guardian. (2018, January 12). *The Guardian view on tech bosses and kids: Time for parents to wake up.* https://www.theguardian.com/commentisfree/2018/jan/12/tech-bosses-kids-time-smartphones-parents-mental-health(Accessed March 10, 2024)

58 Demo, D. H. (1992). The self-concept over time: Research issues and directions. *Annual Review of Sociology,* 18, 303–326. p. 307.

59 U.S. Department of State. (n.d.). *What is modern slavery?* https://www.state.gov/what-is-modern-slavery/(Accessed

November 18, 2024)
60 CNN. (2022, July 3). *Jayland Walker: Police release video of fatal shooting*. https://edition.cnn.com/2022/07/03/us/jayland-walker-police-shooting-video/index.html(Accessed November 18, 2024)
61 Global Justice Now. (2021, June 5). *Black History Month Series: Abolishing the slave trade – History belongs to Black rebels*. https://www.globaljustice.org.uk/2019/10/black-history-month-series-abolishing-slave-trade-history-belongs-black-rebels/(Accessed November 18, 2024)
62 Symons, A. (1907). *William Blake*. E. P. Dutton and Company, p. 14.
63 Symons, A. (1907). p. 14.
64 The HyperTexts. (n.d.). *William Blake: Influence, references, and popular culture*. http: // www.thehypertexts.com/William%20Blake%20Influence%20References%20Popular%20Culture.htm(Accessed November 18, 2024)
65 Oxford Mail. (n.d.). Blake's Heaven. https://www.oxfordmail.co.uk/news/9049885.blakes-heaven/(Accessed November 18, 2024)
66 The HyperTexts. (n.d.). *William Blake: Influence, references, and popular culture*. http: // www.thehypertexts.com/William%20Blake%20Influence%20References%20Popular%20Culture.htm(Accessed November 18, 2024)
67 Norton, C. E. (1909). A biographical sketch. In M. E. Burt & W. T. Chapin (Eds.), *Kipling stories and poems: Every child should know*(pp. xix–xx). Doubleday, Page & Company.
68 Norton, C. E. (1909). p. xxviii.
69 Varley, H. L. (1953). Imperialism and Rudyard Kipling. *Journal of the History of Ideas*, 14(1), 124–135. p. 124.
70 Hitchens, C. (1990). Burdens and songs: The Anglo-American Rudyard Kipling. *Grand Street*, 9(3), 203–234. p. 203.
71 Sowerby, R. (n.d.). What was the real purpose of writing The Jungle Book? *Ranker*. https://www.ranker.com/list/purpose-of-the-jungle-book/rachel-souerby(Accessed November 18, 2024)
72 The Conversation. (n.d.). Jungle Book: Look closely, there's more to Rudyard Kipling than colonial stereotypes. https://theconversation.com/jungle-book-look-closely-theres-more-to-rudyard-kipling-than-colonial-stereotypes-122078(Accessed November 18, 2024)
73 Caesar, A. (1993). *Taking it like a man: Suffering, sexuality and the war poets, Brooke, Sassoon, Owen, Graves*(p. 117). Manchester University Press.
74 Owen, W. (1967). *Collected letters*(H. Owen & J. Bell, Eds., p. 421). Oxford University Press.
75 Owen, W. (1967). p. 452
76 Hipp, Daniel. D. (2005). *The poetry of shell shock: Wartime trauma and healing in Wilfred Owen, Ivor Gurney, and Siegfried Sassoon*(p. 24). McFarland & Company.
77 Owen, W. (1963). *The collected poems of Wilfred Owen*(C. Day Lewis, Ed., p. 31). A New Directions Book.
78 Owen, W. (1967). *Collected letters*(H. Owen & J. Bell, Eds., pp. 533–534). Oxford University Press.
79 Poets.org. (n.d.). I'm happiest when most away. https://poets.org/poem/im-happiest-now-when-most-away(Accessed July 24, 2025)
80 Poetry Foundation. (n.d.). I am. https://www.poetryfoundation.org/poems/43948/i-am(Accessed November 18, 2024)
81 Academy of American Poets. (n.d.). Inward morning. https://poets.org/poem/inward-morning(Accessed November 18, 2024)
82 Mill, J. S. (1901). *On liberty*(pp. 112–113). Walter Scott.
83 Smiles, S. (n.d.). *Self-help*. https://archive.org/details/in.ernet.dli.2015.220299(Accessed May 27 2021, p. 1.)
84 Emerson, R. W. (1855, July 21). *Letter to Walt Whitman*. The Vault at Pfaff's. https://pfaffs.web.lehigh.edu/node/56381 (Accessed November 18, 2024)
85 Cornford, L. C. (1913). William Ernest Henley(p. 22). Constable and Company.
86 Cornford, L. C. (1913). p. 23.
87 Cornford. L. C. (1913). p. 25.
88 History.com Editors. (n.d.). Nelson Mandela released from prison. *History*. https://www.history.com/this-day-in-history/nelson-mandela-released-from-prison(Accessed November 18, 2024)
89 Ellevate Network. (n.d.). Quotes about the power of community. https://www.ellevatenetwork.com/articles/8538-quotes-about-the-power-of-community(Accessed November 18, 2024)
90 Malloch, D. (1922). Good timber. *The Journal of Education*, 95(6), 146.

Answer sheet

Chapter 1

Unit 1A: Bernard Shaw

■ Pre-Reading 2. Vocabulary

1. **famine** → **D.** (n) extreme shortage of food
2. **self-taught** → **B.** (a) acquiring skills or knowledge by oneself without instruction
3. **setbacks** → **E.** (n) something delaying or impeding progress
4. **stubbornness** → **A.** (n) the quality of refusing to change your opinion or behavior
5. **satirizes** → **C.** (v) to use humor, irony, or exaggeration to criticize people or ideas

■ Post-Reading 1. Review

1. **Who is George Bernard Shaw?**
→ George Bernard Shaw was an Irish playwright and critic (1856–1950), known for over 60 plays and his sharp social commentary. He won the 1925 Nobel Prize in Literature.
2. **What is the main plot of Shaw's play *Pygmalion* (1912)?**
→ It's about Henry Higgins, a phonetics professor, who teaches Eliza Doolittle, a poor flower girl, to speak "proper" English so that she could pass as a lady.
3. **How is the story of the movie *My Fair Lady* (1964) different from *Pygmalion* (1912)?**
→ The film gives a romantic ending between Eliza and Higgins, while Shaw's play ends with Eliza gaining independence and not marrying Higgins.

■ Post-Reading 2. Paraphrasing

<Example>
I wandered through Africa's wild forests,
With Dr. Livingstone leading the way.
Then I slipped off to America,
Hiding with Huckleberry Finn all day.

Unit 1 B: Phillis Wheatley

■ Pre-Reading 2. Vocabulary

1. **innate** → **B.** (a) existing naturally from birth; not learned
2. **prolific** → **D.** (a) producing many works or results; very productive
3. **self-evident** → **E.** (a) clearly true and needing no proof
4. **suffocating** → **C.** (v) making it hard to breathe or feel free
5. **undeniable** → **A.** (a) something that is definitely true and cannot be denied

■ Post-Reading 1. Review

1. **Who was Phillis Wheatley?**
→ She was the first published African American female poet and a former slave who gained fame for her literary talent.
2. **What is the main idea of the Declaration of Independence?**
→ All people are created equal and have natural rights to life, liberty, and the pursuit of happiness, and governments exist to protect these rights.
3. **How was Phillis Wheatley's life and experiences as a slave different from those of other enslaved people in her time? What factors contributed to these differences?**
→ Wheatley's life was unusual because she was educated and supported by her owners, which allowed her to read widely and write poetry. This was rare for enslaved people in her time. Her exceptional ability and her environment made her accomplishments possible.

■ Post-Reading 2. Paraphrasing

<Example>
Flying through the sky to reach God's bright home,
The heavenly palace of the powerful God,
With His wings we can fly faster than the wind
And leave the world far behind us.

Unit 2A: William Butler Yeats

■ Pre-Reading 2. Vocabulary

1. **illustrious** → **B.** (a) highly distinguished; famous; renowned
2. **tarnished** → **A.** (v) To make something lose its

shine or good reputation

3. **wavered** → **E.** (v) to become unsteady; begin to give way
4. **betrayed** → **D.** (v) to hurt (someone who trusts you) by not helping or doing something morally wrong
5. **profound** → **C.** (a) having or showing great knowledge or insight; deep; very thoughtful

▪ Post-Reading 1. Review

1. **Talk about the historical background in which William Butler Yeats lived.**

→ Yeats lived during a time of Irish cultural revival and political struggles for independence from Britain. Ireland faced uprisings against British rule, and Yeats was involved in the Irish independence movement, inspired by its folklore and mythology.

2. **Talk about the women Yeats loved.**

→ Yeats first loved Maud Gonne, an Irish independence activist and actress, but she rejected his proposals multiple times and eventually married John MacBride. After Maud's rejection, Yeats later married Georgiana Hyde-Lees. His deep love for Maud never completely disappeared.

3. **What do you think had the most significant influence on Yeats' literature?**

→ Yeats' literature was deeply shaped by Irish myths, legends, and his country's fight for independence. His love for Maud Gonne also inspired many of his poems. These influences gave his work a mix of personal emotion and national identity, making him one of the most important poets of the 20th century.

▪ Post-Reading 2. Paraphrasing

<Example>

I will get up and go to Innisfree.
I will build a small cabin from clay and branches.
I will grow nine rows of beans and keep a beehive.
I will live alone, surrounded by the buzzing of bees.

Unit 2B: Lewis Carroll

▪ Pre-Reading 2. Vocabulary

1. **unfold** → **D.** (v) to become known, revealed, or developed
2. **restrictive** → **C.** (a) limiting one's freedom to act or think; placing controls or constraints on behavior
3. **norms** → **A.** (n) a standard of behavior or mindset that is considered normal or expected
4. **extraordinary** → **E.** (a) having very special, unusual, or remarkable talent or quality
5. **insurmountable** → **B.** (a) too great or difficult to overcome

▪ Post-Reading 1. Review

1. **Briefly summarize the characteristics of the era in which Carroll was born.**

→ He was born in the Victorian era, which valued morality, religion, and social order but often restricted freedom, especially in boys' schools. It was also a time of scientific curiosity and exploration.

2. **Describe Carroll's life, highlighting the differences between his childhood and school life.**

→ Carroll had a happy and free childhood, spending time with his large family and enjoying creative activities. However, his school life at Rugby School was strict and challenging, with heavy academic pressure and strict discipline, which he later recalled with little fondness.

3. **Why have Carroll's novels remained popular for so long?**

→ Carroll's books are unique because they are original, playful, and free from the heavy moral lessons common in his era. The imaginative characters and philosophical questions in Alice's Adventures in Wonderland and Through the Looking-Glass continue to inspire readers to think and dream.

4. **What key themes did Carroll intend to convey in his poem "Life is but a Dream"?**

→ The poem reflects on the passage of time, the innocence of childhood, and the dreamlike nature of life. It suggests that life, like a dream, is fleeting and precious.

▪ Post-Reading 2. Paraphrasing

<Example>

In a Wonderland they lie,
Dreaming as the days go by,
Dreaming as the summers end.

Always floating down the stream,
Staying in the golden light,
Life—what is it but a dream?

Unit 3A: Emily Brontë

■ Pre-Reading 2. Vocabulary

1. **companions** → **A.** (n) people or animals with whom one spends a lot of time or travels
2. **infer** → **E.** (v) to deduce or conclude something based on evidence and reasoning, not explicit statements
3. **pseudonyms** → **C.** (n) fake names used by writers instead of their real ones
4. **reclusive** → **F.** (a) tending to keep away from other people; preferring solitude
5. **masterpiece** → **D.** (n) an artist's or writer's greatest and most outstanding piece of work
6. **evoked** → **B.** (v) to bring a memory, feeling, or image into the mind

■ Post-Reading 1. Review

1. **According to reviews at the time, how did readers react to Emily Brontë's novel *Wuthering Heights*?**

→ Readers were shocked and disturbed by its violence, dark emotions, and depictions of cruelty and revenge. It felt unlike anything published before and challenged the moral expectations of the time.

2. **Emily Brontë used the pseudonym Ellis Bell. Why do you think she did this?**

→ She wanted to avoid prejudice against female writers and keep her work from being judged by her family's social or religious reputation.

■ Post-Reading 2. Paraphrasing

<Example>

When the long day leaves me tired,
And life moves from pain to pain,
Lost and nearly in despair,
Your gentle voice calls me again.
Oh, my true and faithful friend!
I am not alone at all,
As long as you can speak to me
With such a tender call.

Unit 3B: William Wordsworth

■ Pre-Reading 2. Vocabulary

1. **overload** → **C.** (n) a condition where there is too much to handle; an overwhelming burden
2. **liberate** → **F.** (v) to set someone or something free
3. **distinctive** → **D.** (a) easy to recognize because it is different from others; special
4. **radical** → **E.** (a) very different from the usual, especially in political or social views
5. **grind** → **B.** (n) hard, repetitive, and boring work or routine
6. **conviction** → **A.** (n) a strong belief or firm opinion about something

■ Post-Reading 1. Review

1. **Define Romanticism based on the reading.**

→ Romanticism emphasizes spiritual liberty, equality, and fraternity, opposing anything that suppresses these values. It involves deep emotional expression and often seeks inspiration from nature and imagination.

2. **Why did Wordsworth think a new type of poem was needed?**

→ He believed that poetry should be enjoyed by ordinary people, not just intellectuals, and that new poetry could break away from rigid language rules and reach everyone.

3. **What effect did Wordsworth want his poetry to have on his readers?**

→ He wanted his poetry to restore inner peace, heal the human mind, and inspire spiritual renewal through nature and imagination.

4. **How long did it take Wordsworth to complete *Prelude; or, Growth of Poet's Mind*?**

→ He completed the first version in 1805 and kept revising it until 1850, shortly before his death.

■ Post-Reading 2. Paraphrasing

<Example>

We will not grieve, but instead find
Strength in what is left behind,
In the deep, first sympathy
That, once it lived, will always be.

Chapter 2

Unit 4A: D. H. Lawrence

■ Pre-Reading 2. Vocabulary

1. **confronted** → **D.** (v) to face the challenge
2. **discord** → **E.** (n) disagreement between people, ideas, etc.

3. **excessive** → **A.** (a) beyond the ordinary, normal, reasonable; immoderate
4. **eclipses** → **B.** (v) to make (something) less important or popular
5. **restore** → **C.** (v) to return someone or something to the original condition or position

■ Post-Reading 1. Review

1. **What was Lawrence's home environment like when he was a child?**

→ He grew up in a small mining village in Nottinghamshire, England. His father was an uneducated coal miner and his mother was a middle-class former teacher. His home was filled with conflict because of his father's drinking habits, which caused discord between his parents.

2. **Why did the editor replace some words in *Sons and Lovers* when it was first published?**

→ The editor replaced some words to make the novel more "decent" and less sensational, because words about the human body were considered shocking at that time.

3. **What message did Lawrence aim to convey about human relationships in his novel?**

→ He wanted to show that modern civilization and capitalism made human relationships shallow and mechanical, and that human beings should return to their true energy and nature.

■ Post-Reading 2. Paraphrasing

<Example>

It is enough, you are near—
The mountains stand in calm.
Dandelion seeds float halfway in the grass.
You and I together,
Holding our love with pride and joy.
We stand tall with our love.
Everything begins with us,
We are the source.

Unit 4B: Elizabeth Barrett Browning

■ Pre-Reading 2. Vocabulary

1. **talent** → **E.** (n) the ability of a person to be naturally good at something
2. **severe** → **A.** (a) very bad, serious, or unpleasant; causing pain or suffering
3. **led to** → **D.** (v) to cause or bring about a particular result
4. **captivated** → **C.** (a) strongly attracted to or fascinated by someone or something
5. **probable** → **B.** (a) likely to happen; expected

■ Post-Reading 1. Review

1. **Who was Elizabeth Barrett Browning?**

→ She was a renowned 19th-century English poet, celebrated for her literary talent and the deep emotions expressed in her poems.
She was born into a wealthy family, and because of her fragile health, she spent much of her life at home, reading and writing poetry.

2. **What was the major challenge in her life?**

→ Her greatest challenge was chronic illness, which caused severe headaches, back pain, and physical weakness.
This illness limited her social activities, confined her to her home, and led her to rely on pain relievers such as opiates.

3. **How did Elizabeth first meet her husband, Robert Browning?**

→ She first met Robert Browning through her poetry.
He was captivated by her poems and sent her an admiring letter, which began a long correspondence of over 570 letters and eventually led to their meeting and marriage.

■ Post-Reading 2. Paraphrasing

<Example>

I love you in countless ways.
I love you as much as my soul can, reaching as far as it can go,
even beyond what I can see or feel.
I love you with the fullness of my being, in the purest and most perfect way.

Unit 5A: Edgar Allan Poe

■ Pre-Reading 2. Vocabulary

1. **oddities** → **B.** (n) the quality or condition being strange or unusual
2. **excessive** → **A.** (a) going beyond what is necessary, ordinary, or desirable
3. **eerie** → **E.** (a) strange, mysterious, and scary
4. **fatal** → **C.** (a) leading to death
5. **spiraled** → **D.** (v) to move in a twisting, circular pattern; to increase or decrease continuously and

often uncontrollably

■ Post-Reading 1. Review

1. **Why did he drop out of the University of Virginia?**

→ Poe dropped out of the University of Virginia mainly because of conflicts with his foster father, Allan. Poe had little financial support from Allan, and the strict lifestyle of the university did not suit him. Unable to pay for his education, he eventually left the school.

2. **Why were Poe's works not well received by American literary circles?**

→ Poe is well known for his dark, gloomy poems and mysterious short stories, such as "The Raven," "The Black Cat," and "The Murders in the Rue Morgue." His works created eerie and emotional atmospheres that were unique for his time. However, American literary circles, dominated by conservative Puritan traditions, were not ready to accept such dark and psychological themes, so his genius was not fully appreciated in his own country.

3. **Talk about the relationship between Poe and Virginia.**

→ Poe loved his young cousin Virginia deeply, and their relationship brought him brief happiness despite their poverty. Sadly, Virginia suffered from a long illness and died at a very young age, which left Poe devastated. Her death deepened his sorrow and inspired some of the most emotional and tragic elements in his poetry, including "Annabel Lee."

■ Post-Reading 2. Paraphrasing

<Example>

The angels up in heaven
Were jealous of our love.
So one cold night
They sent a chilling wind
That took my Annabel Lee away.

Unit 5B: Thomas Hardy

■ Pre-Reading 2. Vocabulary

1. **architecture** → **F.** (n) designing and making buildings
2. **apprentice** → **E.** (n) a beginner who works under a skilled person to learn a trade
3. **sensibility** → **C.** (n) inner ability to understand and feel emotions and the outside world
4. **clashed** → **A.** (n) fighting or creating conflicts on opposing issues
5. **preferred** → **B.** (v) to like one more than other things
6. **enshrined** → **D.** (v) to protect a person or thing in a special place so it will be remembered

■ Post-Reading 1. Review

1. **Who is Thomas Hardy?**

→ Thomas Hardy was a prominent English novelist and poet of the late 19th and early 20th centuries. He grew up in rural Dorset, England, and his works often reflect the struggles of ordinary people against social norms and fate. Hardy became famous for his realistic novels like *Tess of the d'Urbervilles* and *Jude the Obscure,* as well as for his later poetry that expressed deep emotions and philosophical reflections on life.

2. **Why did Hardy first choose architecture as a career?**

→ Hardy initially pursued a career in architecture because he showed talent in drawing and design, and it was a practical profession that could provide financial stability. His family encouraged this choice, and he trained as an apprentice to a church architect and later worked as an assistant in a London architect's office before fully turning to literature.

3. **What inspired Hardy to pursue novel writing seriously?**

→ Hardy began to take novel writing seriously after meeting Emma Gifford, who encouraged his literary talent. Her support and his desire to achieve both recognition and financial security pushed him to write and publish novels that soon gained public attention, despite some attracting criticism.

■ Post-Reading 2. Paraphrasing

<Example>

I felt so sad and full of sorrow
When the moment I had been waiting for arrived,
And you still did not come to me.

Unit 6A: Joanna Baillie

■ Pre-Reading 2. Vocabulary

1. **protagonist** → **C.** (n) the main character in a story
2. **ethical** → **A.** (a) morally right or wrong according to accepted rules or principles
3. **anticipated** → **E.** (v) to expect or predict something before it happens

4. **governed** → **B.** (v) to control and direct (a group of people)
5. **deficiency** → **D.** (n) the state of not having enough of what is needed

■ Post-Reading 1. Review

1. **Who was Joanna Baillie? Briefly describe her life and achievements.**
→ Joanna Baillie was a Scottish poet and playwright born in 1762 in Bothwell. She became one of the most respected female playwrights of the Romantic era and wrote 26 dramas and several volumes of poetry, though her works were not widely popular during her lifetime.
2. **What were her parents like when she was a child?**
→ Her father was a Presbyterian pastor and a professor at the University of Glasgow, known for his deep moral foundation and emotional temperance. Her mother provided warm love and affection, creating a nurturing childhood environment.
3. **In what genre did she leave most of her works? How are her works evaluated?**
→ Most of her works were dramas, focusing on human passions and moral struggles. Critics praised her as one of the most capable female playwrights of the Romantic period, and her works were later respected for foreshadowing psychological insights and moral complexity.

■ Post-Reading 2. Paraphrasing

<Example>
Your body has no clear shape,
You cannot walk with beauty or grace.
There are only a few small things you can do,
But still, I love you deeply.

Unit 6B: William Shakespeare

■ Pre-Reading 2. Vocabulary

1. **unparalleled** → **E**. (a) being without equal or match; incomparable in quality or extent
2. **adapted** → **D**. (v) to change something so it fits a new situation or purpose
3. **collaboration** → **C**. (n) working together
4. **subject** → **A**. (n) a topic or theme that is discussed or studied in detail
5. **granted** → **B**. (a) considered to be deserved or expected without appreciation

■ Post-Reading 1. Review

1. **What new things did you learn about Shakespeare?**
→ I learned that Shakespeare's works are still adapted for film and theater today and that he invented around 1,700 English words. I also learned that much of his life remains a mystery, which has led some people to question whether he actually wrote all the works attributed to him.
2. **What is the most clearly known historical fact from Shakespeare's life?**
→ The most clearly known historical fact is that he was born in 1564 and died in 1616. At the age of eighteen, he married a woman eight years older than him, with whom he had three children.
3. **Why did some people assume that someone else wrote Shakespeare's works?**
→ Some people assumed that someone else wrote his works because Shakespeare never attended college. Yet his plays display detailed knowledge of law, history, foreign landscapes, and manners, which led to doubts about his authorship.

■ Post-Reading 2. Paraphrasing

<Example>
I feel so sad because I cannot
Speak the love I have for you.
I care for you as I am supposed to,
Not more, not less.

Unit 7A: Alfred, Lord Tennyson

■ Pre-Reading 2. Vocabulary

1. **excessive** → **C.** (a) too much; more than is reasonable or necessary
2. **invaluable** → **B.** (a) extremely valuable; too valuable to measure
3. **devastated** → **D.** (a) completely shocked or destroyed
4. **suppress** → **E.** (v) to hold back (emotion or emotional expression)
5. **skeptical** → **A.** (a) doubtful or having distrust

■ Post-Reading 1. Review

1. **How did Tennyson and Hallam become such close friends?**
→ Tennyson and Hallam met in a literary group at Cambridge University. Hallam wrote an article about

Tennyson's poetry. They became close friends, and Hallam even fell in love with Tennyson's sister, Emily. Their friendship deepened as Hallam sincerely comforted Tennyson during his times of grief with warmth and kindness.

2. What is *In Memoriam* about?

→ *In Memoriam* is a collection of poems that expresses Tennyson's mourning for Hallam's death. It reflects his deep grief, his thoughts on human existence, and his doubts about science and faith. Ultimately, it conveys a journey from despair to hope, proposing that the human soul transcends death.

3. What did the immense popularity of his books bring to him?

→ The immense popularity of Tennyson's books brought him great fame and recognition. He became the most famous English poet of his time and was eventually appointed Poet Laureate, achieving significant literary prestige.

■ Post-Reading 2. Paraphrasing

<Example>

Once again, I stand by this dark house,
On this long and lonely street.
These doors, where my heart once raced,
Waiting eagerly for a hand to greet.

Unit 7B: George Gordon, Lord Byron

■ Pre-Reading 2. Vocabulary

1. **represented** → **E.** (v) to serve as a symbol or example of something, especially in art or literature
2. **indifference** → **C.** (n) a lack of interest, concern, or sympathy
3. **rebellious** → **B.** (a) refusing to obey the authority of existing social norms and fighting against them
4. **misbehavior** → **D.** (n) improper or unacceptable conduct by social or moral standards
5. **entrusted** → **A.** (v) to give someone responsibility for something because you fully trust them

■ Post-Reading 1. Review

1. Describe the main events and key aspects of Lord Byron's life.

→ Lord Byron was a celebrated Romantic poet who became famous for his passionate poetry and adventurous lifestyle. He traveled through Europe on the *Grand Tour*, gained a reputation as a Casanova because of his romantic affairs and scandals, and eventually joined the fight for Greek independence. He died at the age of thirty-six, admired as both a poet and a revolutionary.

2. How did Byron's childhood hardships influence his life and work?

→ Byron grew up in a neglectful and unstable family, facing indifference and emotional hardship. These experiences made him feel lonely and rebellious, which strongly influenced his poetry, giving it a dark, emotional, and defiant tone that reflected his personal struggles.

3. Why do you think Byron entrusted his handwritten manuscripts to Thomas Moore?

→ Byron trusted Thomas Moore as a loyal friend who could protect his personal writings. He may have wanted Moore to manage how the manuscripts were published or preserved, especially to avoid scandal or misuse after his death.

■ Post-Reading 2. Paraphrasing

<Example>

With this water and this wine,
I would lift my cup to you.
May there be peace between us,
And good health to you, Tom Moore!

Unit 8A: Oscar Wilde

■ Pre-Reading 2. Vocabulary

1. **aesthetics** → **F.** (n) the study or appreciation of beauty, especially in art and design
2. **pinnacle** → **E.** (n) the highest or best point of something; the peak
3. **hideous** → **D.** (a) extremely ugly or disgusting to see
4. **corruption** → **C.** (n) bad or dishonest behavior, or losing a sense of what is right and wrong
5. **blissful** → **A.** (a) characterized by or experiencing extreme happiness, joy, and contentment
6. **hostility** → **B.** (n) intense opposition or dislike

■ Post-Reading 1. Review

1. Discuss Wilde's first major success, *The Picture of Dorian Gray*. What themes are explored in this novel?

→ The novel shows the danger of being too proud of one's beauty and the problem of living only for pleasure. It also tells how people often care more about how things look than what they really are.

2. **Why was *The Picture of Dorian Gray* so well received? How does it differ from novels written before its time?**

→ The novel was special because it showed a new way of thinking about beauty and moral freedom. Unlike older novels, it focused on people's inner feelings and free choices instead of strict social rules.

3. **Who are the main characters in the story "The Happy Prince"?**

→ The Happy Prince and the Little Swallow.

■ Post-Reading 2. Paraphrasing

<Example>

It's enough to have been loved,
Even just for a little while.
To hold love's hand and see
Its wings flash in your smile.

Unit 8B: John Addington Symonds

■ Pre-Reading 2. Vocabulary

1. **prosperous** → **F.** (a) experiencing success, wealth, or growth in a positive and often financial aspect
2. **deteriorated** → **D.** (v) to become worse in condition, quality, or health
3. **devoted** → **B.** (v) to sincerely dedicate your time and effort to something or someone
4. **memoir** → **E.** (n) a written account of someone's personal experiences and memories
5. **blackmail** → **C.** (n) the act of threatening to reveal secrets to get money or force someone to do something
6. **mourned** → **A.** (v) to feel or show sadness after someone's death

■ Post-Reading 1. Review

1. **Beyond internet search, what new insights did you gain about John Addington Symonds?**

→ Symonds was a 19th-century scholar who focused on Hellenism and the study of homosexuality in ancient Greece. His own homosexual tendencies influenced his academic focus and writings.

2. **What were Symonds' main areas of academic interest?**

→ His main interests were Hellenism, Platonism, and Renaissance culture, with a special focus on the moral and philosophical aspects of homosexuality in ancient Greece.

3. **Why were Symonds' academic achievements overlooked or under-appreciated?**

→ His achievements were underappreciated because his focus on homosexuality conflicted with the moral standards of his time, leading to accusations, social rejection, and delayed publication of his works.

4. **Discuss characteristics of same-sex relationships in ancient Greek society.**

→ In ancient Greece, same-sex relationships, especially the bond between older and younger males, were often seen as a spiritual and intellectual relationship. Philosophers like Plato discussed it as an ideal form of love, and it was integrated into cultural and ethical discussions of the time.

■ Post-Reading 2. Paraphrasing

<Example>

I met him in a humble place.
He sang beautiful songs that moved me to tears.
At night, he filled my dreams.
During the day, I couldn't stop thinking of his face.

Chapter 3

Unit 9A: Sir Walter Scott

■ Pre-Reading 2. Vocabulary

1. **recognition** → **C.** (n) the act of showing official appreciation for (something)
2. **contracted** → **E.** (v) to become sick or fall ill with a disease
3. **regaled** → **D.** (v) to entertain someone with talks such as stories, jokes, etc.
4. **hounds** → **B.** (n) dogs that are trained and used for hunting animals
5. **legacy** → **A.** (n) something passed down from the past, such as achievements, ideas, or traditions

■ Post-Reading 1. Review

1. **What did Sir Scott study at the University of Edinburgh?**

→ He studied the classics, which was considered the most intellectually demanding discipline at the time.

2. **What changes in the 1800s helped novels become more popular?**
→ Advancements in printing technology and the growth of people's new intellectual needs in the early 1800s contributed to the popularity of novels.
3. **How was his way of writing novels different from other writers of his time, and which historical event is central to *Waverley*?**
→ He differed by pioneering the historical fiction genre, tying moral lessons and imagination to real events, unlike many contemporaries who focused more on moral tales. The central historical event in *Waverley* is the Battle of Culloden, a bloody conflict between the English soldiers and the Scottish Jacobites.

■ Post-Reading 2. Paraphrasing

<Example>

Wake up, happy lords and ladies!
The sun is rising over the mountain.
It's time for a joyful hunt.
Horses, hawks, and hounds are ready.
The dogs bark in pairs,
Hawks whistle, and horns blow.
All the sounds mix together cheerfully.
Wake up, happy lords and ladies!

Unit 9B: Christopher Smart

■ Pre-Reading 2. Vocabulary

1. **steward** → **C.** (n) a person who manages another person's property, land, or estate
2. **sponsored** → **A.** (v) to pay for or support someone's education, activity, or project
3. **established** → **E.** (v) to start or set up something important, such as a system, movement, or institution
4. **mental institution** → **D.** (n) a hospital or facility where people with mental illnesses are treated and cared for
5. **eccentric** → **B.** (a) showing behavior or ideas that are unusual or different from what is normal

■ Post-Reading 1. Review

1. **Explain why Christopher Smart dropped out of school and how he could continue his education.**
→ Christopher Smart dropped out of Maidstone Grammar School because his father died, leaving the family in financial difficulty. He continued his education at Pembroke College, Cambridge University, with the sponsorship of the Duke and Duchess.
2. **What was Smart's occupation?**
→ Christopher Smart was a poet and also a publisher, often using the pseudonym "Mrs. Mary Midnight."
3. **Find instances that highlight Christopher Smart's uniqueness or exceptional qualities in his writings or personal life.**
→ Christopher Smart showed his uniqueness through his deep love for nature and animals, especially cats, his strong religious devotion expressed in hymns like "I Sing of God." His irregular and original poetic style, along with the unusual aspects of his life—including the rumors of madness and his temporary stay in a mental institution—also highlight his exceptional qualities.

■ Post-Reading 2. Paraphrasing

<Example>

He is both serious and playful.
He trusts that God is his Savior.
Nothing is more comforting than his peaceful rest.
Nothing is more lively than his life when he is active.

Unit 10A: Henry Wadsworth Longfellow

■ Pre-Reading 2. Vocabulary

1. **cradle of gold** → **B.** (idiom) being born into wealth and privilege
2. **constrained** → **C.** (v) to limit or control something, especially by rules, conditions, or circumstances
3. **authentic** → **A.** (a) real or genuine
4. **abated** → **D.** (v) to become weakened or less intense
5. **replete** → **E.** (a) filled or well-supplied with something

■ Post-Reading 1. Review

1. **Explain why Longfellow wanted to study European culture.**
→ He admired European culture for their sophistication and richness. His travels there were full of cultural surprises, and those experiences helped shape his literary sensibility.
2. **Describe his family background.**
→ Longfellow was born into a wealthy and prestigious family. His grandfather was among the founders of Bowdoin College, and his father served as a trustee. His family background allowed him to receive an

excellent education.

3. **What were the main themes of his poems?**

→ He mainly sang about the emotions of the human heart—especially sorrow, loneliness, and people's inner life.

■ Post-Reading 2. Paraphrasing

<Example>

I feel a spark of life run through my mind,
Flowing through my nerves and veins.
It's an exciting, almost overwhelming feeling.
I hear the wind moving through the trees,
As if it were playing heavenly music.
The branches bend downward,
Like the keys of a giant musical instrument.

Unit 10B: Gerard Manley Hopkins

■ Pre-Reading 2. Vocabulary

1. **entrepreneurial** → **B.** (a) involved in running their own businesses and pioneering new opportunities in the market
2. **bane** → **A.** (n) someone or something that causes ongoing problems
3. **urban expansion** → **D.** (n) the growth or increase of urban areas and industries
4. **aptitude** → **E.** (n) a person's innate ability or skill in a field
5. **conversion** → **C.** (n) the act of changing beliefs, habits, or ways of thinking

■ Post-Reading 1. Review

1. **Who is Gerard Manley Hopkins?**

→ He was a renowned English poet and a Jesuit priest, known for his innovative poetry.

2. **Talk about Hopkins' school days.**

→ He attended a boarding school where he excelled academically, gained fame for his artistic talent, and was often subjected to physical punishment for disobedience. He later studied at Oxford University, where he was admired for his intellect and friendships.

3. **What is the most critical turning point in Hopkins' life? Why?**

→ His conversion to Catholicism was the most critical turning point. It led him to abandon his previous plans, join the Society of Jesus, and devote his life to faith and poetry. This decision reshaped his personal and professional path entirely.

■ Post-Reading 2. Paraphrasing

<Example>

We seal her cracks but make them worse,
We carve into her until she bleeds.
Those who come after will not see
The beauty she once showed us.

Unit 11A: Alfred Edward Housman

■ Pre-Reading 2. Vocabulary

1. **Moderations** → **C.** (n) preliminary examinations in certain fields of study, assessing a wide range of knowledge
2. **pursue** → **E.** (v) to follow or engage in a particular path or career over a period of time
3. **unparalleled** → **A.** (a) unmatched or without equal in quality or reputation
4. **atheist** → **B.** (n) someone who does not believe in the existence of God or any gods
5. **mass casualties** → **D.** (n) a very large number of people killed or injured at the same time, usually because of war, disaster, or violence

■ Post-Reading 1. Review

1. **Who was Alfred Edward Housman?**

→ Alfred Edward Housman (1859–1936) was an English classical scholar and poet who read Classics at Cambridge and later served as Professor of Latin at University College London and Trinity College, Cambridge.

2. **How did he prepare for a career as a classical scholar while working as a civil servant?**

→ He spent his free time studying in libraries while working as a civil servant in London, preparing himself to succeed in classical studies.

3. **What experiences influenced the main themes of his poems?**

→ The deaths of his mother and his younger brother deeply influenced his poetry, shaping its themes of sadness, loss, patriotism, and the lives of soldiers.

■ Post-Reading 2. Paraphrasing

<Example>

He gives up all and becomes
What he was born to be—
A humble soldier for the king,

Yet ever dear to me

Unit 11B: Jane Taylor

■ Pre-Reading 2. Vocabulary

1. **vitality** → **C.** (n) energy and strength; the quality of being full of life and active
2. **household** → **D.** (a) familiar to most families or people
3. **posthumously** → **A.** (adv) after a person's death
4. **economic monopoly** → **E.** (n) a situation where one group completely controls trade or resources
5. **deprivation** → **B.** (n) a state in which people lack what they need

■ Post-Reading 1. Review

1. **What insights or previously unknown facts did you discover about Jane Taylor?**

→ I learned that her brother collected and published five volumes of her handwritten manuscripts after her death, that she collaborated with her sister Ann on an 1806 poetry volume, and that her prose and essays addressed a wide range of social issues beyond children's rhyme.

2. **Provide a concise summary of Jane Taylor's career.**

→ Jane Taylor (1783–1824) was an English poet and essayist best known for writing "Twinkle, Twinkle, Little Star"; she first published with her sister Ann, then, five volumes of poetry and prose were posthumously published by her brother, and she explored both children's literature and serious social commentary.

3. **What themes or issues was Jane Taylor most concerned with as a writer?**

→ While celebrated for her children's rhymes, she also engaged deeply with themes of freedom, slavery, justice, war, private judgment, voluntarism, and the welfare of marginalized people.

■ Post-Reading 2. Paraphrasing

<Example>

They live in warm, rich homes,
Never knowing life's hard side.
But in this small clay cottage,
They learn what real struggle is.

Unit 12A: Christina Georgian Rossetti

■ Pre-Reading 2. Vocabulary

1. **movement** → **D.** (n) a collective effort by a group of people to achieve artistic or social objectives
2. **contracted** → **A.** (v) to become infected with a disease
3. **discipline** → **E.** (n) the practice of following rules or controlling one's behavior, often to achieve improvement or maintain order
4. **contemporary** → **B.** (a) existing or occurring at the same time period as another event or person
5. **deprived** → **C.** (a) lacking basic needs like food, housing, education, or social opportunities

■ Post-Reading 1. Review

1. **Discuss Christina Georgina Rossetti and her family background. What were the main fields of work they were involved in?**

→ Christina (1830–1894) was the youngest child of Gabriel Rossetti, an Italian-born poet and scholar. Her brother Dante Gabriel Rossetti co-founded the Pre-Raphaelite Brotherhood as a painter and poet; her sister Maria and mother Frances were also writers; and her uncle John William Polidori wrote Gothic fiction.

2. **What stage of life did Rossetti consider the most innocent or pure?**

→ Rossetti considered childhood to be the most innocent and pure stage of life. She believed that childhood was "the purest period of life," a time untouched by corruption or moral weakness. Because of this, she thought that children should be protected from abusive or harmful environments, and her sympathy for them is clearly reflected in her poetry, such as "Is it Well with the Child?"

3. **What social issues did she care about, and what volunteer work did she do for many years?**

→ Deeply concerned about women rejected by society, child exploitation, and slavery, Rossetti volunteered for over a decade at the St Mary Magdalene Home in Highgate, providing refuge and practical help to former prostitutes and other marginalized individuals.

■ Post-Reading 2. Paraphrasing

<Example>

Sheltered from frost and snow,
Hidden from storm and sun,

Seeds lie still in the earth,
Waiting one by one
To wake and burst in bloom.

Unit 12B: Matthew Arnold

■ Pre-Reading 2. Vocabulary

1. **renowned** → **E.** (a) famous and respected for a particular skill, achievement, or quality
2. **derived** → **B.** (v) originated from or based on something
3. **halt** → **C.** (n) a stop or pause in progress or movement
4. **atomized** → **A.** (v) to be separated from others and feel alone in society
5. **appeal** → **D.** (n) a strong request for help or agreement on something important

■ Post-Reading 1. Review

1. **What did you learn about Matthew Arnold that you didn't know before?**

→ Beyond poetry, he was also an educator and critic, briefly taught at Rugby School to satisfy his father, and later became a leading social commentator in works like *Culture and Anarchy*, warning against the "atomization" of society.

2. **Who was Matthew Arnold's father, and what was he known for?**

→ Matthew Arnold's father was Thomas Arnold, a renowned educator and the headmaster of Rugby School in England. He was known for reforming traditional education and emphasizing moral and religious instruction in schools.

3. **What were Mathew Arnold's school days like?**

→ At Rugby and later at Oxford, he won a scholarship but lived rebelliously—mixing study with play, resisting solemn discipline, and behaving with such flair that he both irritated and impressed his peers.

■ Post-Reading 2. Paraphrasing

<Example>

We got more than we ever dreamed,
Yet life isn't what we hoped in youth.
Growing old in sunset's glow
Is not a peaceful end to our days.

Unit 13A: Coventry Patmore

■ Pre-Reading 2. Vocabulary

1. **outdated** → **D.** (a) no longer current or considered; old-fashioned; behind the times
2. **legitimately** → **C.** (adv) in a manner that is fair, justified, and in accordance with accepted practices or standards
3. **virtuous** → **E.** (a) having high moral standards; behaving in a morally good and honest way
4. **converted** → **B.** (a) to change one's religious faith or beliefs to another
5. **self-sacrificing** → **A.** (n) showing a willingness to give up your own interests or happiness so that other people can be helped or benefit

■ Post-Reading 1. Review

1. **Discuss the reasons for the popularity of his poems among the public during his lifetime.**

→ Patmore's *The Angel in the House* captured the Victorian ideal of marriage with a vivid, heartfelt celebration of wedded devotion and domestic harmony. Its moral seriousness and clear Christian values struck a chord with readers who saw family virtue as the bedrock of society, driving sales across Britain and America.

2. **Why do his poems no longer appeal to critics and ordinary readers today?**

→ Modern audiences find his depiction of the "angelic" wife overly sentimental and restrictive, reflecting outdated gender roles that clash with today's emphasis on equality and individual freedom. The prescriptive tone and moral earnestness now feel archaic rather than uplifting.

3. **What were the primary sources of inspiration for his poetry?**

→ Patmore drew directly on his own happy marriage to Emily Augusta—whose piety, intellect, and devotion embodied his poetic ideal—and on the broader Victorian Christian belief in self-sacrificial love. These personal and religious influences shaped both his themes and his earnest, didactic style.

■ Post-Reading 2. Paraphrasing

<Example>

My purpose now is simple: to celebrate her virtues as both maiden and wife,
I can think of no greater honor than to praise her all

my days.
Lifted by the wings of love and made noble by her gentle spirit,
I will show what kind of man is worthy of such a beautiful partner.

Unit 13B: Sir Henry Newbolt

■ Pre-Reading 2. Vocabulary

1. **barrister** → **D.** (n) a lawyer in some countries who is qualified to provide specialist legal advice and represent individuals in higher courts
2. **recognition** → **C.** (n) the act of officially acknowledging someone's achievements or services, often leading to honors such as knighthood
3. **intense** → **B.** (a) showing a high level of energy, enthusiasm, or effort; very strong or serious in quality
4. **strengthen** → **A.** (v) to make something stronger or more effective; to improve in power, ability, or firmness
5. **casualties** → **E.** (n) people who were injured or killed in an accident, war, or other event

■ Post-Reading 1. Review

1. **What new information about Henry Newbolt did you learn from this article compared to what you found online?**
→ I discovered that his father's death at age four led to a move to Bristol, that he abandoned a legal career after publishing *Admirals All*, and that he spent years on community service—campaigning to improve English usage and helping found his academic committee—before being knighted in 1915.
2. **How would you describe Newbolt's personality?**
→ He combined boundless enthusiasm and warmth with disciplined rigor, inspiring others through both his sociable optimism and his steadfast moral commitments.
3. **What made Newbolt's poetry widely admired in his time?**
→ His verse—celebrating duty, courage, and fair play in an accessible, stirring style—perfectly captured the patriotic and imperial values of Victorian and Edwardian Britain.

■ Post-Reading 2. Paraphrasing

<Example>
Though death has swept across the land
And England's honor seems at risk,
A schoolboy's cry—"Play up! Play up! And play the game!"—
Still unites and spurs everyone to persevere.

Chapter 4

Unit 14A: William Blake

■ Pre-Reading 2. Vocabulary

1. **flocked** → **C.** (v) to gather in a large group
2. **harsh** → **A.** (a) very severe, unpleasant, or difficult to endure
3. **throughout** → **B.** (prep) in every part of (something or a place)
4. **challenging** → **E.** (v) to question, dispute, or call into doubt; to test the strength, skill, or truth of something
5. **compassion** → **D.** (n) a deep awareness of and sympathy for another's suffering, coupled with a desire to alleviate it

■ Post-Reading 1. Review

1. **Describe in detail the impact that the Industrial Revolution had on British society during Blake's lifetime.**
→ In Blake's London, steam-powered factories and mechanized looms drove farm families into overcrowded cities, where low pay and dangerous, repetitive work in cramped mills bred widespread poverty and despair. Workers injured or ill from the harsh conditions were cast aside without support, and entire neighborhoods became slums of misery that deeply troubled Blake and informed his critique of industrial society.
2. **In what ways did Blake's illustrations for his poetry collections differ from the typical ones of his era?**
→ Rather than relying on standard, uniform engravings, Blake personally created hand-colored prints filled with bold, unconventional compositions. He wove symbolic figures and surreal landscapes into the margins, turning each page into a visionary experience rather than a simple illustration of the text.
3. **What message did Blake aim to convey through**

his illustrations?

→ Blake used his art to reveal spiritual truths hidden beneath the era's materialism and injustice. By placing scenes of human suffering alongside angels, demons, and radiant visions, he urged viewers to see beyond industrial progress and recognize the divine spark within humanity.

■ Post-Reading 2. Paraphrasing

<Example>

I was born out in the southern wild,
My skin is dark, but my heart shines bright—
As pure as any English child,
Though my body wears the night.
Before the sun could climb the sky,
My mother sat me underneath a tree,
Held me close, kissed my cheek,
And pointed east as she spoke.

Unit 14B: Rudyard Kipling

■ Pre-Reading 2. Vocabulary

1. **suitable** → **B.** (a) appropriate or fitting for a particular purpose, person, or situation
2. **pursue** → **E.** (v) to follow or try to achieve something over a period of time, such as a goal, dream, or career
3. **devaluation** → **C.** (n) A reduction in the value, importance, or reputation of something
4. **jingoistic** → **A.** (a) characterized by extreme patriotism, especially in the form of aggressive or warlike foreign policy
5. **propaganda** → **D.** (n) information, especially of a biased or misleading nature, used to promote a political cause or point of view

■ Post-Reading 1. Review

1. **What did you learn about Kipling from the article?**

→ The article showed that Kipling spent his childhood moving between India and England, that his first years in Staffordshire and later education at Clifton College and Oxford shaped both his literary tastes and career choices, and that despite early acclaim he faced mixed critical reevaluations for his imperialist views.

2. **How did Kipling's childhood influence his work?**

→ Growing up in India left Kipling with a lifelong fascination for its landscapes, peoples, and stories, while his frequent returns to England gave him the bicultural perspective that fueled the exotic settings and complex characters in poems like "The White Man's Burden" and stories such as *The Jungle Book*.

3. **Why have people loved *The Jungle Book* for such a long time?**

→ Readers have cherished *The Jungle Book* because its blend of adventure and moral lessons—embodied by Mowgli's struggle, his friendships with Baloo and Bagheera, and the thrilling jungles—speaks to universal themes of courage, belonging, and the triumph of innocence over fear.

■ Post-Reading 2. Paraphrasing

<Example>

Take up the White Man's burden,
Send your strongest young away,
To help the people you now rule,
Working hard through every day.
They seem wild and troubled—
Part child, part storm, in need of care.

Unit 15A: Wilfred Owen

■ Pre-Reading 2. Vocabulary

1. **audited** → **C.** (v) to attend a class informally (not for credit)
2. **rear** → **B.** (n) an area relatively far back from the front line; the back part of something
3. **numbness** → **A.** (n) the state of being not able to feel sensations
4. **traumatic** → **E.** (a) causing emotionally disturbing or distressing problems
5. **touted** → **D.** (v) to promote or praise actively; to put forward one's strengths

■ Post-Reading 1. Review

1. **Explain why he was unable to continue his higher education.**

→ Although Owen passed the University of London matriculation in 1911, his family lacked the funds to cover tuition and living expenses, and no scholarship was available. Forced to earn his keep as a pastor's assistant and by auditing classes, he ultimately had to abandon formal study entirely.

2. **What kind of person do you think he was?**

→ He was a sincere and responsible person with strong courage and a sense of duty. Despite financial hardship and mental suffering, he continued to study, serve as a tutor, and later fought bravely as a soldier, showing dedication and self-discipline.

3. **How would you describe the challenges he faced in the hospital, considering both his physical and psychological struggles?**

→ In the hospital, he faced both physical and psychological challenges. Physically, he suffered from shell shock symptoms such as nightmares, numbness, and paralysis. Psychologically, he struggled with guilt and depression because people at the time misunderstood shell shock, seeing its victims as weak or cowardly. Despite treatment, his trauma continued to haunt him.

■ Post-Reading 2. Paraphrasing

<Example>

At dawn the sorrow only grows deeper.
All we know is that war drags on,
rain soaks the ground, and heavy clouds hang overhead.
The new light seems to gather its gloomy weapons against the trembling sky—
yet in the end, nothing ever changes.

Unit 15B: John Donne

■ Pre-Reading 2. Vocabulary

1. **persecution** → **C.** (n) the act of systematically discriminating against or mistreating individuals based on their political beliefs or religious practices
2. **suitable** → **A.** (a) ideal or appropriate for particular circumstances or conditions
3. **dishonoring** → **E.** (v) to bring shame or disgrace upon someone, especially by violating their dignity or honor
4. **allegiance** → **D.** (n) a formal promise of loyalty to a sovereign or government
5. **correspondent** → **B.** (n) a journalist who reports from areas of conflict or warfare, providing firsthand accounts of events

■ Post-Reading 1. Review

1. **What did you learn about John Donne from the reading?**

→ The article reveals that John Donne led an unusually dramatic life for his era. Born into a devout Roman Catholic family in 1572, he nonetheless attended both Oxford and Cambridge, where his sharp intellect flourished even though he could not take a degree. Donne then trained for the law and served as secretary to Sir Thomas Egerton, Lord Keeper of the Great Seal, before embarking on a literary career that included poetry, sermons, and eventually ordination. Along the way he suffered financial hardship, personal loss, and the turmoil of religious conflict, all of which deeply informed his work.

2. **What kept Donne from getting his degree?**

→ Though Donne completed the required coursework at Oxford and Cambridge, he was unable to swear the required oaths of allegiance to the Church of England. As a devout Roman Catholic, he could not renounce papal authority, and at that time adherence to the Anglican settlement was a formal prerequisite for graduation. His faith therefore blocked the final step to an official degree.

3. **Why did Donne get married in secret?**

→ Donne's clandestine marriage to Anne More was driven by social and familial pressure. Anne was the niece of Sir Thomas Egerton, Donne's employer and patron, and their union lacked the consent of her family. Fearing Egerton's wrath—and knowing a public ceremony would end his own prospects—Donne and Anne exchanged vows in secret, a choice that led to temporary disgrace and financial penalties but which they both ultimately upheld.

■ Post-Reading 2. Paraphrasing

<Example>

When anyone dies,
I feel a little smaller,
because we are all part of the same human family.
So do not ask whose death the bell announces;
it is a warning for you too.

Unit 16A: Walt Whitman

■ Pre-Reading 2. Vocabulary

1. **persistence** → **E.** (a) continuous and determined effort over time
2. **pursuit** → **D.** (n) the act of striving toward or seeking out a specific goal or objective
3. **wellspring** → **B.** (n) a source or origin from which something continually flows or develops
4. **centers on** → **C.** (v) to have something as the main subject, focus, or interest

5. **plain** → **A.** (a) simple and ordinary in appearance; not decorated or elaborate

■ Post-Reading 1. Review

1. **What was Whitman's lifestyle?**

→ Whitman lived a simple and independent life. He spent his time reading and meditating on life, collecting materials for writing, and working persistently on his own. Many people thought he was lazy because he often seemed to be resting, but in reality, he was quietly developing his ideas and spirit.

2. **Although *Leaves of Grass contains only a dozen poems, why does it remain a lasting legacy of American literature to this day?***

→ Although it has only a few poems, *Leaves of Grass* reflects Whitman's deep thoughts, wisdom, and the American spirit of democracy, freedom, and individuality. It was highly praised by writers like Emerson and became widely recognized in both the U.S. and Britain, leaving a lasting influence on American literature.

3. **Which movie quotes Whitman's poem which was written in honor of Lincoln's death?**

→ The movie *Dead Poets Society* quotes Whitman's poem "O Captain! My Captain!" which he wrote to mourn President Abraham Lincoln's death.

■ Post-Reading 2. Paraphrasing

<Example>

I rejoice in who I am,
and sing the song of myself.
My thoughts can be your thoughts,
and all the good in me is yours too.

Unit 16B: William Ernest Henley

■ Pre-Reading 2. Vocabulary

1. **plague** → **E.** (a) to cause persistent pain or distress
2. **sympathized** → **B.** (v) to feel the same way about another person's feelings or opinions
3. **character** → **A.** (n) a person's natural abilities and qualities
4. **amputated** → **D.** (v) to surgically remove a limb or part of the body
5. **segregation** → **C.** (n) a system that keeps people of different races separate and treats them unequally

■ Post-Reading 1. Review

1. **What caused the greatest suffering in Henley's life?**

→ Henley suffered greatly from recurring tuberculosis, which eventually forced him to have one leg amputated. In addition, he endured extreme poverty and long periods of physical pain, which made his life very difficult.

2. **What role did Thomas Edward Brown play in Henley's life?**

→ Brown provided Henley with great moral support and encouragement at a time when he was losing hope. He inspired Henley to believe in his own literary talent, helped him open his mind to new ideas, and became a lifelong friend.

3. **What effect did Henley's poem quoted in the movie *Invictus* have on the main character?**

→ The poem gave Nelson Mandela the strength to endure the hardships of his long imprisonment. It motivated him to stay resilient and overcome challenges, eventually inspiring his leadership in uniting South Africa.

■ Post-Reading 2. Paraphrasing

<Example>

It doesn't matter how difficult life is
or how many hardships I face.
I am the one who controls my life,
and I decide the direction of my own soul.

Unit 17A: Douglas Malloch

■ Pre-Reading 2. Vocabulary

1. **untouched** → **E.** (a) in its natural (original) conditions, unspoiled
2. **reflected** → **D.** (v) to show or express (properties of things, people's attitudes or emotions)
3. **timber industry** → **C.** (n) the business of growing, cutting, and selling trees for wood products
4. **paradigm** → **A.** (n) a model, a distinctive pattern, or an example of something
5. **metaphor** → **B.** (n) a way to describe something by saying it is something else

■ Post-Reading 1. Review

1. **What was Malloch's occupation?**

→ Malloch worked as a journalist and poet. He wrote articles for the *Muskegon Chronicle* and the

American Lumberman, and he also published poems in magazines.

2. **What was the central theme of his poetry?**

→ His poetry often used trees and nature as symbols to teach life lessons. He showed that, like trees growing strong through wind and storms, people become stronger through hardships.

3. **Why were his poems so loved?**

→ His poems were simple, touching, and easy to understand. They encouraged people to live bravely, value community, and grow stronger through life's difficulties.

■ Post-Reading 2. Paraphrasing

<Example>

If you can't do something great,
Do the small thing well.
If you can't shine like the sun,
Be a star that lights the night.
Winning is not about being big,
But about doing your best
In whatever you are.

Unit 17B: T. S. Eliot

■ Pre-Reading 2. Vocabulary

1. **heritage** → **A.** (n) an object or culture passed down from previous generations
2. **naturalized** → **B.** (v) to acquire the nationality of another country and become a citizen of that country
3. **prominent** → **C.** (a) standing out or important; easily noticeable
4. **representative** → **D.** (n) a person who speaks or acts for others, or a typical example of a group or quality
5. **insights** → **E.** (n) the ability to clearly understand the true nature of something or someone

■ Post-Reading 1. Review

1. **Talk about Eliot's family environment in which Eliot grew up.**

→ Eliot grew up in a wealthy and intellectual family. His father was a brick company owner who provided him with financial support, and his mother was a poet who inspired his literary interests. This family environment allowed him to focus on his studies without worrying about money.

2. **What unique qualities or approaches set Eliot apart from other modernist writers?**

→ Unlike many other modernist writers, Eliot combined Western and Eastern traditions in his works and approached modern problems with deep intellectual reflection. He used his wide knowledge of literature, religion, and philosophy to explore modern civilization critically. This blending of traditions and his philosophical depth made his modernism unique.

3. **What is the common theme in Eliot's "The Waste Land" and *Four Quartets*?**

→ Both works focus on the problems of modern civilization and the spiritual emptiness of people. They search for solutions to life's difficulties, suggesting that true renewal and meaning come from moral discipline, tradition, and inner reflection.

■ Post-Reading 2. Paraphrasing

<Example>

Every word and every line
is both an ending and a new start.
Every poem is like a farewell,
and every action leads us forward—
toward challenge, toward risk,
toward the unknown—
and that is where life begins again.

Hyangil Kim (김향일)

Professor, Division of Creative Convergence Liberal Arts, Sahmyook University
M.A. in TESOL, University of Leeds
Ph.D. in TESOL (English Education), Hankuk University of Foreign Studies

Her main research interests include L2 motivation, affect, and learner differences in second language learning. She has published several SSCI-indexed papers in the field of English language teaching and learning.

Yeongyu Kim (김연규)

Ph.D. in English Literature, Gangneung-Wonju National University
Research Professor (Type A) supported by the National Research Foundation of Korea
Special Research Fellow at the Institute for the Humanities, Gangneung-Wonju National University
Lecturer in the Division of Liberal Arts and General Education at Gangneung-Wonju National University

Her research focuses on nineteenth-century English poetry, particularly religious verse. She has published several articles and books on figures such as John Henry Newman and Gerard Manley Hopkins. Currently, she is conducting a five-year research project on the narrative structure of John Keats's long poems.

Reading the Lives of Poets:
Discovering the Self and the World

1판 1쇄 _ 2025년 10월 25일
1판 2쇄 _ 2026년 2월 25일

저　　자 · 김연규 · 김향일
발 행 인 · 정현걸
발　　행 · 신아사
인　　쇄 · 한승문화사
출판등록 · 1956년 1월 5일 (제9-52호)
주　　소 · 서울특별시 은평구 통일로 59길 4
전　　화 · 02)382-6411 · 팩스 02)382-6401
홈페이지 · www.shinasa.co.kr
E-MAIL · shinasa@daum.net

ISBN 979-11-7342-111-2 (93840)
정가 23,000원